CRIP TIMES

CRIP: NEW DIRECTIONS IN DISABILITY STUDIES

General Editors: Michael Bérubé, Robert McRuer, and Ellen Samuels

Committed to generating new paradigms and attending to innovative interdisciplinary shifts, the Crip: New Directions in Disability Studies series focuses on cutting-edge developments in the field, with interest in exploratory analyses of disability and globalization, ecotheory, new materialisms, affect theory, performance studies, postcolonial studies, and trans theory.

Crip Times: Disability, Globalization, and Resistance
Robert McRuer

Crip Times

Disability, Globalization, and Resistance

Robert McRuer

NEW YORK UNIVERSITY PRESS

New York

NEW YORK UNIVERSITY PRESS
New York
www.nyupress.org

References to Internet websites (URLs) were accurate at the time of writing. Neither the author nor New York University Press is responsible for URLs that may have expired or changed since the manuscript was prepared.

Library of Congress Cataloging-in-Publication Data
Names: McRuer, Robert, 1966– author.
Title: Crip times : disability, globalization, and resistance / Robert McRuer.
Description: New York : New York University Press, [2017] | Series: New directions in disability studies | Includes bibliographical references and index.
Identifiers: LCCN 2017012917| ISBN 978-1-4798-2631-5 (cl : alk. paper) | ISBN 978-1-4798-7415-6 (pb : alk. paper)
Subjects: LCSH: Sociology of disability. | People with disabilities. | Homosexuality—Social aspects. | Culture and globalization.
Classification: LCC HV1568 .M372 2017 | DDC 306.76/6087—dc23
LC record available at https://lccn.loc.gov/2017012917

New York University Press books are printed on acid-free paper, and their binding materials are chosen for strength and durability. We strive to use environmentally responsible suppliers and materials to the greatest extent possible in publishing our books.

Manufactured in the United States of America

10 9 8 7 6 5 4 3 2 1

Also available as an ebook

CONTENTS

ACKNOWLEDGMENTS

I cannot put into words how much it has meant to me, over the course of completing this book, to share my life with Cristhian Soto-Arévalo, Joseph Choueike, and Andrew Glaspie. Like many other misfits, we use the word family to describe what we might be, even as we recognize the inadequacy of available languages to describe the sustaining, queer and crip, ways of thriving in the world that we've collectively shaped. As always for me, Tom Murray and Angela Hewett have also been at the center of it all, contributing to that thriving; Tom has the distinction of being part of my life and supporting me from the very first time I published an article in queer theory, in the early 1990s. I love you all and thank you for the laughter, companionship, and sheer joy with which you surround me; I thank Cristhian in particular for shaping a home with me. Thais Austin, Karen Rodríguez, and Nate Swift-Erslev are also part of the sustaining network of our life, and I am grateful to each of you. Over the course of writing this book, my collaborations with Merri Lisa Johnson, Kateřina Kolářová, and Anna Mollow have enriched my life and work; the deep friendships and queer, crip, and feminist connections I have shaped with each of you as we have presented, written, edited, or taught together have profoundly shaped the way I approach the world. You are present in so many ways in the pages of this book.

David Mitchell and Sharon Snyder's arrival in Washington, D.C., in 2013 was transformative; I still cannot believe that they are just around the corner. I am honored to be your friend and colleague and love the fact that we have presented together on disability and political economy from Washington to Moscow to Byron Bay, Australia. I hope it is clear to readers of *Crip Times* how much it has been shaped in conversation with your own groundbreaking scholarship. David and Sharon have been part of a Washington, D.C.-area disability studies writing group; the emergence of that group as I was producing the final draft of this book has been a lifeline. I am so grateful to the rigorous commentary of the other members of that group over the past few years: Julia Watts Belser, Jeff Brune, Jonathan Hsy, and Sara Scalenghe.

Anna Mollow and Holly Dugan deserve special mention here, as they read the entire manuscript during the final year of revisions. I have taken so many of Anna's suggestions in the pages ahead; I have no doubt that the clarity of the arguments in every chapter is in part due to her careful reading and thinking about the material. My only regret is that I have not been able to incorporate more of her invaluable suggestions. Holly's enthusiasm for the project and capacity for connecting it to the things we teach and think about in George Washington University's Department of English are much appreciated, as are the ways in which she has consistently underscored the project's timeliness and even urgency.

I am so fortunate in general to have the most amazing group of colleagues at GWU; special thanks to Jeffrey Jerome Cohen for his support and friendship and for reading portions of *Crip Times* over the years. I have also received incisive commentary on particular chapters from Daniel DeWispelare, Jonathan Hsy, Ayanna Thompson, and Gayle Wald. In English and across the university, I have benefited from innumerable conversations about this work and related material and want to thank especially Marshall Alcorn, Jennifer Chang, Patricia Chu, Manuel Cuellar, Joseph Fisher, Wade Fletcher, Randi Gray Kristensen, Antonio López, Dan Moshenberg, Dara Orenstein, Lisa Page, Rachel Riedner, Tara Wallace, Gail Weiss, and Abby Wilkerson. My students continue to inspire me and I want to particularly acknowledge Gabrielle Bychowski, Tyler Christensen, Dora Danylevich, Brady Forrest, Ian Funk, D. Gilson, Peyton Joyce, Molly Lewis, and Sam Yates. Constance Kibler continues to work some sort of queer magic to keep the Department of English afloat; working with her over the past several years has kept me grounded. Connie, your friendship means so much to me.

It has been an extreme privilege to engage with and write about the work of Livia Radwanski and Liz Crow, the two artists who are at the center of the second half of *Crip Times*. I encountered Livia's work and the global project "El Museo de los Desplazados" in July 2013, and made contact with Livia herself the following year. I am so grateful to her for putting me in contact in turn with a range of artists and activists thinking about culture, housing activism, and disability in Mexico City, including Mariana Delgado, Ricardo Nurko, and Javier Toscano. Ricardo gave me a long walking tour of Colonia Roma and was able to provide a great deal of insight into the shifting architecture of the neighborhood; my long discussion with Javier about housing and disability activism in Mexico City in general was indispensable. By the time I met Livia in person in October 2015, I felt like we were old friends. We walked the streets of Colonia Roma together and most importantly, went together into Calle Mérida, Number 90, where she introduced me to many of the residents who had struggled for more than five years to return to their home. Livia also connected me to the Left Hand Rotation collective, which originated El Museo de los Desplazados in Spain and Portugal, and I appreciate their enthusiasm for my work and help in understanding their global project. Liz met with me on short notice for the first time in July 2014 in Bristol; our conversation ultimately changed the shape of the project, making it clear to me that I needed to have a chapter on her 2015 performance piece *Figures*. During the 2015 performance, it was an honor to be part of the project for a few days as Liz sculpted alongside the banks of the Thames in London; Liz's production team, including Matthew Fessey, China Blue Fish, and Jessie Edge were amazing and so welcoming. Livia and Liz are very different artists working in very different locations in the world, but their critical thinking on class, gender, embodiment, and social justice harmonizes in so many unexpected ways. I am grateful to both artists for reading and commenting on the chapters that focus on their work.

This book is also about crip and queer activism, and Bethany Stevens deserves special notice in that regard. I appreciate how open she was to working with me as I wrote about This Is What Disability Looks Like. I am also grateful to her for being so much fun and such a good friend.

A University Facilitating Fund grant from GWU provided much needed support for this project at a crucial moment in 2014, in particular making possible a research trip to the UK. The fact that *Crip Times* centers on the UK means that many colleagues and friends there have been indispensable. During my research trip in 2014, I spoke with Liz Carr, Jo Church, Kaliya Franklin, Sue Marsh, and others; as should be clear in the pages ahead, Kaliya's beautiful photograph "Left Out in the Cold" quickly became an iconic image for me over the completion of this project. Lucy Burke deserves special mention for all that she has done over the past several years keeping me apprised on the nuances of British politics and austerity's impact on disabled people. I am very grateful to Richard Seymour for sending me his book *Against Austerity* when it was still in manuscript. His work has influenced my own thinking in so many ways; I can only hope to approach the level of nuance he brings to analyses of class, austerity, and British politics. I have never met Samuel Miller in person but I found countless articles on disability, austerity, and the UK thanks to him. I was fortunate to meet Matthew McQuillan in early 2015, and am grateful to him for connecting me to a range of housing activists in London. A hearty thanks as well to other UK-based colleagues and friends who provided invaluable insights or simply moral support: Clare Barker, David Bolt, Marie Clare, Dan Goodley, Catherine Long, Stuart Murray, Simon Wales, and Philippa Willitts. My friendship and collaboration with Margrit Shildrick extends beyond our many UK-based conversations; I am particularly grateful to the ways in which she has made possible conversations about my work in Sweden and Norway.

Portions of what eventually became this book were initially presented in Spain in July 2011, in the weeks and months following the initial occupation by activists of the Puerta del Sol in Madrid, protesting the government's austerity measures. My interactions with activists and thinkers in Spain in that summer and in subsequent visits have been life-changing. Melania Moscoso's friendship, deep knowledge of Spanish history and disability activism, and anticapitalist politics animate every page of this book that is focused on Spain. I'm grateful as well to my friends Sara María Morón, Lucas Platero, Soledad Arnau Ripollés, Javier Romañach, and the late, sorely missed Paco Guzmán Castillo. In July 2015, Andrea García-Santesmases made it possible for me to present portions of this project for the first time in Spanish, in Barcelona. I want to thank Andrea and the amazing group of Barcelona-based disability activists, including Antonio Centeno and Raúl de la Morena.

In Mexico, Jhonatthan Maldonado Ramirez has been key in disseminating the work of crip theory in general and in providing a venue for me to discuss *Crip Times*; I also want to thank Elsa Muñiz Garcia, Mauricio List Reyes, and other members of the scholarly network Cuerpo en la Red. I'm deeply grateful to Cristián Iturriaga for meeting with me in

Santiago in June 2015 and for his ongoing updates on student activism and disability activism in Chile. Matthew Durington sent me his work on securitization and South Africa, which helped to shape the section of the manuscript on Oscar Pistorius. *Crip Times* is not directly about Brazil, but Marco Gaverio, Anahi Guedes de Mello, Michelle Lage, and Amanda Muniz have made possible conversations and presentations about the project that have helpfully linked the project to disability and antiausterity activism there, and I thank them for it.

Gina di Grazia is one of the finest readers of my work, and I was fortunate to have her as a research assistant during part of the time I was completing this book. So many colleagues have read parts of this manuscript directly or rigorously engaged with it as I have presented it publicly over the past six years. In addition to those I have already noted, I want to thank Rachel Adams, Stacy Alaimo, Susan Antebi, Claire Barber, Cynthia Barounis, Elizabeth Bearden, Liat Ben-Moshe, Pamela Block, Fiona Kumari Campbell, Peter Campbell, Mel Y. Chen, Eli Clare, Christina Crosby, Ann Cvetkovich, Lennard Davis, Jay Dolmage, Lisa Duggan, Jill Ehnenn, Julie Passanante Elman, Bengt Elmén, Nirmala Erevelles, Ramzi Fawaz, Roderick Ferguson, Anne Finger, Margaret Fink, Kevin Floyd, Kelly Fritsch, Ann Fox, Rosemarie Garland-Thomson, Macarena Gomez-Barris, Kim Q. Hall, Christina Hanhardt, Cassandra Hartblay, Louise Hickman, Morgan Holmes, Michelle Jarman, Benjy Kahan, Anastasia Kayiatos, Ann Keefer, Katie King, Christopher Krentz, Riva Lehrer, Marilee Lindemann, Dana Luciano, Josh Lukin, Nina Mackert, Micki McGee, Patrick McKelvey, Rod Michalko, Julie Avril Minich, Sophie Mitra, José Esteban Muñoz, Kevin Murphy, Mimi Thi Nguyen, Robert Dale Parker, Catherine Prendergast, Margaret Price, Alyson Patsavas, Jasbir Puar, Sangeeta Ray, Zahari Richter, Rebecca Sanchez, Carrie Sandahl, Sami Schalk, Susan Schweik, Alexis Shotwell, Martha Nell Smith, Karen Soldatic, Susan Stryker, Nikki Sullivan, Carly Thomsen, Tanya Titchkosky, Karen Tongson, Amy Vidali, Salvador Vidal-Ortiz, Jeremy Wade, Linda Ware, Margot Weiss, Melissa Autumn White, Kathi Wiedlack, and Cindy Wu. A special thanks to Margaret Price, Ann Fox, and Johnna Keller for a much-needed conversation about anxiety at a key moment of completing final revisions.

J. Jack Halberstam and an anonymous reader for NYU Press provided enthusiastic commentary that made the final version of this book so much better. Jack read the revised manuscript as well and I am very grateful for his care in doing so, his great suggestions along the way, and his friendship. As always, it is a pleasure to work with NYU Press, and with Alicia Nadkarni and Eric Zinner, in particular. Ellen Samuels and Michael Bérubé, a final thanks to you. As we inaugurate Crip: New Directions in Disability Studies, I look forward to thinking with you about the expansive and transformative ways in which disability is shaping and reshaping our world.

Introduction

Crip Times

It was the summer of 2011, and for seven weeks in July and August I watched an embodied movement in motion. I was living in Madrid one block away from the Puerta del Sol [Gate of the Sun], the plaza that had been occupied since May 15 by Los Indignados, an eclectic group whose name ("the indignant ones") marked and marks their sharp opposition to the dominant economic and political order. Members of the movement insisted that the Spanish political establishment was protecting finance capital through global economic turmoil, even as it simultaneously put into place a wide range of extreme cost-cutting measures (a program of so-called "austerity") that made the lives of ordinary Spanish people more vulnerable and precarious. On any given day that summer, beneath the at times scorching heat of the Madrid sun, thousands of bodies came together, sweating, chanting, clapping, sitting, standing, embracing, laughing, and—at times—crying in frustration, fear, or pain.

The name "Los Indignados" was in part inspired by the Spanish translation of a 2010 French essay by Stéphane Hessel, *Indignez-vous!* calling in its very title for indignation and for action against injustice. Hessel, a ninety-three-year-old concentration camp survivor and member of the French Resistance against the Nazis, wrote in *Indignez-vous!* about a variety of topics: the vast income inequality sustained by the ruling class under capitalism; police brutality; the mistreatment of immigrants and the poor; and the struggle of Palestinians for self-determination, a struggle that Hessel perceived as linked to the historical struggles of the French Resistance itself and the fight for Algerian independence (Glass). If "indignation" sometimes connotes in English a relatively cerebral opposition to an idea, person, or event that is, as the *OED* puts it, "unworthy of regard or notice," from 2011 onward, Los Indignados insisted, on the contrary, that the world take notice of what was happening in Spain.

Moreover, as Míriam Arenas Conejo and Asun Pié Balaguer make clear, their indignation was far from merely cerebral and was in fact expressed through "una experiencia de militancia encarnada" [an experience of embodied militancy] (239). "The outraged," conjuring up images of anger, tensed bodies, and clenched fists, is thus a more forceful and visceral translation of "Los Indignados," and indeed the English translation of Hessel's book is *Time for Outrage*. In Spain itself, the occupation of the Puerta del Sol and dozens of other locations across the country represented the beginning of an embodied popular movement that came to be known by the day and month it originated: 15-M—or #15M, as news of the May 15 occupation traveled across Twitter and other social networks. Internationally, "Los Indignados" was (and remains) the more recognized descriptor for the activists who took the plaza that summer.

The Puerta del Sol is located a block away from the Plaza Mayor in Madrid and is, in a literal or official sense, the center of Spain. Km. 0 (the space from which distances are measured in Spain) is located in the Puerta del Sol and Calle Mayor [literally, Main Street] and other important streets and avenues—many of them busy pedestrian walkways lined with bustling shops and restaurants—radiate outward from the plaza. Given its geographical centrality in the city and country, the Puerta del Sol has often served as the symbolic location for Spanish citizens making public statements or participating in what Michael Hardt and Antonio Negri might describe as "the political project of instituting the common" (*Commonwealth* ix), with the elements of the "common" understood expansively and democratically as "those results of social production that are necessary for social interaction and further production, such as knowledges, languages, codes, information, affects, and so forth" (viii). In the symbolic public space of the Puerta del Sol, Los Indignados announced through words and actions their opposition to the political and economic establishment, denouncing the privatization of public resources and other maneuvers that, in Hardt and Negri's words, secure "regimes of property that exclude the common" (ix). In direct contrast to such exclusions, one prominent banner across an entrance to the Puerta del Sol essentially declared a welcome to anyone who might join the struggle. "Bienvenida Dignidad" [Welcome Dignity], the banner read, materializing through that invocation a space free from what activists identified as the indignity of austerity [Figure 1.1].

Figure 1.1. "Welcome Dignity," Puerta del Sol, Madrid. Photo by Author.

In a Crip Time and Place

I had come to Madrid in 2011 to immerse myself in Spanish-language study. Like any serious student of language, however, I was acquiring in the process not only words and phrases that might reproduce the world as I knew it in English, but whole new ways of thinking that had the power to alter that world, or to make it strange. In many ways, it was a perfect year for that pursuit, given the rapidly shifting syntax and morphology of struggle not only in Spain but around the world. Revolutionary uprisings against despotic governments had swept across Tunisia, Egypt, and other locations from December 2010 onward and had been dubbed the "Arab Spring." Not long after plazas and squares across Spain were occupied, students took to the streets in Santiago and other cities in Chile to demand free and accessible education at all levels; related movements in Mexico City and Quebec would emerge within a year. In London and across the United Kingdom in August 2011, protests erupted after the police shooting of Mark Duggan, an unarmed black man, in the North London neighborhood of Totten-ham. The UK protests drew attention to racism and police violence, as well as to poverty and rising levels of inequality in the country. The UK government in general at the time was implementing cuts that I will spotlight in great detail in the pages to follow; the general program of cost-cutting and privatization was not unlike what was taking place in Spain.

Neither these struggles nor the politics of neglect and scarcity that necessitated and animated them were explicitly focused on disability. Indeed, the main contention of *Crip Times: Disability, Globalization, and Resistance* is that the absolute centrality of disability to a now-global pol-itics of austerity has rarely been theorized explicitly or comprehensively, even if increasing numbers of disabled activists and artists globally are recognizing and calling out the disproportionately negative impact of austerity on disabled people. The UK is one place where that calling out has been most amplified, and it is for that reason that I focus centrally, in what follows, on that location. *Crip Times*, however, is in many ways a product of the embodied promise and the profound disappointment of 2011, and the book thus of necessity reverberates to Spain, where it began for me, as well as to other locations where echoes of the promise of that year can still be discerned.

Los Indignados are often positioned as one of the main inspirations for the Occupy Wall Street movement that erupted in Fall 2011; working groups in occupied plazas in Madrid, Barcelona, and across Spain, as in New York and across North America later that year, focused on imagin-ing alternatives to the dominant form of capitalism known as neoliberal-ism, as well as on rethinking a range of more specific issues structured by it, including health care, immigration, and education. Some working groups in Spain emphasized aspects of culture or employment, while others specifically emphasized justice for women, prisoners, or disabled people. Decisions regarding courses of action were reached through a consensus of the entire group present in the plaza at a given moment. The Puerta del Sol was covered in graffiti that summer and filled with pictures and signs declaring "La crisis que la paguen ellos" [Let them pay for their crisis!] or "Sin pan no habrá paz" [Without bread there will be no peace] [Figure I.2]. Makeshift shacks filled the area; in addition to space for resting or sleeping, these shacks provided services such as a

Figure I.2. "Without Bread There Will Be No Peace," Puerta del Sol, Madrid. Photo by Author.

people's free library for both borrowing and donating books and space for some basic community medical care. One manifesto makes clear that Los Indignados did not accept donations of money; they did, however, accept objects with use value, including chairs and tables, sleeping bags, food, and medicine (Álvarez et al. 29).

It was a crip time and place, to rework J. Jack Halberstam's now-famous description of the "strange temporalities, imaginative life schedules, and eccentric economic practices" that characterize queer times and places (*In a Queer Time* 1). As I hope will be clear throughout *Crip Times*, I am building on the work of a range of contemporary theorists who are attempting to locate (in the sense both of finding *and* describing spatially) what Halberstam identifies as "the alternatives to capitalism that already exist and are presently under construction" (12). In contrast to the work of Halberstam and many others in queer theory, however, my project is explicitly disabled, or crip.[1] Exactly how this project might be comprehended as *crip*—drawing on the activist and theoretical analytic derived from the word *cripple*—will be clearer as this Introduction continues. On a very basic level, however, *Crip Times* is simply more centrally concerned with what Sharon L. Snyder and David T. Mitchell term "cultural locations of disability"—"locales that represent a saturation point of content about disability" (*Cultural* 3). Such saturation points are not always immediately legible or tangible; few commentators beyond Arenas Conejo and Pié Balaguer read the Spanish 15-M movement of 2011 through disability, for instance (and virtually no commentators writing about the movement in English). This book in part attempts to theorize crip ways of reading for and across the saturation points.

As "La crisis que la paguen ellos" suggests, throughout the summer of 2011 Spanish activists were protesting the government's reactions to the global economic crisis that had begun more than three years prior. In Spain, in the financial sector predatory and speculative lending practices generated a bubble with banks and property developers borrowing at a rate that inflated real estate values across the country (before the crisis, even though individuals were also being given predatory loans by Spanish banks, ordinary citizens were generally left far behind by the financial speculation among wealthy investors that produced the bubble). In 2008 the bubble burst, causing a sudden crash in the housing and construction sector. Construction prior to the crisis had been booming; the industry's precipitous collapse, with thousands of construction companies declaring bankruptcy from 2008 onward, significantly contributed to the deep recession which the country entered. A state-financed bailout fund to protect the banks was established in 2009. Los Indignados quite rightly interpreted the government's reaction as one that privileged bankers and pushed the majority of the population (which had essentially funded the bailout) even further into crisis. One of the initial slogans of the movement directly marked the defiance of Los Indignados against this official reaction, "No somos mercancía en manos de políticos y banqueros" [We are not commodities in the hands of politicians and bankers].[2] The centrist Partido Socialista Obrero Español (PSOE) [Spanish Socialist Workers' Party], led by then-Prime Minister José Luis Rodríguez Zapatero, imposed harsh austerity measures on the general Spanish population to combat the crisis, slashing government spending and raising the retirement age from 65 to 67. The cuts to government spending were particularly punishing as the unemployment rate had risen above 20 percent by early 2011. For young adults, those whom friends and teachers were already describing to me as *una generación perdida* [a lost generation], the rate was closer to 45 percent. The bodies and minds of that generation were quickly registering the crisis: even before the occupation of the Puerta del Sol, a 2010 survey of primary care clinics noted a sharp increase in patients being treated for anxiety or for alcohol dependency; the same study noted a decided link between unemployment or the inability to pay personal debt and the risk of major depression (Fernández-Rivas and González-Torres 585).

The official political landscape in Spain has been dominated by two different parties for most of the past forty years. Los Indignados were outraged with both parties, and with good cause, given subsequent events: for ordinary citizens, the crisis in Spain generally accelerated in the years following 2011. The conservative Partido Popular (PP) [People's Party] retook power at the end of the year, and between 2011 and 2015 Prime Minister Mariano Rajoy proved to be one of the most faithful executors of austerity in the Eurozone. A third-party, Left alternative in Spain, Podemos [We Can], emerged to great fanfare in early 2014 and in the space of four months propelled five candidates to seats in the general European Parliament (a popularly elected parliamentary body of the European Union). One of those members was Pablo Echenique, a wheelchair user who previously had no plans to enter politics, but who joined Podemos because he "was indignant because in Spain and other countries there are growing numbers of poor people, while we see more and more millionaires and politicians involved in corruption cases" (qtd. in Catanzaro). Podemos, however, could not achieve a majority in the December 2015 national elections. The PP received the most votes nationally but also did not receive a majority; a second national election was thus held in June 2016. The PP in the second election received even more votes but remained shy of a majority. In a parliamentary vote in October 2016, Rajoy was finally confirmed again as Prime Minister after a sufficient number of PSOE representatives agreed to abstain, essentially allowing his confirmation to move forward and avoiding a third election. A year earlier, Podemos-supported candidates were elected mayor in Barcelona and Madrid in May 2015; municipal success, however, has not yet translated into a sustained challenge to the PP at a national level, not least because of the PSOE's ongoing complicity with Rajoy and his austerity agenda.

While living near the Puerta del Sol during that summer of 2011, I became friends with a number of activists—particularly queer and disability activists, but also members of the 15-M movement more generally. I participated in some of the marches, including a massive one on July 23, 2016, retaking the plaza after it had been cleared by police. I witnessed such a clearance by police twice, the second time later in August in advance of then-Pope Benedict's arrival. Catholic youth from around the world were descending on Madrid for World Youth Day, and Los Indignados were angry that Spanish taxpayers were essentially subsidizing the event. Moreover, as harsh cuts to social services were being imposed on the citizenry, visitors for World Youth Day were receiving transportation discounts on the Madrid Metro. Happy Catholic youth waving flags from around the world and marching through the streets singing songs about the life to come were welcomed by the officially secular state in Madrid that summer (Roman Catholicism has protections in the Spanish Constitution but is not a state religion). To make that welcome clear, Los Indignados were evicted from the plazas they had been occupying/living in across the country. And indeed, *desalojo* or *desalojamiento* [eviction] were the Spanish words most frequently used (by both activists themselves and the mainstream media) to describe the police clearance of plazas across the country.

Throughout this period, I was compelled by the ways in which bodies and bodily imagery emphasizing precarity were being used to send messages of outrage and resistance. Unruly bodies occupying public spaces, bodies—as it were—out of bounds, were challenging the guardians of capital and short-circuiting the official consensus that those guardians urgently needed to forge about the "necessity" or inevitability of drastic austerity measures.[3] For the July 23 march, I was with disability activists Melania Moscoso Pérez and Javier Romañach. The march began near Parque Retiro (the large park on the eastern side of central Madrid) and wound through the financial center to the Puerta del Sol, with the intention of retaking the plaza after the eviction. As we moved slowly forward, we noticed that some activists had stripped down to their panties, bras, and briefs in front of the Ministry of Equality and Social Affairs (later,

Figure 1.3. Activists protesting austerity cuts, Ministry of Equality and Social Affairs, Madrid. Photo by Author.

under the PP, renamed simply the Ministry of Social Affairs). Their embodied action was intended to signify that "these cuts are stripping us to nothing" [Figure 1.3]. Later, as we passed the Banco de España heading into the Puerta del Sol, we saw that activists had written "CULPABLES" on its walls, peppering those walls with red hand prints. The banks, in other words, were perceived as "GUILTY" and as far as the people were concerned, they had blood on their hands [Figures 1.4 and 1.5].

The fascist dictatorship of Francisco Franco, which ended upon Franco's death in 1975, is still experienced as *casi ayer* [almost yesterday] in Spain, and that memory of a decades-long state repression inevitably circulates around contemporary police violence (some would say that the memory of brutal repression held police violence in check, for a time). Clearly, however, especially in the days leading up to the Pope's arrival, these embodied messages against austerity were increasingly perceived as too intense and too extreme by the powers that be, and violent police attacks on activists and activist spaces across the country

Figure 1.4. "Guilty," Banco de España, Madrid. Photo by Author.

Figure 1.5. "The Government Has Blood on Its Hands," Banco de España, Madrid. Photo by Author.

Figure 1.6. Police beating, August 2011, Puerta del Sol, Madrid.
Photo by Author.

commenced as the summer continued (the police reaction that summer was not unlike the reaction against Occupy Wall Street later in the
year in the United States, as the state moved in to clear occupied spaces
across the country). During the two *desalojamientos* that I witnessed
in Madrid, as 15-M activists were evicted from the plaza, I observed
quite harsh police violence (mainly fierce beatings with police batons)
against activists [Figure 1.6]. Bodies out of bounds, instituting the common in opposition to the financial and state institutions identified as
culpables, as responsible for the crisis, apparently needed to be moved
out of sight.

In the years that followed the birth of the movement, in the opinion
of many activists police violence against them intensified almost continuously. Rajoy's Partido Popular began to impose measures designed
to curtail the kinds of protests and occupations the world witnessed
in Summer 2011. By 2015 Spain's Civil Protection Act, more popularly
known as the "Ley Mordaza" [Gag Rule] was in effect, criminalizing any
unauthorized photography of the police (such as the photos I myself
took) and putting into place strict restrictions on how, when, and where
protests in Spain could take place. In the very week that I am completing a first draft of this Introduction in Fall 2014, fourteen of nineteen

activists detained for their role in generating the movement—all of them between 18 and 26 years old in 2011—received a total of seventy-four years in prison for disorderly conduct, resistance, provocation or attack against agents of authority, and a range of other offenses. Moscoso Pérez told me of a friend who had to flee to Chile rather than face eight months in prison. The friend's "crime," apparently, was singing in an assembly while the Puerta del Sol was occupied.

Cripping Austerity

My own circle of friends and acquaintances that summer was a disabled and queer one.[4] The bodies and body imagery I have thus far described, however, are not obviously or explicitly disabled, even if the capacity to write on the walls of the Banco de España in blood does, at the very least, suggest a wound or injury, with "blood" serving as the trace of a body that has been hurt or damaged in some way. The connections between disability and the 15-M movement were nonetheless quite explicit for some activists. The Foro de Vida Independiente y Divertad (FVID) [Forum for Independent Living and Diversity/Liberty] had emerged in Spain a decade earlier and put into circulation the concept of "Diversidad Funcional" [Functional Diversity], now used by many activists in numerous Spanish-speaking locations as the preferred term for talking about disability. Romañach described the emergence of FVID as "un mini 15M diez años antes de aquel" [a mini 15-M movement ten years before the fact] (qtd. in Arenas Conejo and Pié Balaguer). In 2011, significant efforts were made to ensure that the encampments in Madrid and Barcelona were accessible, and the global disability activist phrase "nada sobre nosotros, sin nosostros" [nothing about us without us] helped fuel the general "proceso de construcción del nuevo 'nosotros'" [process of construction of the new "we"] that Los Indignados were defiantly putting forward; "nada sobre nosotros sin nosotros" became, in this new context, "no nos representan" [they don't represent us] (Arenas Conejo and Pié Balaguer 236, 239). As the 15-M movement in general attempted to theorize precarity and vulnerability, the already established disability movement became a site for understanding those concepts as central and textured components of human experience (Arenas Conejo and Pié Balaguer 239).[5]

Most studies of austerity, however, have noted neither disability's centrality to a global austerity politics nor the nuanced ways, as in Spain, that disability might serve as a site from which to understand and resist that politics. Mark Blyth's important book *Austerity: The History of a Dangerous Idea* makes no mention of disability, and even David Stuckler and Sanjay Basu's *The Body Economic: Why Austerity Kills*, while focusing on public health in various locations, and opening with very personal illness narratives, has no entry for "disability" in the index.[6] *Crip Times* thus in many ways simply aims to make explicit and central what is implicit and peripheral in other studies. The project "crips" contemporary capitalist globalization, or more precisely, crips the global economic crisis that is largely offered up as justification for the austerity we are now enduring and which does not promise to go away any time soon. *Crip Times* crips this crisis by specifically adding crip and queer perspectives to studies that are seeking to analyze the cultural logic of neoliberalism and the austerity that is now part and parcel of it. Analyzing the "cultural logic of neoliberalism" more generally, simply entails asking how cultural formations and movements circulate around, emerge from, and resist the hegemonic global political economy of neoliberal capitalism.[7]

"Creeping privatization" and "crippling austerity" are phrases that currently travel rather freely through global media (although not necessarily or consistently through the mainstream media); "cripping austerity" (my subheading in this section, and a phrase I have often used during the completion of this book to describe its central aim), not so much.[8] Indeed, I have sometimes been "corrected" by interlocutors hearing me use crip as a verb to describe an action that might be performed *upon* austerity. "Surely when you said 'cripping austerity,' you meant 'crippling austerity,'" one writer from the right-wing Heritage Foundation informed me condescendingly. It's not a misunderstanding that bothers me particularly (although members of the Heritage Foundation are definitely not the presumed audience for this book), as I do believe it's useful to imagine that we are living in what I will call crip times, and I welcome the opportunity to think about what that might mean and to translate some of the edgy and powerful valences of *crip* (as noun, verb, and adjective) to readers or listeners unfamiliar with the term. *Crip Times* is obviously concerned from start to finish with disability (even as it hopes to open up capaciously the many generative ways the term *disability* has functioned or might function). Nonetheless, some discussion of the other central terms of my analysis (on a basic level, *neoliberalism* and *austerity*, but even more importantly, *crip* and *crip times*) is important at the outset, particularly for readers outside crip culture, disability activism, or the interdisciplinary field of disability studies. I define my key terms in the remainder of this section before decidedly pivoting, in the remaining sections of this Introduction, to the UK.

Neoliberalism

Neoliberalism has been the dominant political economy since the 1980s; the architects of neoliberalism emphasized both the centrality of an unencumbered "free" market and the state's complex role in vouchsafing that centrality. The neoliberal state is often imagined, or positioned rhetorically, as a small, supposedly noninterventionist and nonregulatory state, but as Richard Seymour quite rightly explains, and as my Spanish examples from 2011 underscore, "the neoliberal state is a big interventionist state," especially in its penal, police, or military forms; the neoliberal state, as Seymour puts it in his important study *Against Austerity: How We Can Fix the Crisis They Made*, "is *ever more involved* in organising corporate dominance" (10, 11). In Chile under Augusto Pinochet (followed quickly by other repressive regimes in the Southern Cone), in the United Kingdom under Margaret Thatcher, and in the United States under Ronald Reagan, neoliberalism was consolidated and slowly globalized through the state-driven privatization and deregulation of forces that would block the sacrosanct "free flow" of capital. In the process, the state was indeed, in one very specific sense, downsized through profound cuts to public social services, but it has been, in some ways paradoxically, deeply interventionist states around the globe that have managed that downsizing.

Especially in Chile and the Southern Cone, the consolidation of new regimes of private property and the control of vibrant, democratic public cultures were often secured through violence, repression, and the literal, state-sanctioned disappearance of dissidents. Naomi Klein, in her landmark book *The Shock Doctrine: The Rise of Disaster Capitalism*, argues more generally that the engineers of neoliberalism have consistently relied on or actively deployed "shock" to push their ideas through. Klein looks to both "natural" and human-made disasters in *The Shock Doctrine*, recognizing of course that even "natural" disasters such as Hurricane Katrina in 2004 are simultaneously "human made" in many ways (through callous disregard for the environment, through neglect of infrastructure, through underfunding of state-supported emergency services, and so forth). The point for Klein is that not only military coups and wars, but also earthquakes and hurricanes, and of course economic "crises," have provided both a shock and a "blank slate" for imposing usually quite unpopular ideas on suffering populations already reeling from the disaster at hand. For example, after the violent September 11, 1973 coup that brought Pinochet to power (and that deposed and drove to suicide the democratically elected president Salvador Allende), Klein writes that the University of Chicago-trained economists ("Chicago boys") around Pinochet were experiencing "giddy anticipation and deadline adrenaline" (94). The coup and its aftermath were to provide, finally, a laboratory for putting into place the ideas of economist Milton Friedman that they held sacred: "privatization, deregulation and cuts to social spending—the free-market trinity" (94). Similar giddy anticipation would erupt repeatedly among the power brokers of neoliberalism following countless shocks around the world over the next four decades.

Neoliberalism institutes "flexible" production, or "just in time" production, that is often outsourced to locations with cheaper labor costs, usually in the Global South. Having resources for production "just in time" means that the materials needed for production are never (inefficiently) stockpiled; the demand for products in various locations, moreover, is assessed more continuously and rigorously to avoid overproduction. David Harvey explains that the " 'just-in-time' principle . . . minimises the cost of idle inventories": "producers deal with suppliers directly and, with optimal scheduling and supply models, transmit orders for components directly back down their supply chain" (*Enigma* 68). The flexible efficiency of this globalized model of production stands in stark contrast to the Fordist mass production of the mid-twentieth century, which (with its innovative factories) was efficient in its moment but depended upon less than "optimal" forms of communication and delivery to and from its assembly lines. This efficiency of production has been coupled with an "efficiency" of sorts, of consumption; in and through its flexibility and speed, as neoliberalism has congealed, it has relied on or produced "new forms of niche consumerism" (Harvey, *Enigma* 131), constructing or hypostasizing target markets or identities—particular, defined groups to whom a streamlined "just-in-time" production could cater.[9]

Niche consumerism is one of the ways in which individualism has been reinvented or repackaged for our times (consumption, in other words, has been hyper-individualized). The other dominant way in which individualism has been repackaged is more obviously punitive, as neoliberalism depends not only upon fetishized notions of consumer "choice" but also upon related notions of "personal responsibility" (Duggan, *Twilight* 12). The neoliberal mandate for "personal responsibility" implicitly calls for and explicitly generates a constant monitoring of both self and others. Lisa Duggan writes that "social service functions are *privatized* through *personal responsibility* as the proper functions of the state are narrowed, tax and wage costs in the economy are cut, and more social costs are absorbed by civil society and the family" (*Twilight* 15–16). Rhetorics of personal responsibility, perhaps unsurprisingly, have been particularly pronounced in the United States, but they are increasingly central in other locations such as Britain.

Austerity

Despite its different valences in different locations, contemporary *austerity* is a response to the crises of twenty-first century neoliberal capitalism, and is in many ways simply neoliberalism intensified, even as the fantasy of consumer choice is positioned as out of reach for more and more people. Like neoliberalism more generally, austerity is characterized by a lowering of government spending, an increasing of labor hours for workers (hence, the raising of the retirement age in Spain), cuts to benefits and social services, and—wherever possible—privatization of those social services. All these measures, in the age of austerity, are imposed to again spur capitalist growth that has stalled and to protect thereby the profits of capitalists through the crises. Austerity is generally wrapped up in rhetorics of emergency, whether the topic is reducing a national debt, paying for an International Monetary Fund (IMF) loan, or protecting banks from catastrophic loss. The supposed need for "emergency" austerity measures in so many locations was so pronounced in the years after 2008, that National Public Radio in the United States (now simply called "NPR") reported that *austerity* had been named word of the year in 2010 by Merriam-Webster's dictionary. NPR has itself since been a victim of austerity politics, as its budget has been slashed, a range of diverse programming cut, and staff reduced (Goldstein; Carney).[10]

Like Klein in her general overview of disaster capitalism, Mark Blyth—in his own history of what the subtitle of his book terms that "dangerous idea," austerity—focuses on multiple locations, noting at the current moment that "German ideals of fiscal prudence clash with Spanish unemployment at 25 percent and a Greek state . . . slashing itself to insolvency and mass poverty while being given ever-more loans to do so" (2). The United States, meanwhile, has been marked by "a hollowing out of middle-class opportunities, and a gridlocked state" that, despite its gridlock (which might suggest fractures in a consensus), has generally not advanced alternatives to the economic order that has been dominant for more than three decades (2). "If we view each of these elements in isolation, it all looks rather chaotic," Blyth writes, but "what they have in common is their supposed cure: austerity, the policy of cutting the state's budget to promote growth" (2). Ongoing loans for Greece have come on the condition that harsher and harsher cuts be imposed on citizens (even though the Greek population voted overwhelmingly in 2015 to reject those conditions); the gridlocked state in the United States has often resulted from Republican refusals to act until more austere budgets are pushed through the legislature; and so forth. Post-2008, austerity has been the ubiquitous neoliberal cure for the global economic crisis.

Even if a consensus that austerity does not actually work is legible in many economic analyses and (clearly) in popular opinion, in most locations some form of austerity politics is still nonetheless put forward as "common sense" across the mainstream political spectrum.[11] This seeming-consensus has certainly been evident for more than thirty years in the United States, with the Democrats and the Republicans, but also until recently in Spain, with the PSEO and the PP; it is evident, as we shall see, in the UK, with the Conservative (Tory) Party on one side, and "New Labour" as it emerged at the turn of the century under Tony Blair and Gordon Brown on the other. That consensus has shown multiple fractures over the course of writing this book, with emergent parties of the Left (Syriza for a time in Greece, Podemos in Spain) or the left wing of the Labour and Democratic parties in the United Kingdom and the United States openly, if very unevenly, critiquing the consensus around austerity and imagining alternatives.[12] However, given how thoroughly austerity has succeeded as what Richard Seymour rightly calls a "class strategy," it is not likely "that the Left will be able to simply stop austerity in its tracks, and immediately reverse its successes thus far" (*Against* 29, 152).

As a transnational class strategy responding to the global crisis, austerity has served well as the pretext for managing "crisis," and it has had as its effect the ongoing (and indeed astronomical) upward redistribution of wealth. Following the September 2015 election, by party members, of the socialist Jeremy Corbyn as leader of the Labour Party in the UK (and thus as the official leader of the opposition party), the editors of *Salvage: A New Quarterly of Revolutionary Arts and Letters* (including Seymour), observing that class strategy suddenly thrown into sharp relief through Corbyn's challenge to the New Labour consensus, wrote that the struggle against austerity, and neoliberal capitalism more generally, "will refract through its own institutional and ideological character the conflict that cleaves society as a whole, that between exploiter and exploited, between oppressor and oppressed. And the odds in that conflict remain stacked heavily in favour of the habitual victors" ("Pessimism"). Although *Crip Times* turns repeatedly toward generative activist and artistic responses from 2011 forward, to a global austerity politics, I share Seymour's (and his coeditors') caution and pessimism about the ease with which austerity might be countered, given the immense political and economic power of those who would sustain it and who have profited immensely from its implementation, *regardless* of whether it has "succeeded" or "failed" (on its own ostensible terms) as an economic strategy.[13]

Crip

Austerity bites, as one recent title out of the UK would have it; Mary O'Hara's *Austerity Bites* details stories of the current hardship faced by poor and working-class populations in the country.[14] Partly because of that bite, however, *austerity* is probably the most readily accessible (and widely disseminated) keyword in my study. The terms *crip*, or *cripping*, however, as I suggested, could use more framing. In some ways, like *queer*, *crip* as a noun has had a variegated history. *Crip* has clearly been a derogatory term (derived in English again, from the word *cripple*) and will always, I contend, carry traces of a painful history of stigma and derision. *Crip* has, however, in the face of this, been a term that has been reclaimed by many disabled people and groups themselves. Even more than *disability* itself (which also has been reclaimed and resignified to mean something different from, or in excess of, lack or loss), *crip* has functioned for many as a marker of an in-your-face, or out-and-proud, cultural model of disability. As Snyder and Mitchell explain, a cultural model of disability recognizes "disability as a site of phenomenological value that is not purely synonymous with the processes of social disablement" (*Cultural* 5). Given that disabled people themselves have done the labor of resignifying *crip*, *crip* is not opposed to *disability* (far from it; *crip* arguably revels in disability). *Crip* does, however, generally stand in opposition to both the medical model, which would reduce disability to the univocality of pathology, diagnosis, or treatment/elimination, and to some forms of the well-known social model, largely developed in the UK, which suggest that *disability* should be understood as located not in bodies per se but in inaccessible environments requiring adaptation. *Crip*'s excessive, flamboyant defiance ties it to models of disability (and to uses of the term *disability*) that are more culturally generative (and politically radical) than a merely reformist social model.

Although the historical connections of *crip* to *cripple* seem to tie the term to mobility impairment, it has actually proven to be far stretchier. A recent set of two special issues of the *Journal of Literary and Cultural Disability Studies*, coedited by Merri Lisa Johnson and me and focusing on "Cripistemologies" (a term coined by Johnson), positions *crip* as describing well what we might see as non-normative or nonrepresentative disabilities—disabilities, shall we say, that would never be legible beneath the universal access symbol for disability. Several essays included focus on what Anna Mollow terms "undocumented disabilities" ("Criphystemologies" 185); others focus specifically on borderline personality, anxiety, chronic pain, HIV/AIDS, trans identity, and a range of other forms of embodiment or impairments at times not always adequately or easily comprehended by the signifier *disability*. Likewise, throughout her important study *Feminist, Queer, Crip*, Alison Kafer at times uses the term to think carefully about issues, mental states, behaviors, or forms of embodiment that might not, on the surface, appear to be about disability at all. For Kafer and others, *crip* has the capacity to encompass forms of embodiment or states of mind that are arguably in excess of the able-minded or able-bodied/disabled binary. Not unlike *queer* at its most radical, *crip* often has the fabulous potential to be simultaneously flamboyantly identitarian (as in, we are crip and you will acknowledge that!) and flamboyantly anti-identitarian (as in, we reject your categories or the capacity of languages saturated in ableism to describe us!).[15] As my use of "we" here suggests, and as Kafer's study explicitly affirms throughout, the politics of *crip* have generally been actively collective or coalitional.

There have certainly been necessary debates about the limited or situated value of the word. I myself sought to encourage such debates when, in 2006 in *Crip Theory: Cultural Signs of Queerness and Disability*, I listed a range of terms that have performed similar critical work and insisted that *crip* should be "permanently and desirably contingent: in other queer, crip, and queercrip contexts, squint-eyed, half dead, not dead yet, gimp, freak, crazy, mad, or diseased pariah have served, or might serve, similar generative functions. . . . Crip is a critical term [that] in various times and places must be displaced by other terms" (40, 41). Both *Crip Theory* and *Feminist, Queer, Crip*—as this list of varied, contingent, and shifting queercrip contexts hopefully affirms—situate *crip* itself as generally emergent from activist and artistic cultural locations of disability, even as it has been taken up at this point in a wide range of transnational academic locations (which can, of course, themselves be activist and/or artistic).

Eli Clare is one artist and activist who has written thoughtfully about *crip*; in *Exile and Pride: Disability, Queerness, and Liberation*, Clare explicitly uses the first-person plural to explain how "we in the disability rights movement create crip culture, tell crip jokes, identify a sensibility we call crip humor" (68). For Clare, creative deployments of *crip* differentiate it from the more individualistic *supercrip*. Supercrips have often been critiqued for participating in ableist "overcoming" narratives, as though disability represented an adversity over which one must "triumph" (through athletic competition or daring adventures, for example).[16]

Clare appeared with numerous other disabled artists in Mitchell and Snyder's groundbreaking 1995 documentary *Vital Signs: Crip Culture Talks Back*, with the very title suggesting that *crip* is connected to disability community, solidarity, outspokenness, and defiance. *Crip*, in all these senses, has not been limited to the United States; in the UK the cartoonist Crippen has generated biting critiques of both ableist ideas generally and austerity in particular, and performer Liz Carr has created "crip radio" through a podcast called "Ouch!" available on the BBC's disability website. In Australia, comedienne and disability activist Stella Young produced a comedy performance called "Tales from the Crip" aimed at affirming disabled people's sexuality while mocking ableist notions that disabled people should be "inspirational" (she even wore a T-shirt that read "Inspiration Boner Killer"). "I identify with the crip community," Young said in a 2012 interview, "I didn't invent the word—it's a political ideology I came to in my late teens and early 20s. People often say to me 'You can't say that!' and I say, 'Well, my people have been saying it for decades so I reckon I probably can'" (Northover). Back in the United States, Mike Ervin has blogged as "Smart Ass Cripple" since 2010 on the "official site for bitter cripples (and those who love them)." Leroy Moore has invented an African American, disabled, and genderqueer cultural form called Krip-Hop—with the K, for Moore, marking a distance from the C of the Los Angeles–based gang called the Crips. Aiming to bring hip-hop artists and poets with disabilities to a wider audience, Krip-Hop has been integrated into some of the performances of Sins Invalid, a troupe celebrating the beauty, desirability, and diversity of queer and disabled people of color.

Usage of the term as an adjective in cases such as these underscores its generative character: when combined with a noun (crip community, crip culture, Krip-Hop), "crip" as adjective is not simply additive. Describing something like culture as "crip" remakes the substance in question: "crip culture" is not simply crip + culture (as if we all agreed in advance what the latter term might mean). In the same ways that "crip" as noun does not simplistically mark a form of existence that can be known in advance, "crip" as adjective cannot be reduced to a mere descriptor. The term's power when used as a verb in turn emanates from its uses as a noun or adjective. Queer disability theorist Mel Y. Chen has written about "animacy," which he describes as the degree of "liveness" associated with an entity or term. Animacy hierarchies, for Chen, have generally fixed, or deadened, that which has been understood as queer or disabled. For Chen, "a queer-crip approach to disability" is marked, in contrast, by an enlivening or "disentangling of the discourses . . . that contain and fix dis/abled bodies" (215). Whether as noun, adjective, or verb, *crip* has participated in what Chen identifies as "reworldings that challenge the order of things" (237).

To crip or not to crip is not the question for many writers, artists, and activists as the crip times I describe below demand action. We are, however, still collectively discovering what it might or can mean "to crip" and, as a verb, the term is still perhaps best defined by what it might potentially become (as a process) than by what it is. Two important conferences in Prague, the Czech Republic, that postdate the global economic crisis—Cripping Neoliberalism in 2010 and Cripping Development in 2013—implied in their titles that *cripping* entails radically revisioning, from committed anti-ableist positions, the taken-for-granted systems in which we are located. "Cripping Neoliberalism" and "Cripping Development" interrogated fetishized notions of capitalist growth and highlighted how bodies and minds are unevenly caught up in, or differentially materialize around, global processes of uneven development. The location of the 2010 and 2013 conferences outside the United States or western Europe notably indicated a desire to find new languages useful for thinking about disability and impairment in the Global South or postsocialist countries.[17]

Crip and *cripping* can certainly be positioned alongside a range of terms that represent the need for new or multiple languages for thinking about disability. For some scholars, such as Julie Livingston and Jasbir K. Puar, *debility* has played a key role in the development of new, critical vocabularies. *Debility* is useful, in particular, for Livingston's work in Botswana, where no word translates easily into "disability," but where a concept is nonetheless needed for encompassing a range of "experiences of chronic illness and senescence, as well as disability per se" (113). I am very sympathetic to this work, and *debility* arguably describes well many of the bodily experiences I consider in the pages ahead. Puar, however, often explicitly offers up *debility* as part of a supersession narrative, or what she describes as "a move from disability to debility" ("Prognosis" 166).[18] *Crip* and *cripping*, in contrast, do not assume in advance that *disability*, especially as it is worked on and across by artists and activists and not just by state and capital, is always and everywhere exhausted.

Crip has crossed some borders relatively easily and has, at this point, moved in and out of various languages. One of the first special issues of an academic journal on crip theory (titled *Cripteori*) was a bilingual (English and Swedish) special issue out of Scandinavia; the issue carefully examined both the multiple *and always contested* ways in which the term had been taken up by a range of subjects in Norway, Finland, Sweden, Denmark, and Iceland. The activist, anticapitalist newspaper or zine *Crip Magazine*, out of Vienna, Austria, was also bilingual (English and German). *Crip* resonates strongly with some radical queer and disability activists in Spanish-speaking and German-speaking locations generally (in German, the contemporary history of *crip* partially intersects with the longer history of the *Krüppel* Movement, although the ways in which the term currently travels in German-speaking locations, perhaps especially in connection to radical groups in Vienna, seems to me to be semiautonomous from that movement).[19] In Spain, Moscoso Pérez and others have begun to talk about "cripwashing" as a complicated process of state control or domestication of disability liberation, using the very language of disability activism (170). "La teoría *crip*," Lucas Platero suggests, is potentially translated as "literalmente teoría tullida" ("Políticas" 11); in Spanish contexts, la teoría tullida or crip has been used as a tool for naming or exposing neoliberal appropriations of radical visions of disability activism and coalition.[20] Theorizing similar appropriations in a Czech context, Kateřina Kolářová uses the idea of "the inarticulate post-socialist crip" to describe impaired or disabled (and socialist) modes of being that have been silenced by celebratory neoliberal uses of disability during the transition to capitalism in eastern Europe (257).

"To crip," like "to queer," gets at processes that unsettle, or processes that make strange or twisted.[21] *Cripping* also exposes the ways in which able-bodiedness and able-mindedness get naturalized and the ways that bodies, minds, and impairments that should be at the absolute center of a space or issue or discussion get purged from that space or issue or discussion. Such purging has tended to be in the service of the smooth functioning of a globalized neoliberal capitalism, which is (as should be clear from my Spanish and Czech examples above) one reason why the term has had such resonance with more radical disabled activists (since it exposes or disrupts that smooth functioning).

Cripping always attends to the materiality of embodiment at the same time that it attends to how spaces, issues, or discussions get "straightened." The critical act of cripping, I argue, resists "straightening" in a rather more expansive sense than we might think of straightening, at the moment, in queer studies, activism, or art. This is in part because the radical power of *queer* has been diluted by global commodification processes that have not (yet) domesticated *crip* or contained and commodified what Mia Mingus terms "crip solidarity" ("Wherever You Are"). For disability radicals, *crip* is a keyword that currently connects to what queer of color and crip of color theorists such as Mingus have begun to call "disability justice" ("Changing"). Disability justice moves beyond mere rights-based and nation-state–based strategies (represented most prominently by the Americans with Disabilities Act). It also forges anti-neoliberal coalitions in the interests of a global crip imagination, which can invent new ways of countering oppression and generate new forms of being-in-common.

Crip Britain

Crip Times, the book, as I have indicated, largely centers on one location, the UK. It repeatedly spins out, however, to other places as it traces both the globalization and resistance of my subtitle. For many disabled people living there, the UK has certainly felt like ground zero for austerity since the early 2000s. Crip times, the concept, thus attempts to capture what has been happening, during that time, in the UK. Some readers will note echoes of "New Times" in my title; those echoes are deliberate.[22] "New Times" was a phrase used by Stuart Hall, Martin Jacques, and other cultural studies writers associated with the journal *Marxism Today* in the 1980s. Jacques edited *Marxism Today* between 1977 and 1991, when the journal stopped publication. A volume called *New Times*, collecting a series of articles published in *Marxism Today* and selected other pieces (including, importantly, critiques), was published in 1989 and was edited by Hall and Jacques. Some of the articles in the volume had first appeared in a special issue of *Marxism Today* published in late 1988. During its existence, *Marxism Today* was the official journal of the Communist Party of Great Britain, although during the time of Jacques's editorship, contributions (and readership) came from the Left more broadly, including eventually the liberal or center-Left that would become associated with New Labour. Many of the pieces associated with the special issue and the 1989 collection emerged from direct conversations held in May 1988, as the writers gathered to make sense of contemporary Britain.

In the *New Times* volume and special issue, writers exploring the concept of "New Times" were attempting to account for shifts in the economic, political, cultural, and critical landscape under Thatcherism (a term coined by Hall himself), although they were also attempting to think beyond Thatcherism (Hall, "Great Moving" 14). Thatcherism and neoliberalism more broadly were positioned as phenomena marking a decisive shift, a new hegemonic formation, and the writers in *New Times* were interested in theorizing how popular consent to that formation had been secured. Hall himself considered various ways that the shift was being described ("'post-industrial,' 'post-Fordist,' 'revolution of the subject,' 'postmodernism'"), recognizing at the time that none of these terms was "wholly satisfactory" for describing what was taking place ("Meaning" 117).

The Labour Party had faced dramatic losses in 1983, as Thatcher was reelected, although Klein (and others) would later argue that the manufactured "shock" of the Falklands War altered Thatcher's fortunes and allowed her to continue pushing through unpopular ideas and policies (in particular, defeating striking mine workers in the two years that followed the general election) (Klein 163–176). A critique of Labour Party politics in the UK, and of a politics focused solely on class and located largely with labor unions, emerged from this turbulent period and was a component of the *New Times* debates and anthology; Hall, Rosalind Brunt, and others were emphatic that the Left needed to account more actively for the changes wrought by "the politics of identity" (Brunt 150) and a wide variety of social movements (feminism most specifically, but also movements focused on race, sexuality, and the environment).

Disability as such (as a substantive entity that, even potentially, might be part of these new social movements) is only mentioned a handful of times in the 463-page volume. David Marquand points out that post-Fordism has generated a "growing underclass of the handicapped and unskilled" (374). Beatrix Campbell, interviewing a range of people across the UK living in what she calls "New Times Towns" (279), mentions "disabled access" as part of a changing urban landscape and specifically identifies Chris Sharp, who ran the Pinehurst Training Initiative in Swindon and advised business owners there on "facilities for the disabled" (292, 294). Geoff Mulgan, in another essay on the changing face of cities, suggests that new communications infrastructures allow for new forms of communication, such as "teleshopping for the old and disabled" (267); a page later, he notes that city cards (allowing access to various urban spaces) allow for "discounts to the unemployed, pensioners or the disabled" (268). Sarah Benton gestures somewhat vaguely toward actual "movements" formed by "those disabled by injury, illness, or addiction" (343). Earlier in the volume, Robin Murray calls for new spatial organizations and "designs that take into account those needs which have no power in the market (like those of the disabled)" (61) and Charlie Leadbeater mentions "responsibilities to the poor and sick" (144). The latter two comments in particular identify "the disabled" in passing as subjects of concern in *New Times*, but in doing so, unintentionally imply that the disabled cannot really be subjects in their own right. The very grammar of these phrases, positioning disability and sickness as objects of prepositional phrases, underscores the illegibility of disability subjectivity in *New Times*.

In general, "disability" only appears in the *New Times* collection occasionally as a negative metaphor. Leadbeater, for instance, later suggests that, despite the changes that might be associated with *New Times*, nothing "disables the Left from having a powerful and coherent critique of Thatcherite individualism" (144). Other writers, including Hall himself, at the time and later, likewise considered how various elements of *New Times* might or might not "disable" the Left: "The conventional culture and discourses of the Left, with its stress on 'objective contradictions,' 'impersonal structures' and processes that work 'behind men's (*sic*) backs,' have disabled us from confronting the subjective dimension in politics in any very coherent way" ("Meaning" 120). Hall's *sic* in relation to "conventional" discourses of the Left is particularly ironic in this passage, calling attention to the ways in which our languages are always

saturated in masculinism immediately before deploying language inescapably saturated in ableism. The cosmopolitan knowingness of *sic erat
scriptum*, "thus was it written" (even if, of course, *we* would never write
it that way), colludes in blocking access, in *New Times*, to new ways of
knowing (and knowing with) disability.

Disability, however, is arguably present on a spectral theoretical level,
as Brunt, Hall, and others turn to the writings of (disabled) Italian Marxist Antonio Gramsci to develop a vocabulary adequate to the moment.
"Unless and until we have an adequate recognition of the ways identities
work," Brunt wrote, "we are not going to be effective at world-changing.
Antonio Gramsci, the pre-war Italian communist leader, was particularly acute on this point, as on many others, of how to make a politics
that was subjectively relevant" (153). It did not occur to the *New Times*
writers (or most other commentators since) that Gramsci's disability
(a curved spine and diminutive stature) might have influenced his insights into the role of identity in shaping and reshaping hegemonic cultural formations, despite the fact that Brunt points out that

> he was developing a different revolutionary vocabulary based on what
> he called "a critical awareness" that took as its first injunction the ancient
> Delphic wisdom, "Know thyself." Gramsci's point was that if revolution-
> aries were to develop a clear and coherent conception of the world they
> wanted to change they should make a start by asking how people expe-
> rienced the world as it was, how they got by and coped with it on a daily
> basis. (153–154)

Anne Finger, Tom Coogan, and a few others have since begun the process of thinking through, in ways *New Times* writers did not, Gramsci's
relevance for disability studies (and I will engage Finger's work momentarily, as well as in the Epilogue to *Crip Times*).[23]

New Times writers perhaps most controversially attempted to theorize
not just relations of production but of consumption and choice, working
to find languages that did not simply see consumers as duped by ideology but as actively participating in forging cultural forms and shaping
identities through their consumer choices. This was controversial because, even though Hall and others were trying to open up a generative
"gap, analytically, between Thatcherism and new times," they were still

taking some of the changes under Thatcherism (or aspects of Thatcherism) very seriously in order to ask whether "it *may* become possible to resume or re-stage the broken dialogue between socialism and modernity" (Hall, "Meaning" 127). According to many critics, then, the *New Times* thinkers appeared to be too captivated by the power, popularity, and spectacle of Thatcherism; their effort to discern new ways of thinking, these critics suggest, prepared the way for Blair and New Labour (and by analogy on the other side of the Atlantic, for New Democrats and Bill Clinton). Prior to his own ascension to power, Blair himself wrote a piece for *Marxism Today*. Mulgan would later work as an adviser to Brown.

After their losses in 1983, the British Labour Party did not win a general election until Tony Blair's victory in 1997. "New Labour," however, was a descriptor first used to describe a reinvented party in 1994, and a manifesto of New Labour's positions was published in 1996, with the title *New Labour, New Life for Britain*. The manifesto reflected the party's new commitment to the "third way" politics legible in other locations. This politics was dubbed "third way" because it supposedly reconciled right wing economic policies with more liberal social policies; third way thinking defined both Labour under Blair and Brown and the US Democratic Party under Clinton. As Lisa Duggan and others have shown clearly, "'third way' parties and leaders labored to combine pro-market, pro-business, 'free trade' national and global policies with shrunken remnants of the social democratic and social justice programs of Western welfare states" (*Twilight* 9–10). The "third way" politics of New Labour and of Clintonism really only continued neoliberalism in new guises, often in guises that *appeared* to validate or celebrate "difference" and diversity. For his part, Hall was quick to distance himself from the "change" Tony Blair and New Labour represented in the UK, and Hall's own cultural studies effort to develop new vocabularies for thinking about the transition, "from one regime of accumulation to another, within capitalism, whose impact has been extraordinarily wide-ranging" (Hall, "Meaning" 127), can hardly be blamed for the rise of third way thinking. Still, some *New Times* writers (such as Mulgan) were more directly implicated in the rise of third way thinking and (by extension) the dissolution of a rigorous analysis of class in Britain. Jacques himself expressed some enthusiasm at the moment of Blair's emergence, but even before he became prime minister, Hall and Jacques had published an article arguing that "Blair embodies the ultimate pessimism—that there is only one version of modernity, the one elaborated by the Conservatives over the last 18 years" (qtd. in Harris). The journal returned for one issue in 1998 to denounce "the Blair project," with a cover picturing Blair with the word "Wrong" written below his face (Harris).

Crip Times looks back to this history to look forward; I intend the title to signify in at least three ways. First, given the traces of pain and stigma that, as I indicated, *crip* always and inevitably carries, "crip times" can hardly convey any straightforward or simplistic cheeriness about the possibilities before us. I would argue, against some of its critics, that "new times" also was not simplistically optimistic (indeed, Hall and Jacques explicitly said as much in their Introduction [17]), while conceding that optimism is nonetheless more obviously or inescapably written on the surface of the "new times" 1980s phrase. "Crip times," in contrast, are obviously harsh times, even—we might add—virtually Dickensian "hard times," and my title thus in some ways allows me to have it both ways, agreeing with *New Times* theorists that a new and decisive shift has taken place with the emergence of neoliberal capitalism while also recognizing and partially agreeing with other contemporary Marxist thinkers who want to foreground not a shift but rather the deep similarities between our moment and say, the worst ravages of industrial capitalism in Victorian England.[24] Second, nonetheless, "crip times" sustains and extends the insistence that we must think about what Hall terms the revolution of the subject—extending that insistence, in particular, given that, as I suggested, *disabled* subjectivities, experiences, and social movements were not obviously central to the *New Times* project (and even though, significantly, radical AIDS activism on both sides of the Atlantic was coming into its own, and Hall himself would write a few years later about how the HIV/AIDS pandemic was one reason why we so desperately needed the work that cultural theory and cultural studies could do) ("Cultural Studies" 272–273). Finally, "crip times" does mark, in and through the harsh and austere moment we inhabit, promise and possibility. To adapt the words of crip artist Riva Lehrer (as she describes "these people I'm falling in love with"), a group of "really amazing crips" has materialized since the late twentieth century (qtd. in Snyder and Mitchell, *Self-Preservation)*. To judge by the sheer amount of cultural production and consciousness they have generated, these really amazing crips are arguably a collectivity that had not existed before in exactly the same way. That crip collectivity is now being (transnationally) radicalized by austerity, and collectively generating resistance to the inadequate resolutions to economic, political, and social "crises" preferred by the guardians of neoliberalism, or by any single state. I contend that the paradoxical ways in which "crip times" carries both harshness and potentiality, along with the simple fact that the crip radicalization traced in this book is the direct result of an age of austerity, should demand a consistent focus on *both* "identity" (in its complex and ever-shifting valences) and on the class dynamics and analysis that critics of *New Times* worried was in danger of being lost.

In many ways, although the chapters ahead have many layers, my theses in *Crip Times* are relatively straightforward and, I hope, consistent across the cultural locations of disability I survey in this book. Disability, as I have suggested, is one of the undertheorized central issues of a global austerity politics. Surveying the ways in which activists and artists are responding to crip times, I contend that crips *themselves* are globally putting forward this thesis about disability's centrality and that, in some locations, their demand for disability justice is starting to register. Disability in our neoliberal moment, however, simultaneously exists as never before as a niche, an identity, even a market that is potentially quite useful (in varied ways that I will detail) to the guardians of austerity politics. Disability, in that dangerous situation, has *some* circumscribed potential to go the way of a globalized, commodified queerness, even if, as I have intimated, *disability* and *crip* both retain in our moment a certain critical possibility or promise not always palpable (any more, or as much) around *queer*. Finally, the path that cripping takes (that is, which way "disability" pivots in this dangerous moment) is wrapped up in affect, or rather a vacillation between the politics of affect (deployed quite effectively by state and capital to sustain the class strategy of austerity) and what Jasbir K. Puar and others have theorized as affective politics (*Terrorist* 215). Deborah Gould uses "the term *affect* to indicate nonconscious and unnamed, but nevertheless registered, experiences of bodily energy and intensity that arise in response to stimuli impinging on the body" (19). Affect in social movements, Gould argues, is indicative of potentiality; "affective states can shake one out of deeply grooved patterns of thinking and feeling and allow for new imaginings" (27). A crip affective politics is discernible, I will argue in this book, in and through various forms of excessive and flamboyant, activist and artistic, crip resistance.

What has been happening since 2010 in the UK (and in the Eurozone) is in many ways not necessarily new, even if it is legible as a reaction to a new (post-2008) crisis in neoliberal capitalism. The cure for the current crisis in the United States and the UK, as well as in countries across Europe, is akin to the "structural adjustment" policies imposed on heavily indebted poor countries in the Global South by global financial institutions such as the World Trade Organization (WTO), International Monetary Fund (IMF), and World Bank (with centers of power in the United States and western Europe) since the 1970s. Austerity in the UK, and elsewhere in Europe and North America, in a way thus represents crip times coming home to roost, as it were.

From 2010 to 2015 in the UK, austerity was implemented by a coalition government, the first to exist in Britain since World War II. In the 2010 general election, the Conservative Party, led by David Cameron, did not receive enough seats in Parliament for an outright majority and during five days of negotiations in May 2010, it was not entirely clear that a new government could be formed. Although the centrist Liberal Democrats, under the leadership of Nick Clegg, had prior to the 2010 elections appeared to favor a rather different political and economic agenda, they agreed to enter into a coalition government with the Tories. After his loss, Gordon Brown, the New Labour leader who had been prime minister since 2007, resigned from that position a day after resigning as Labour Party leader. In the new coalition government, Cameron became prime minister and Clegg, deputy prime minister. Ed Miliband was subsequently elected as the new Labour Party leader.

Soon after the formation of the coalition, the Tories embarked on one of the most intense austerity agendas in the world, *ostensibly* to address the immense budget deficit that had been generated in Britain by the global economic crisis. Cameron appointed George Osborne as his chancellor of the exchequer (akin to the secretary of the treasury in the United States); Osborne would become one of the primary architects of the Tory–Liberal Democrat austerity plan. Iain Duncan Smith was appointed the secretary of state for work and pensions; Smith would execute the austerity plan by "reforming" welfare benefits in the UK. Although the coalition claimed repeatedly after 2010 that it did not plan to privatize the wildly popular British National Health Service (NHS), many commentators found this claim to be absolutely specious, as more and more elements of the NHS were altered, outsourced, or trimmed. The Health and Social Care Act of 2012 allowed for a dramatic restructuring of the NHS, devolving what had been organized by public Primary Care Trusts (PCTs) to local Clinical Commissioning Groups (CCGs). The CCGs would be responsible for deciding how health care would be organized and paid for; private organizations would be allowed to compete for the opportunity to provide care. The Health and Social Care Act explicitly used the (privatizing) language of choice and competition to describe the restructuring of the NHS that was being legislated.

In addition to these shifts in the ways in which national health care would be organized, the cuts to social services and benefits that emerged from Osborne's and Smith's program of austerity have been extreme. Moreover, in the general election of 2015, in an upset that few had predicted, the Tories won outright, and thus continued their austerity agenda without their coalition partners. In his 2010 budget, Osborne had laid out his intention of cutting £11 billion per year in benefits (following a drastic initial cut that was to be even larger) (Vale). In his 2015 budget, delivered a month after the Tories began governing alone, he announced that an additional £12 billion would be cut from the benefits budget. Osborne's 2015 budget was approved by Parliament in October that year. It in some ways made austerity in the UK permanent, as a component of the budget mandated that the government run a surplus in so-called "normal" years. Such a target, which accepted without question that deficits and deficit spending are signs of an ongoing "crisis," essentially precluded the possibility that the austerity cuts from 2010 to 2015 might be reversed. Although Corbyn as the new Labour leader rallied the opposition to vote against Osborne's budget, twenty-one New Labour members of Parliament abstained from the vote, tacitly affirming an ongoing cross-party common sense that some form of permanent austerity is necessary.

Cameron continued to govern as prime minister until July 2016, when he resigned following the results of a popular referendum he had called on British membership in the European Union. In a move dubbed "Brexit" (British exit), the country voted to leave the EU. Cameron, who had argued strongly against that result, stepped down and was shortly thereafter replaced by his former home secretary, Theresa May. Although I discuss Brexit briefly in my epilogue, *Crip Times* is largely about the Cameron years, when the Conservative austerity agenda was secured.[25] The politics of affect that has accompanied this agenda has been multivalent—a limited but spectacular celebration of disability and disability identity (most obvious around the London 2012 Olympic and Paralympic Games that I consider in chapter 1) having coexisted with a concerted campaign to cast recipients of benefits as "scroungers" or "spongers" or "shirkers." Although Thatcher herself rode to power as early as May 1978 rhetorically introducing phrases such as "we should back the workers and not the shirkers" (qtd. in Jones, *Chavs* 62), phrases such as "benefit scroungers" or "shirkers" did not appear with frequency in the British press prior to the Tory–Liberal Democrat coalition; they are now ubiquitous.[26] "Shirkers" are generally opposed to "strivers" in the contemporary scenario, and "strivers" take a US-style, neoliberal "personal responsibility" for their actions. Popular culture has disseminated the idea of "scroungers," who supposedly *don't* take personal responsibility and who cheat the system, in numerous venues, most infamously perhaps in the series *Benefits Street* that aired on Britain's Channel 4 in January 2014. *Benefits Street* followed the lives of residents of James Turner Street in Birmingham, supposedly a location with one of the highest number of benefits recipients in the country. Those living "life on the dole" (and *Benefits Britain: Life on the Dole* was in fact the title of yet another television "exposé," that aired on Channel 5) have been subject to a constant suspicion that turns attention *away from* class inequalities and *toward* (individualized) behavior. Owen Jones's *Chavs: The Demonization of the Working Class* makes clear that the stereotyping of poor people, especially poor youth, as dirty "chavs" (a derogatory term used to mock supposedly antisocial behavior and outlandish dress) has been a largely successful rhetorical strategy materializing what Cameron called in a key 2010 campaign speech a "Broken Britain" that needs behavioral change (and of course, "personal responsibility") more than anything like class solidarity or economic justice (which, from Thatcher's Britain to Cameron's, has been cast as completely anachronistic) (Jones, *Chavs* 78).

Cripping Gramsci is useful for understanding this harsh project of rhetorical disqualification. In her brief analysis of Gramsci's "Some Aspects of the Southern Question," Anne Finger notes that Gramsci offers "a granular dissection not only of how the interplay among class, religion, regional, and social differences maintained capitalism's power, but also for offering a sketch of how revolutionary alliances might be formed to contest capitalist hegemony." "Some Aspects of the Southern Question" was an unfinished piece left behind by Gramsci at the time of his imprisonment; it attends to the ways in which the gap between the North and South of Italy is sustained *discursively*, in ways that block revolutionary alliances. The implication Finger puts forward in her analysis of Gramsci's piece is that it is a sort of disability theory *avant la lettre*, in that Gramsci critiques the ways in which *both* "the propagandists of the bourgeoisie" *and* the Socialist Party disqualify Southerners by appealing, even "scientifically," to a supposedly innate corporeal inferiority: "if the South is backward, the fault does not lie with the capitalist system or with any other historical cause, but with Nature, which has made the Southerners lazy, incapable, criminal and barbaric" (qtd. in Finger). For Finger, this unfinished critique of bourgeois and Socialist Party rhetoric provides "in 'embryonic form' a reading of disability politics, one moreover that offers tantalizing hints about the links between disability and race." As *Crip Times* hopefully will make clear (especially in my Epilogue, but also, in varied ways, in the chapters that precede it), these links between disability and race are very much active in the contemporary disqualification of benefit scroungers.

In contrast to Gramsci's embryonic disability theory excavating how the Italian South was cast as essentially disabled (with its implicit critique of the ways in which what we might comprehend as disabled difference was *indirectly* targeted for scorn), the contemporary politics of affect stigmatizing recipients of benefits in the UK has often *directly* targeted disabled people. Liberals in general, New Labour, and also those much further on the Left have generally criticized this conservative campaign of rhetorical demonization. The critique of this stigmatizing rhetoric, however, has often quite interestingly come with a caveat. The caveat goes something like this: although no one denies that there are *some* people who have cheated the system in some way, the vast majority of benefits recipients are not trying to do so.[27] Critics of sponger or scrounger rhetoric often, quite earnestly, point to how *very small* the number of people is who have "cheated the system." Even Jones, for example, positions his sharp critique of the ways in which the Conservatives have mobilized the figure of the fraud on benefits alongside an acknowledgment that (of course) a small amount of fraud does happen (Jones, *Chavs* 196).

Crip Times avoids all caveats in this regard, in part drawing on a logic from AIDS cultural theory and activism. In *Melancholia and Moralism*, Douglas Crimp urges that we "recognize that every image of a PWA [Person with AIDS] is a *representation*, and formulate our activist demands not in relation to the 'truth' of the image, but in relation to the conditions of its construction and to its social effects" (99). Every image of a scrounger in crip times (even the scrounger who materializes in a caveat temporarily acknowledging that yes, a small percentage of poor people do take advantage of benefits) is likewise a representation, and *Crip Times* attends not to the argument about whether scroungers exist but to the conditions of construction of such representations and their social effects. Or, in the spirit of the crip playfulness and artistry that will be on display throughout this book, I will suggest that *if* scroungers *do* exist, they're fierce, fabulous, and committed to social justice for disabled people and opposed to their neoliberal spectacularization. As I put *those* scroungers before you, however, I'm explicitly putting forward a counter-representation, or arguing, as Hall does, for an ongoing attention not to the truth of a given representation but to the "politics of representation" ("New Ethnicities" 442). To illustrate what I mean, I turn in the next section to a brief and critical reading of a filmic representation, Tom Hooper's *The King's Speech*, which was produced in the same year (2010) that brought us the coalition and their austerity agenda.

The Crip's Speech in an Age of Austerity

In the UK itself, *The King's Speech* was specifically released, to great acclaim, in January 2011. It screened throughout much of that spring. In the United States, it went on to win Academy Awards for Best Picture, Best Director, Best Actor, and Best Screenplay. In this section, I use *The King's Speech* to reflect on what I will term *emergent disabilities*, or on emergent uses of disability in our moment. By "emergent uses of disability," I'm referring *both* to the ways in which disability is currently not repressed but managed by neoliberal biopower and indeed useful to its operation *and* to the ways in which disability exceeds that management.[28] By using Raymond Williams's term "emergent" to talk about disabilities *themselves*, I'm tentatively tracing the materialization of disabilities that I want to mark as somewhat different from the residual or dominant forms we think we know (Williams 121–127). The materialization of disabilities I consider took place in a range of locations, including onscreen in Hooper's film, in journalism in circulation around it, and in communities responding to those textual representations. As many disability studies analyses would have it, dominant forms of disability in cinema, in the words of Jay Dolmage, "make it sound scary and clinical." In the face of that clinical approach, however, most cinematic representations of disability, as Dolmage points out, "want to keep the disabled character cheerful. If that's not possible, the disability turns the character completely evil. It has to be one or the other" ("Hollywood"). While not entirely disagreeing with this recognizable critique, and while I will examine here a character who does, I concede, work his way toward a type of cheerfulness, I argue that his cheeriness (or evil) may be beside the point. I'm not sure, any longer, that it has to be one or the other. A crip politics of representation must attend to what Puar might term "the convivial relations between" the emergent neoliberal utility of certain disabled figures and disability identity, representation, and rights (*Terrorist* 117).[29]

Outside the theater, throughout the first half of 2011 various groups were mobilizing (or, we might say, keeping Hall's contestatory politics of representation in mind, were *scrounging together*) an initial response to the Tory-Liberal Democrat coalition's punishing program of cuts to social services. A range of protests, marches, and actions in 2011 brought together students, workers, pensioners, and—indeed, as part of all these actions—disabled people. A massive public sector strike, for example, was held in the UK on June 30, 2011, to protest the coalition government's cuts in general and specifically to protest changes to public sector pension plans, such as raising the retirement age from sixty to sixty-six. A "Unite the Resistance" meeting was held on June 22, in preparation for the strikes of June 30. A report on the meeting quoted a disabled activist whose name was given only as "Andy," and who insisted that disabled people would be "front and centre" of the movement against austerity cuts. Disabled people would take that position, Andy continued, "by right, not by charity" (qtd. in S. Robinson). There are many things I like about Andy's June 22 assertion; it is, to use the language with which I closed the previous section, fierce, fabulous, and committed to social justice. It also importantly conjures up, however, *tactical maneuvering at a specific historical moment*: "front and centre" implies positioning in relation to forces that are themselves, similarly, not fixed but rather constantly shifting.

Although in relation to the emergent disabilities I will trace in circulation around *The King's Speech*, I'm going to argue *against* disability rights, representation, and identity, I simultaneously want Andy's forceful words to reverberate throughout the rest of this Introduction in order to (of course) argue for them. I will work my way in conclusion toward what I hope is both an *amplification* and *resignification* of Andy's assertion that is still true to his militant intent. Put differently, in an effort to partially negate what I will theorize as "the crip's speech," I focus in this section on the complex ways that disability rights, representation, and identity currently function and circulate, and how they are, to stick with the language of positioning, corralled. Ultimately, though, I'm *not* exactly seeking to nullify any of them. This section of my chapter is necessarily paradoxical (or perhaps, more properly, dialectical), negating "the crip's speech" while simultaneously discerning within it the articulation of another world, one that might be comprehended as depending upon the inventive forms of transnational queer-crip activist and artistic relationality that are the primary subjects of this book. I attempted to foreground (and work through) similar seeming paradoxes throughout *Crip Theory*. For instance, in a consideration of the chunks of concrete dislodged by disability activists with sledgehammers at inaccessible street corners in the 1980s (activists whom I identified as "crip theorists in the street"), I wrote that the concrete is "simultaneously solid and disintegrated, fixed and displaced. . . . If from one perspective that chunk of concrete marks a material and seemingly insurmountable barrier, from another it marks the will to remake the material world" (35). Similarly, the "crip's speech" that I will trace in *The King's Speech* (and the rights, representation, and identity that subtend it) in many ways appears solid and inert, while the crip's speech that will emerge as this Introduction and project conclude is generatively disintegrated and displaced.[30]

Although *Crip Times* is almost entirely about disability, important, field-transforming work in queer studies, as I have suggested, provides one of its conditions of possibility—work such as Licia Fiol-Matta's *A Queer Mother for the Nation*, Lisa Duggan's *The Twilight of Equality?* or Puar's *Terrorist Assemblages*. These studies and many others in their wake have arguably shifted the starting line for queer theory—in other words, these theorists may have argued their way *toward* the ideas I will spotlight in this section, but now I would say a critical queer theory *begins* with them. They demonstrate not simply that queer relationality at times fails to usher in a more just social order but also that it can actively collude with exploitation and hierarchization—with, for instance, patriarchy, racism, imperialism, class oppression—to shut down queer possibility, becoming, or world-making. As Fiol-Matta looks critically at the political and literary career of Chilean Nobel laureate Gabriela Mistral, for example, analyzing aspects of Mistral's life that might be understood as "queer" (a decidedly non-normative gender presentation, a series of affairs with women, a very public and yet spectacularly nonreproductive maternal identity), she argues that these non-normative, and even incoherent, aspects of Mistral's life were actually deployed to buttress racialized nationalisms, patriarchy, and state-sanctioned heteronormativity throughout the Americas. Structures of racism and heteronormativity, in other words, congealed *in and through* Mistral's queerness.[31] Other theorists, Duggan and Puar perhaps most prominently among them, have outlined similar queer problematics—marked in Duggan by the concept of "homonormativity," in Puar by concepts such as "homonationalism" (Duggan, "New Homonormativity" 175; Puar, *Terrorist* 2). For Duggan, a "new homonormativity," at the turn of the twenty-first century, emerges from third way politics and works with and not against "dominant heteronormative assumptions and institutions . . . while promising the possibility of a demobilized gay constituency and privatized, depoliticized gay culture anchored in domesticity and consumption" ("New Homormativity" 179). Homonationalism, for Puar, can be understood as a kind of "national homosexuality" that is in many ways sanctioned by state and capital and that colludes in the securitization and imperialism required to sustain and extend the reach of neoliberal capitalism (*Terrorist* 2). These latter analyses, of course, are more directly specific to our own moment and to the workings of queer relationality in and through neoliberal capitalism. They demonstrate, arguably, that neoliberalism can function very efficiently *with* queerness, and no matter how far back we intuited that fact (some *New Times* writers were already talking about gay niche markets emerging in the 1970s), this foundational early twenty-first century queer work fleshed it out.

As should be clear from my opening sections, I'm interested in theorizing how neoliberalism and the austerity that now undergirds it similarly work, in queer ways, in relation to disability and to crip forms of relationality. Of course, *The King's Speech* is not necessarily the most likely text to bring forward for such a project: 1930s Britain, when the film takes place, might have been an austere time for ordinary Britons; not so much (then as now) for the Royal Family. Still, perhaps surprisingly, I'll start by not trashing the film. *The King's Speech* tells the story of King George VI (Colin Firth), who assumes the throne in England in December 1936 after his brother Edward VIII abdicates in order to marry his mistress, a divorcee. "Bertie," as King George is known to his intimates, is a reluctant monarch represented by the film as doing what is necessary for the British Empire at a time of looming war with Germany (although the historical Edward VIII was a Nazi sympathizer, this complication is completely avoided in the film). Bertie's reluctance to rule is wound up with his fear of public speaking and a lifelong stammer (or stutter, as it is known in the United States). With the help of an Australian speech therapist named Lionel Logue (Geoffrey Rush), however, Bertie learns to speak more confidently with minimal stammering, and *The King's Speech* concludes with his nine-minute September 1939 radio address to the nation declaring that Britain is at war with Germany. As the film's thematic string music crescendos in the background, Britons of all social classes (and indeed around the globe) are represented gathering in front of radios to hear Bertie speak: "In this grave . . . hour . . . perhaps the most fateful in our history . . . I send to every household of my uh-peoples, both at home . . . and overseas, this message . . . speaking with the same depth of feeling for each one of you as if I was able to cross your threshold and speak to you myself."

I say "perhaps surprisingly" in relation to what I'll initially say about Hooper's film, because of my goal in this section of considering "emergent disabilities." If I were to simply trash *The King's Speech*, I would essentially be identifying it as more of the same, as we have in fact learned to identify the "same old, same old" for a few decades now in disability studies. *The King's Speech*, that is, is a sentimental, inspirational "overcoming" movie (meaning that it is clearly about the "triumph" *over* disability); it seems rather clearly designed for nondisabled consumption (disability activists and disability studies scholars have long critiqued the idea that one needs to "overcome" disability); it largely locates the problem not in the social context in which the disabled person finds himself but in his impairment (the problem is, in other words, King George VI of England's stammer); and it joins a very, very long list of films that present audiences with an actor (in this case Colin Firth) who is ultimately showered with awards for playing crip—the message being, "good for you Colin Firth [or Daniel Day Lewis, or Sean Penn, or Jack Nicholson, or Dustin Hoffman, or Tom Hanks, or or . . .], you can play this incredibly challenging role; here's your Golden Globe, your Oscar, your global admiration."

But crip times don't call for simply the same old, same old representation. It's Lewis, Penn, Nicholson, Hoffman, and Hanks that I contingently mark here as "residual"—in Williams's terms, "effectively formed in the past, but . . . still active in the cultural process" (122). I'm going to suggest that *The King's Speech* might be approached differently. In an effort to think in new ways about the uses of disability rights, representation, and identity in our moment, I'll start by examining some of the innumerable positive spins on the film (positive readings of the film that can be easily located both outside and inside disability cultures). The BBC's blogger Disability Bitch, for example, is a writer who usually, as she confesses, "tackles . . . controversial disability topics with all the subtlety of a hammer cracking a nut." Yet Disability Bitch finds herself quite surprised by *The King's Speech*, noting,

> Readers, I must be ill. . . . I went to the cinema and saw a film where a non-disabled man played a disabled monarch, and I didn't find myself overcome with hatred. . . . [The film] was scripted by a bloke who stammers himself and it was, y'know, kinda quite good, actually. . . . It's become a boring cliché. Yet again a Normal actor's going to win big prizes

for playing Abnormal. I'm Disability Bitch. I'm supposed to be throwing popcorn at the screen in protest, I think. Instead, I merely shrugged and noted that there are informative articles about stammering in every single newspaper in the world this week. And I'm only slightly exaggerating.

Indeed, Disability Bitch might have added, the bloke in question—screenwriter David Seidler—himself provided one of the presumably informative articles, weaving his personal story with Bertie's, and answering his question of "Why tell the story at all?" with "Well, one percent of the population stammers. That's an awful lot of stuttering. A great deal of living in silence." A recognizable disability identity thus *materialized* in both *The King's Speech* and (even more) in reporting around it—so much so that by early in 2011 there was something of a meme going around: "It's been said that *The King's Speech* will do for stuttering what *Rain Man* did for autism: plant a sympathetic view of disability in the public consciousness" (Wehrwein). As I've been implying, I think *The King's Speech* goes beyond *Rain Man* and earlier films, but for now I just want to signal, first, its *affirmation of disability identity*. The film is undeniably intended to be inspirational (and a critique of inspiration is a major component of my next chapter), but even that inspiration, in this particular context, might be tied to the affirmation of an emergent disability identity. Wendy Chrisman in fact writes that "inspirational narratives can serve a different purpose" for "underrepresented disabilities" (181, 180).

Disability identity is also forged in the film through a particular kind of queerness and I would even say (to update somewhat my own arguments in *Crip Theory*), disability and queerness are not *necessarily* deployed solely in the service of an apotheosis of compulsory heterosexuality and able-bodiedness (*Crip Theory* 19–28). In another positive spin, Melissa Wiginton, in a religiously inflected blog post about *The King's Speech* and feminism (I largely disagree with Wiginton's analysis, but invoke it to solidify a point), argues that this is "a story of men dealing with difficulty through mutual vulnerability." It is, Wiginton insists, "what men have been warned against" and it "points to the possibility of new archetypes, metaphors, models and ways of being through which men of all colors can flourish, for their own souls and for the vitality of the common life." It is, we might say, a kinda queer, kinda crip homosociality for the twenty-first century, structured in part through a playful embrace not only of vulnerability, but also of the libidinal energy passing between the men. This nonhomophobic homosociality was played up not only onscreen, but off, in public appearances with Firth, Rush, and Hooper, who (for example) spoke in his acceptance speech at the Oscars about the "triangle of man love" responsible for the film's success (Hooper, "Acceptance Speech"). Onscreen, just minutes before the king's speech, Lionel says to Bertie softly, in the room where the two are alone with the microphone, "Forget about everything else and just say it to me. Say it to me as a friend." With my earlier point about neoliberalism functioning efficiently with a certain amount of queerness still very decidedly in the background, then, I want to signal via Wiginton, second, that this *"positive representation" of disability* might be read through and not against homoerotics and even crip erotics that can play a role in generating new, twenty-first century masculinities.

Finally, the disabled figure in *The King's Speech* has been positioned by some commentators as an appropriate figure not only for the crisis of 1939 (Britain in its "fateful moment" of confrontation with fascism), but our own. The film was released to a quite positive reception in Britain in 2011 only months after both the general election (and the beginning of austerity) and the announcement that Prince William and Kate Middleton were to wed. The *Guardian's* film blog, in this context, attempted to account for the positive British reception of the film; the title of their account was "What *The King's Speech* can teach Prince William and Kate Middleton." Its subtitle, however, was even more pointed: "The nation has been roused by Tom Hooper's tale of triumph for Windsor publicity in an age of austerity. Sound familiar?" There's something uncannily accurate about how the *Guardian's* analysis sums up what I'm arguing about emergent disabilities and about the cultural work of the film: "What does the applause for *The King's Speech* signify? . . it expresses an appetite for leadership—for a figurehead able to convince us that he or she is a sympathetic human being who feels our pain and will offer principled guidance in times of adversity" (Walters). The piece implies that the organizers of the Royal Collection for William and Kate, marketing souvenirs connected to the nuptials, took the lesson offered by the disabled monarch of *The King's Speech*. The announcement for the Royal Collection specifically referenced "austere times" and in that context, conveyed to every household of Britain's peoples that the contemporary (and benevolent) royal family would absorb for consumers any tax rise from their purchase of wedding memorabilia.

"Today we've come a long way in our dealings with the handicapped," Seidler writes in his own piece on the writing of *The King's Speech* and the role his own stammer played in it. *Disability rights have significantly advanced*, he implies, completing the circle I've been drawing in this section: the film can be read as materializing an underrepresented disability *identity*, providing a positive disability *representation*, and marking an epoch (counterposed to earlier ones) of substantive disability *rights*.

I want, however, to rewrite the *Guardian's* question: what does the applause for *The King's Speech* obfuscate? And what might it mean that in "austere times," or "times of adversity," a disabled figure is not only deployed to represent a feel-good national unity, but even pedagogically offered up to the current House of Windsor, which—the *Guardian* piece suggests—might "earn itself a generation of ovations" if it walks the walk and talks the talk like Bertie? This is the crip's speech that I want to negate—any sort of disability exceptionalism that, *using disability as a vehicle*, both positions threats (to the nation, to national well-being, to the economy and national solvency) as external or simply elsewhere (because "we" as a people, as a group, as a nation, are effectively and affectively united) and masks the redoubled, and *internal*, neoliberal threat to disabled or impaired bodies and minds.

In a different context, Julie Passanante Elman and I have adapted Puar's notion of "sexual exceptionalism" in "queer times," and I'm drawing on that adaptation in what I'm arguing here (*Terrorist* 2; Elman and McRuer). Puar contends in *Terrorist Assemblages* that contemporary geopolitics now target certain gay and lesbian, and even "queer," subjects for life while simultaneously queering "terrorist corporealities" and targeting them for death (so that the "terrorist" body for Puar is always constructed as perverse, excessive, and queer in the broad sense—and through that construction, in need of elimination). Puar positions these queer processes—targeting some for life, some for death—as interrelated: "the deferred death of one population recedes as the securitization and valorization of the life of other populations triumphs [a telling and multilayered word, in the context of "Tom Hooper's tale of triumph"] in its shadow" (*Terrorist* 3). Puar names the bifurcation she traces "sexual exceptionalism," suggesting that "homosexual [and again, even queer] subjects who have limited legal rights within the U.S. civil context gain significant representational currency when situated within the global scene of the war on terror" (*Terrorist* 4). "Currency," in Puar's analysis, might be understood both in its monetary sense, where the term describes units in a system of economic exchange, and in its linguistic sense, where the term describes concepts or ideas that gain acceptance over time as they are repeatedly used or deployed in various contexts.

Disability exceptionalism, as Elman and I theorize it, allows for "the deployment of disability's depoliticization as cultural capital." I'm putting forward disability exceptionalism here as a cousin of sexual exceptionalism that *works particularly efficiently in narrativizing austerity*, or (to reinvoke Klein) the "shock doctrine." Rewriting Puar fairly explicitly, we might say that disabled subjects (or even subjects whom we might read as crip) who have often extremely limited legal rights or access within a given national context, and whose lives are made even more precarious by a global austerity politics, gain *significant representational currency* for the neoliberal establishment when situated within local manifestations of the current crisis of capitalism. "Currency," in this formulation, would again have economic valences, as disabled subjects are situated in an insidious system of exchange that secures or vouchsafes austerity in and through exceptionalized narratives of disability identity (and, in this sense, it's worth underscoring that the *Guardian*'s film blog, imagining how the House of Windsor might *purchase* ovations, explicitly uses language that draws attention to the narrative's current *earning power*). "Currency" would also have linguistic valences, as those narratives increasingly become an accepted part of contemporary vocabularies. The "war on terror" that is Puar's immediate topic is of course part of the current, global crisis of capitalism; hence my positioning of sexual and disability exceptionalism as cousins. I find that *disability* exceptionalism, however, queer as it may be (and indeed, as transparent or two-dimensional as it may be—because, what could be more cartoonish than a "sympathetic human being who feels our pain and offers principled guidance in times of adversity"?), has a particular capacity for narrativizing austerity and the shock doctrine.

Expired Insurance Policies; or, Scrounging Corporealities

I conclude, however, with a return to the promise of the crip's speech amplified otherwise. It's important, in doing so, to clarify how I am arguing against disability identity, representation, and rights, and how I am decidedly not. As with many other projects in disability and queer theory, *Crip Times* consistently puts pressure on "identity," attuned to the dangers that attend its congealing in the neoliberal era. Nonetheless, despite the dangers that circulate around identity, representation, and rights, *crip* and *disability* both have, in the crip times sketched in these pages, also contingently but undeniably marked what Duggan describes as "an expansion of the hopeful moments of actually existing politics" (*Twilight* 86); a unilateral theoretical rejection of either term risks missing *or fixing* the vibrancy of actually existing politics. Duggan herself is rightly critical of what she describes as the "pedagogical tone" that at times accompanies theoretical assessments (and often, abrupt and knowing dismissals) of political movements that deploy "identity" (*Twilight* 86).[32]

Andy, the disabled activist preparing for the June 2011 public sector strikes, makes absolutely clear that avoiding a pedagogical tone and attending to the vibrancy of actually existing politics is crucial. Andy, after all, literally invoked "rights" and suggested that he and disabled comrades would *represent* disability in the struggle; presumably, this representation would be of disability importantly substantialized as an identity. Again, however, Andy's deployment of identity, representation, and rights is a *historical* and *tactical* positioning of them "front and centre." In that specific crip time and place, a time and place of indignation or outrage, disabled people materialize, Marx might say, "not in any fantastic isolation and rigidity, but in their actual, empirically perceptible process of development under definite conditions" (*German* 155). Put differently, the definite conditions of embodied precarity in Crip Britain have necessitated and called forth disabled people's positioning front and center in the struggle against austerity.

As identity, representation, and rights are comprehended by and in neoliberalism (and materialized in fantastic isolation in a text like *The King's Speech*), in contrast, they are contained and domesticated. In that sense, they are worth countering directly and forcefully. In queer theory, the anti-identitarian position, first, is the easiest to grasp: sexual and disability exceptionalism completely depend upon a limited identity politics that incorporates some identities while positioning others (whether "terrorist corporealities" or benefit scroungers) as inadmissible or *incomprehensible*, in all the senses of that term: unintelligible, ungraspable, or even the archaic sense of "having or subject to no limits" (and thus paradoxically in need of intense control) (*OED*).

An antirepresentation position, second, is more specifically a call to attend to emergent disabilities and to move away from the "positive representation"/"negative representation" binary that disability studies and other interdisciplinary fields often traverse. Whether or not *The King's Speech* is a positive representation of stammerers (or any other "underrepresented disability"), it says very little about *how* that good or bad representation (and disability identity more generally) might be discursively useful in the current geopolitical order.

Third, and finally, a contingent and tactical argument "against disability rights" in relation to emergent disabilities should be understood in the Marxist sense, where rights are cordoned off from all that is happening front and center. Costas Douzinas, for example, has described rights as "an insurance policy for the established order" (93). He argues that the "rights of man started as normative marks of revolutionary change" (93). The emergent bourgeois order (and we might think here of Marx's analysis in "On the Jewish Question"), however, substantialized those rights in ways that effectively negated them, so that "positive human rights" became "defence mechanisms against the possibility of resistance and revolution. The removal of the right to revolution was an attempt to foreclose radical change" (93).[33] My point concluding this Introduction is essentially twofold: neoliberal capital can now deploy not just a globalized gayness, not just queerness, but even disability rights and the crip's speech to hang on to its defense mechanism. The insurance policy, however, doesn't cover it for all that's happening at this moment, for all the inventive and slippery ways in which the crip's speech, *understood otherwise*, is stammering its way toward resistance and revolution.

What has been happening on the ground in the UK from 2010 onward, and which I will detail in the chapters ahead, is disability exceptionalism hypostasized. Both the coalition's initial Health Reform Bill and the much more punitive Welfare Reform Bill proposed and put in place cuts that were devastating to countless disabled people across the country. There was almost immediately, for instance, a 20 percent cut to the disability living allowance (DLA). The DLA paid a maximum of £70 a week in care costs and £50 in mobility bills. That payment was capped and the DLA replaced in 2013 with a Personal Independence Payment (PIP) providing an even smaller maximum. By the final year of the coalition government, right before the Conservatives began to govern alone, the number of households with at least one disabled person in the UK in "absolute poverty" (meaning that someone's income is so low that they cannot afford basic needs even before disability needs are taken into account) had increased by 10 percent. In that final year alone, 300,000 more "disabled households" entered absolute poverty (Pring, "Disability Poverty").

But, as I've been suggesting, the austerity shock needs to be narrativized, and the coalition government said, first, that the increase in claimants had become unsustainable: as Smith's plan to overhaul the welfare system was unveiled in 2011, the government reported that 3.16 million people were receiving DLA and that £12.1bn was the predicted expenditure for the previous year. According to their figures, this was a 30 percent increase from 2.4 million recipients eight years previously (Ramesh). However, it said, second, and even beyond the coalition (including, that is, the official New Labour opposition at the time), that "benefit fraud" and (corporealized) benefit scroungers were sabotaging the system, destroying it for the disabled people for whom it was intended. Maria Miller, for instance, while serving from 2010–2012 as UK Undersecretary of State for Disabled People (despite repeated calls for a vote of no confidence from the people she was supposed to represent), said in an interview that it was not right that the UK had "a benefits system where there are more alcoholics and drug addicts in receipt of disability living allowance than the blind" (this is actually an unremarkable assertion in most national contexts, where rehabilitation services of necessity are accessed by those needing help with addiction) (Owen). Miliband, the Labour/opposition leader at the time, in a speech in June 2011 officially "opposing" austerity politics, and "speaking with the same depth of feeling for each one of you as if he were able to cross your threshold and speak to you himself," likewise (adapting Puar rather directly here) marked these crip times by invoking disability identity while conjuring up a benefit-scrounging corporeality: services are being cut by an austerity government, he notes, but ultimately it's because citizens "were not showing responsibility and were shirking their duties. From bankers who caused the global financial crisis to some of those on benefits who were abusing the system" (qtd. in Watt).

I have said I'm not interested in the "reality" of so-called "benefit fraud," but corporate tax evasion, which is far beyond anyone's estimate of "benefit fraud" in the UK, currently runs at £70bn (and the London 2012 Games alone cost a total of almost £9bn, of which £1bn was diverted public funds) (Murphy; Gibson). I'm less interested in the rest of this book, however, in these rather ready-to-hand figures debunking neoliberal uses of disability, than in crip (and queer) networks resisting those uses of disability: from the Hardest Hit marches on May 11, 2011 and October 22, 2011 in London and across the country (on May 11 perhaps the largest disability protest ever) to queer activists turning banks into sexual health clinics and HIV/AIDS education centers, to activists like Andy front and center by right and not charity (but audible now as a crip *reinventing the right to resistance and revolution*), to cyber activists generating the Spartacus Report detailing the effects of cuts on people's lives, to Broken of Britain or any other network reaching for the transnational consciousness Disabled People Against Cuts (DPAC) locates in "everyone that refuses to accept that any country can destroy the lives of people just because they are or become disabled or sick" and that resists "government austerity measures which target the poor while leaving the wealthy unscathed."[34]

"You still stammered on the W," Lionel Logue says immediately after King George's successful speech, rallying the nation in times of trouble (Logue's identification of this imperfection is offered to his student rather lovingly, as the two men smile and gaze at each other). "Well I had to throw in a few," Bertie replies, "so they knew it was me." As disability, like queerness, is remade by and for neoliberalism, cripping austerity entails tracing resistance and revolution—those speeches, marches, encampments, and other creative actions that we mobilize so that they know that it's still us—wherever they appear and however they are embodied.

Mapping Crip Times

As a queer disability studies project, *Crip Times* is interdisciplinary, broadly attentive to the global political and economic shifts I have been tracing in this Introduction while considering through a crip analytic how specific activists and artists, participating in social movements of various kinds, generate change and resistance to hegemonic forms of globalization in an age of austerity. I am indebted throughout to a range of writers focused on critiquing austerity or neoliberalism more broadly from the vantage point of contemporary Marxisms. Certainly my focus on specific texts broadly conceived (film, internet memes, activist performance, photography, sculpture) is grounded in my own training in close reading in literary and cultural studies and in my belief that cripping austerity entails using whatever varied skills or capacities each of us has. Stuart Hall's basic cultural studies understanding of "representation"— "the production of meaning through language" ("Work" 16)—drives my analysis of both dominant and alternative discourses of disability and impairment in crip times. I have, for instance, essentially argued here that the filmic language of *The King's Speech* produces and thereby helps to consolidate new or emergent understandings of/meanings for disability in our moment, and that the language of disability is contested, in turn, by the emergent activist and artistic languages I have begun to put forward and that I will analyze in much more detail in the chapters ahead. I have already suggested that Raymond Williams's understanding of dominant, emergent, and residual discourses animates my thinking in and about crip times. *Crip Times* additionally relies on the Williams of *Keywords: A Vocabulary of Culture and Society*; thus, in and through the textual analyses contained in each chapter, I also pose, as Williams would describe it, "a problem of *vocabulary*, in two senses: the available and developing meanings of known words, which needed to be set down; and the explicit but as often implicit connections which people were making, in what seemed to me, again and again, particular formations of meaning—ways not only of discussing but at another level of seeing many of our central experiences" (15). Each chapter includes, for this reason, not just an analysis of cultural texts and social contexts but a meditation on disability and one keyword: disability and *dispossession* in chapter 1, disability and *resistance* in chapter 2, disability and *displacement* in chapter 3, and disability and *aspiration* in chapter 4. On the surface, this organization seems to pair neatly two negatives (dispossession and displacement) with two positives (resistance and aspiration). My analysis of each keyword, however, will complicate and sometimes explicitly reverse that surface appearance.

Chapter 1 opens with a focus on the hype around the London 2012 Olympic and Paralympic Games as spectacle. I mainly approach this spectacle through a reading of an inspirational meme that circulated at the time—a well-known image of South African sprinter Oscar Pistorius running alongside a disabled little girl from Sussex in the UK. The opening texts for this chapter are thus largely images of incorporation that construct affective (and effective) global images of the UK (and South Africa) as open, tolerant, and accessible. I read these images as consolidating what I call an "austerity of representation" that is part and parcel of an economics of austerity more generally. All the spectacle, however, was happening at the same time that activists outside the Olympic and Paralympic stadiums were protesting the fact that the games were sponsored by Atos, a private French IT company also charged with carrying out tests designed to find disabled benefit recipients "fit to work" (and thus ineligible for benefits). Spectacle and dispossession thus emerge in this analysis as two sides of the same neoliberal coin.

The chapter, additionally, in the wake of Pistorius's killing (in a gated South African community) of his girlfriend Reeva Steenkamp, examines the affective shift around Pistorius's global image. I read the melodrama into which Pistorius has been placed as obscuring the masculinist violence responsible for Steenkamp's murder as well as, more broadly, the actual conditions of securitization, dispossession, and violence in South Africa that disproportionately impacts disabled people, women of color, and queers. I conclude by turning to some of the ways disabled cultural producers have generated what can be understood as critically crip forms of dispossession, materializing images and tactics that contest and dislodge the ways in which disability is caught up in neoliberalism's austerity of representation.

Drawing on Kevin Floyd's analysis, in *The Reification of Desire: Toward a Queer Marxism*, of microlevel forms of queer resistance to neoliberalism (forms of resistance he terms "pornography") (203), chapter 2 examines more closely global crip activism, broadly understood. I open with a meditation on the complex and contradictory life of *resistance* in contemporary queer and crip theory. A politics of resistance, deeply indebted to the work of philosopher Michel Foucault, played a large role in the development of queer theory in the 1990s and disability theory in the early 2000s. In some prominent queer theoretical texts of the past decade, however, resistance has been explicitly dismissed for a number of reasons, such as the problematic ways it is tied to identity or its capacity for easy commodification, including within critical theories that are consciously or unconsciously fueled by the search for new and different figures of resistance. I counterpose these critiques of resistance to queer and crip work on embodiment in global contexts committed to "carrying forward the project of resistance," as Darieck Scott puts it (9). This work has often emerged in the generative space of queer of color or crip of color critique (the work, for instance, of Scott himself or of Nirmala Erevelles). I position such crip/queer theorizing as a tactic of resistance; my overview of this theorizing sets the stage for a brief consideration of five geographically specific locations where *additional* forms of crip activism and distinct tactics of resistance became legible in 2010–2011: California, Chile, Spain, Greece, and the UK.

Chapters 1 and 2 are broadly connected in their attention to activism; the remaining two chapters are directly focused on specific artists. Chapter 3 takes as its text the global and itinerant exhibition "El Museo de los Desplazados" [The Museum of the Displaced] which has generated more than 75 installations on five continents. My particular focus is the photography of Livia Radwanski, a Brazilian photographer living and working in Mexico City who documented the gentrification of Colonia Roma, west of the historic city center. Her photographs represented the displacement of families and the destruction of the buildings in which they live. The Mexican state under President Enrique Peña Nieto has notoriously refused to recognize student movements and other forms of activism; it has, however, officially and with great fanfare "recognized" some disabled individuals. My analysis of Radwanski's work considers how populations that are not recognized come into focus in crip times, and some of the ways in which they resist.

I am especially interested, in this chapter, in the British government's activities during this period in coalition with its Mexican partners. Even as, back in the UK, the coalition government was putting forward a policy that came to be known as the "bedroom tax" (which resulted in a cut in benefits for anyone having a "spare bedroom" in the living space they were renting, and which disproportionately impacted disabled people and their families), it was busy exporting a vision of British openness and accessibility, redesigning street corners in Mexico City and preparing for 2015, which the government had declared the "Year of Mexico in the UK and the UK in Mexico." I use a close reading of Radwanski's photos, alongside a consideration of housing and processes of gentrification in Mexico City, to demonstrate the ways in which the global exchange of neoliberal forms of accessibility works in tandem with ongoing processes of displacement.

Finally, chapter 4 works with and beyond the Thatcherite keyword *aspiration*. I consider how rhetorics of aspiration emerged in Thatcher's England, paying particular attention to the ways in which those rhetorics depended upon both able-bodied and disabled figurations (with those who were not "aspirational" consistently represented as sick and disabled). The rhetorical use of disability continued into the Blair and Cameron years (years sometimes described as Blatcherite or Blameron to mark the neoliberal continuity between the Tories and New Labour) as explicit appeals to an "Aspiration Society" became more ubiquitous. I attend to the material effects generated by the consensus around an Aspiration Society, considering those whom Owen Jones describes as "left behinds" (*Chavs* 61). Those who are not, or cannot be, sufficiently aspirational, have faced material consequences; these consequences have included literal dispossession and displacement.

Aspiration, however, has been conceived in other—Marxist and queer—ways and, through an analysis of a performance piece called *Figures*, by Bristol-based performance artist and sculptor Liz Crow, my final chapter attempts to access those alternative conceptions. An "aspiration to totality," in the Marxist sense, attempts to "approach the universal" from a specific vantage point and grasp the "web of relations" that compose a historical moment (Floyd 12). Floyd argues that, over the course of the twentieth century, queer aspirations to totality make possible complex, situated understandings of, and interventions into, the social relations of capital and heteronormativity. In my final chapter, I contrast Crow's attempt to approach the universal from a specific *crip* location to neoliberal discourses of public art that ideologically deploy the universal to mask the specific. More directly, I consider and critique an art installation produced for Remembrance Day 2014 (November 9, 2014) outside the Tower of London, when 888,246 ceramic poppies were on display for almost a month. In Commonwealth nations, Remembrance Day has been celebrated since World War I to remember members of the armed services who have died in the line of duty. The popular 2014 installation was created by artists Paul Cummins and Tom Piper and was called *Blood Swept Lands and Seas of Red*. Prime Minister Cameron and numerous other public officials showered the piece with effusive praise; attempts to critique *Blood Swept Lands and Seas of Red* were ridiculed or even deemed offensive to the British people.

Crow also worked with numbers in her April 2015 installation *Figures*, but a much smaller number: 650. There are 650 constituencies in the United Kingdom and 650 Members of Parliament. Over a period of twelve consecutive days and nights in April 2015, Crow sculpted 650 human figures from raw river mud, "each one representing an individual at the sharp end of austerity." Sculpted in London on the banks of the Thames and then returned to Bristol, the figures were ultimately burned in a bonfire while actual stories of austerity from across the UK were read aloud. On the day the Tories took full power in May 2015, the dust from the remains of the figures was scattered into the sea from a boat off the coast near Portishead. *Figures*, Crow insists, raises "profound questions about how we treat each other, what kind of society we want to be, and what role we might each of us have in bringing that about." Crow's crip aspiration to totality and burning installation, I contend, undermines from a specific vantage point the smug bourgeois universalism and neoliberal utility of public art such as *Blood Swept Lands and Seas of Red*.

I conclude with an Epilogue that again ties these questions back to the intersection of region, race, and disability, titled, in homage to Gramsci and Finger, "Some (Disabled) Thoughts on the Immigration Question." My Epilogue attempts to do some justice to the ways in which the antidisabled discourses of austerity in Britain are subtended by a racialized anti-immigrant disourse, which is particularly evident in charges that eastern Europeans and others are coming to the UK because of alleged "benefits tourism." The right-wing United Kingdom Independence Party (UKIP), which has increasingly appealed to a segment of the British populace and even achieved some electoral successes, has particularly relied on anti-immigrant sentiment; many would say that Brexit, which I consider briefly in the Epilogue, partly depended on the resentments UKIP repeatedly articulated. I return to Los Indignados in conclusion to contrast their embrace of figures from elsewhere to the inward-looking "UKIPisation of English politics" (Seymour, "UKIPisation"). A politics of austerity, I conclude, will always generate the compulsion to fortify borders and to separate a narrowly defined "us," in need of protection, from "them." *Crip Times*, and crip times, however, can and will only end with an aspiration to the outward-looking vision proferred by the indignant ones.

1

An Austerity of Representation; or, Crip/Queer Horizons

Disability and Dispossession

My Introduction ended on austerity and an inevitable and necessary excess, as I both introduced the UK government's radical post-2010 austerity agenda and gestured toward some of the excessive ways in which resistance has arisen in the wake of that agenda. Resistance can be discerned within a particular, critical valence of what I called "the crip's speech," collectively articulated by "emergent disabilities" in our moment. At times, as my reading of *The King's Speech* should indicate, emergent disabilities are clearly useful for neoliberalism and can even, as with the disability identity represented in that film, be showered with awards by the establishment. I am ultimately more interested, however, in other emergent disabilities in crip times, in crip subjects material-izing in ways that are "radically contrary to being aligned to a state or a dominant discourse," to draw on Andrew Robinson's analysis of the philosopher Alain Badiou. For my purposes in this chapter, Robinson's "state" here should be comprehended *both* as the currently hegemonic neoliberal state administering austerity politics as a near-global common sense *and* as any fixed or static mode of being. Disabled People Against Cuts (DPAC), Broken of Britain, and others I consider throughout this book have come forward with new disabled subjectivities and coalitions actively contesting the insidious ways disability has been made to speak in and for neoliberalism.

The next two chapters introduce varied forms of crip activism in an age of austerity. I sustain a focus throughout on some of the under-standings of "excess" available in Badiou's work on subjectivity. I begin this chapter, however, with a consideration of the more familiar and somewhat predictable dangers of neoliberal capitalist excess, through an analysis of Olympic images of both spectacle and melodrama. Marx and Engels themselves literally predicted and observed capitalist excess, famously noting that the bourgeoisie "has accomplished wonders far surpassing Egyptian pyramids, Roman aqueducts, and Gothic cathedrals" (476). In this chapter and the next, my own analysis eventually moves away from that more recognizable capitalist spectacle and toward an overview of unpredictable and differently excessive forms of resistance to a global austerity politics.

In what follows, I theorize austerity even more comprehensively as both an economic and a broadly cultural phenomenon or strategy. Put differently, the *economic strategy of austerity* in many ways requires a *cultural politics* that I will describe here as an *austerity of representation*. What Tobin Siebers calls an "ideology of ability" has long vouchsafed flattened, nonthreatening representations of disability (7); my contention is that such deadened representations are newly put to use, in crip times, to obscure the workings of austerity. A neoliberal austerity of representation is on display throughout *Crip Times*, but I focus here on how that austerity of representation works to *foreclose* other crip possibilities, both in the sense of ruling out or preventing and in the sense of (more specifically and a bit ironically) taking possession of something that has been the property of another. A literal foreclosure in the economic sense happens when one party "fails" to meet its obligations to pay the bank; the *representational* foreclosure I'll put forward here is more metaphorical, but is likewise essentially a response to those who won't abide by the economic and cultural rules neoliberalism affords us (because they don't feel obliged to, or cannot). A neoliberal austerity of representation disciplines what Lauren Berlant, in a discussion of Brian Massumi, terms "unforeclosed experience" (5); it is a strategic (and ongoing) move that dilutes the power and potentiality of alternative, more radical or resistant, representations.[1]

I also begin in this chapter a sustained attention to four keywords for the crip times we inhabit: *dispossession, resistance, displacement,* and *aspiration. Dispossession* is the focus of the current chapter, and is a keyword that my introduction of a neoliberal "foreclosure" should already anticipate. The activism spotlighted in this chapter and the next aspires to work against, with, and (perhaps most importantly) through a multivalent politics of dispossession that is a necessary component of austerity. David Harvey names neoliberal processes that centralize wealth through privatization and through redistribution of resources away from the public "accumulation by dispossession" (*New* 137). In Harvey's terms, the global austerity politics that escalates super-exploitation of workers globally and protects capitalists while slashing services to the poor would be a clear example of such accumulation by dispossession: wealth is redistributed to/accumulated by those at the top while those at the bottom are dispossessed of resources, public services, or secure networks of care. Without question, we should oppose such neoliberal dispossession—the form of dispossession upon which austerity depends. The varied forms of crip activism I pivot toward in this chapter and the next, however, to draw on Judith Butler and Athena Athanasiou, allow us "to formulate a theory of political performativity" that might materialize *contingent and desirable* versions of dispossession that counter the dominant (and quotidian) forms of dispossession that should be resisted (ix–x). The versions of dispossession that Butler and Athanasiou invoke, writing in their own joint conversation literally titled *Dispossession*, take us out of ourselves in ways that allow for political action with others.

The forms of activist resistance that I introduce in this chapter and that I multiply in the next will be put forward as varied crip tactics. For Michel de Certeau, a *tactic* (which he differentiates from a dominant *strategy*) "makes use of the cracks that particular conjunctions open in the surveillance of the proprietary powers. It poaches in them. It creates surprises in them. It can be where it is least expected. It is a guileful ruse" (37). Not incidentally, for my purposes here, de Certeau's writing on tactics emerges in part from reflections on the varied uses of an accoutrement of disability— Charlie Chaplin's cane, a historical walking stick which we might, in José Esteban Muñoz's sense of "cruising utopia," apprehend by looking toward the past (and toward the utopian promise contained in performances from the past) in order to look forward; for Muñoz, cruising utopia generates "a backward glance that enacts a future vision" (4).[2] Chaplin's cane, in most of the early twentieth-century films in which he appears as "the little tramp," is fascinating to de Certeau because of the proliferating, nonsingular, and inventive possibilities it affords the socially marginal figure Chaplin portrayed: "Charlie Chaplin multiplies the possibilities of his cane: he does other things with the same thing and he goes beyond the limits that the determinants of the object set on its utilization" (98). The tactics of this chapter and the next likewise proliferate crip possibilities, going beyond the austere limits both the state and dominant discourses would impose upon disability (and indeed, upon the objects often associated with it).

In the following section, I turn to some of the limited representations of disability that were in wide—indeed, spectacular—circulation during the first summer Olympic Games to follow the global economic crises of 2008: the London 2012 Olympic and Paralympic Games, held from July 27 until August 12, 2012 and (for the Paralympics) from August 29 until September 9, 2012. Disabled activists, artists, and scholars have long critiqued the ways in which "inspirational" imagery or messages attach to disabled lives and experiences: as disabled individuals supposedly "overcome" what has long been put forward as the "struggle" or "hardship" of disability, they "inspire" nondisabled observers or readers, even by carrying out the quotidian activities of an ordinary life. "A boy without hands bats .486 on his Little League team," Eli Clare writes. "A blind man hikes the Appalachian Trail from end to end. An adolescent girl with Down's syndrome learns to drive and has a boyfriend. A guy with one leg runs across Canada" (*Exile* 2). The critique of this two-dimensional representation of disability is not new, but my contention in the following section is that it was particularly pronounced in 2012 because an inspirational understanding of disability, which activists denounced as "inspiration porn" or "cripspiration," was especially useful to the neoliberal establishment as it sought to detract from the activism outside the Olympic and Paralympic stadiums and across the country. This activism was mobilizing a politicized disability critique of the harsher and harsher austerity policies that were devastating disabled lives in the UK and elsewhere. In my analysis of inspiration porn, I focus particularly on the complex and shifting ways in which the white South African athlete Oscar Pistorius was caught up in, and indeed helped to cement, an austerity of representation during this moment of spectacle.

In the section that follows my survey of inspiration porn in and around 2012 and of the activism that was obscured by it, I turn toward the work of Kevin Floyd, who puts forward other, more generative understandings of "pornography" in *The Reification of Desire: Toward a Queer Marxism* (203). I contend that Floyd's explicitly queer project can lay the groundwork for an analysis of what we might understand as an excessive and "pornographic" crip sociality explicitly opposed to an austerity of representation that would tame, domesticate, or contain disability. In my final section, I read that pornographic crip sociality into a collective 2012 project of counterrepresentation, This Is What Disability Looks Like. This activist photographic project flourished on social media for a time in the wake of, and opposed to, the inspiration porn that was in wide circulation around the London 2012 Games. I argue that This Is What Disability Looks Like put into circulation what I will theorize as a *critically crip dispossession* that can be positioned *as against* austerity and that can arguably be discerned in a range of locations around the world. In the chapter that follows this analysis of representation and counterrepresentation, in the interests of extending the crip theory of political performativity I introduce in my analysis of This Is What Disability Looks Like, I turn directly to the keyword *resistance* and put forward six tactical, geographically dispersed examples of this critically crip dispossession.

Cripspiration and Its Discontents

As is always the case with the Olympics and Paralympics, excess and spectacle, driven by corporate capital, were in evidence around the London 2012 Games. I focus in what follows on a specific image that can be read as marking that excess, in and through disability. As Olympic and Paralympic fever swept the United Kingdom and the globe in July and August 2012, a 2009 photo of Oscar Pistorius and a five-year-old British girl named Ellie Challis resurfaced [Figure 1.1]. In the photo, Pistorius, who is a double amputee, is represented running alongside a cherubic Challis, whose hands and lower legs were amputated after a serious, life-threatening bout with meningitis.

This photo, of course, to virtually any reader of *Crip Times*, means something completely different from what it meant in August 2012 and thus requires some contextualization before I discuss its Olympic and Paralympic circulation. As of this writing in January 2017, Oscar Pistorius has served more than two years of what was initially a five-year prison sentence, handed down by South African Judge Thokozile Masipa. Pistorius had been charged on September 14, 2014, with culpable homicide for the February 14, 2013, killing of his girlfriend Reeva Steenkamp, a white South African model. Culpable homicide is essentially the South African term for manslaughter; after an extended trial, Pistorius was, in other words, initially sentenced by Judge Masipa for unlawfully, but also unintentionally, killing Steenkamp. Pistorius was considered for release by a parole board in August 2015, but that release was temporarily suspended while a higher court considered an appeal of the original

Figure 1.1. "The Only Disability in Life Is a Bad Attitude," Oscar
Pistorius and Ellie Challis meme.

ruling. If the parole board had allowed early release it would have been
because of Pistorius's "good behavior" or rehabilitation while in prison;
under such circumstances, he would have remained on a restrictive pro-
bation. On December 3, 2015, however, the Supreme Court of Appeal
overturned the charge of culpable homicide and found Pistorius guilty
of murder.[3]

When the culpable homicide charge was overturned, a decision on
a more extended sentence for the murder conviction was set for later
in 2016. On July 3, 2016, Judge Masipa amended her initial conviction,
handing down a six-year term to Pistorius for the murder of Steenkamp.
South Africa has one of the highest murder rates in the world, and a
murder conviction generally carries a minimum fifteen-year sentence.
In delivering a lighter sentence, Judge Masipa took into account what
she saw as some "mitigating factors" in Pistorius's case, such as remorse
("Oscar Pistorius"). From 2014 onward, Judge Masipa herself had received numerous verbal threats and attacks, and was placed under police

protection for her own safety. Some prominent legal organizations in South Africa explicitly connected these attacks to Masipa's race and gender. The case, as I will underscore in the next section, was already completely about gendered violence and masculinist rage, and the threats against Masipa reflect the violence and rage so readily aimed at women and at people of color in South Africa. "People may disagree with the judgment," the legal organizations speaking out against the threats levied at Masipa said in an official statement. "However, attacking and threatening Judge Masipa because she is black or because she is female is simply unacceptable" (qtd. in Conway-Smith).

Steenkamp was killed late at night in the couple's home in the gated, almost entirely white, Silver Woods Country Estate, where they lived. Steenkamp was behind a locked bathroom door. By some accounts, Steenkamp had locked herself in the bathroom following a heated argument. As Pistorius's story would have it, however, the couple had been sleeping in the moments leading up to Steenkamp's death, and he feared that an intruder had broken into the house. What was not in contention in either the original trial or the appeal that resulted in the conviction for murder is that Pistorius fired four shots into the locked bathroom door; one of the shots (perhaps the first) ended Steenkamp's life.

Pistorius's sentences for both culpable homicide and murder have largely been served in Kgosi Mampuru II jail in Pretoria, South Africa. Pistorius has mostly been held in the hospital wing of the jail, in a small and cramped single cell. Despite its size, the single cell is a privilege (of sorts) denied most inmates in the country (Raphaely). The "privilege" of a single cell is debatable, but other inmates have described very different experiences in Kgosi Mampuru II jail. A disabled inmate named Eric Viljoen, for example, explained that he lived in a crowded cell with thirty-seven others while incarcerated there and was never given a choice to be in the hospital section. Viljoen, who lost his leg in an accident, said that he also repeatedly needed to maneuver up and down steps as he was moved around the jail (Raphaely).

This extremely complicated post-Olympic geography suggests that the Pistorius-Challis photo now carries very different meanings from when it initially resurfaced at the time of the Games; I contend here that the meanings that have attached to Pistorius at *both* moments are actually part of the larger, limited, representational matrix that is the subject of this chapter. The Pistorius-Challis photo is still in wide circulation and in fact remains Pistorius's profile picture for his official Twitter account, although that account has been dormant for the entire time he has been incarcerated. In the remainder of this section, after analyzing the complex and shifting cultural work of the photograph in 2012 and beyond, I'll fill out—by way of some reflections on visibility—my larger argument about the insidious workings of an austerity of representation, ultimately turning away from Pistorius and from what Floyd calls "the violence of neoliberalism" (195). David T. Mitchell has recently demonstrated the importance of Floyd's *The Reification of Desire* for disability studies (6). This chapter extends that project through a consideration of what I will position in this chapter, via Floyd, as an excessive queer/crip pornographic imagination that resists the violence of neoliberalism.

Pistorius famously qualified for the 2012 Olympics after a long controversy, beginning in 2007, when it was determined that his prosthetic racing legs did *not* give him an "unfair advantage." Initially declared ineligible to compete by the International Association of Athletics Federations (IAAF), Pistorius appealed that decision, and it was subsequently overturned. Although he failed to qualify for the Summer 2008 Olympic Games, he indeed qualified for the competition in London four years later. Over the course of his appeal, Pistorius insisted, in an identity-based assertion that has relevance for my argument in this chapter, "My focus throughout this appeal has been to ensure that disabled athletes be given the chance to compete and compete fairly with able-bodied athletes" ("Pistorius Eligible").

In the resurfaced photo in August 2012 (long after these controversies were at least officially declared over), Challis is wearing custom-fitted prosthetic legs designed by Dorset Orthopaedic; they are specifically designed to be like Pistorius's, which are Cheetah Flex-Run limbs made by the Össur corporation. The image is saturated with nonindividual, corporate interests, even though those circulating this image-cum-meme during the Olympics intended to affirm a "universal" feel-good message of triumph and of individual distinction or personal identity. As I explained in the Introduction, it was possible to apply to the National Health Service (NHS) in the UK for Primary Care Trust funding (PCT), before PCT funding was eliminated in 2010. Current applications now go through 211 Clinical Commissioning Groups (CCGs), ostensibly giving more control to local General Practitioners (GPs). The success of CCGs, however, some of which are now managed by private firms, has been (to say the least) mixed across the UK; an eighty-page report in 2015 determined that the CCGs have basically guaranteed that "nobody is in charge locally" (qtd. in Wintour and Campbell). Privatization of British health care, however, was in evidence well before the demise of PCT funding. From one angle, the funding from the PCT allowed for someone like Challis to access *some* public funds to receive a prosthesis at Dorset Orthopaedic. From another angle, however, the "company" (their term) provides a "market-leading service" (their words) (Dorset, "Company Overview"). Dorset looked to the public option only after taking a sizable portion of private funds. Private funds were arguably Dorset's first target anyway, and in Challis's case, they received such funds, since the Essex community where she lives rallied to raise the money that ultimately allowed Challis to be the youngest person ever fitted with carbon fiber prosthetic legs ("Toddler's Best"; Dorset, "Ellie-May Challis"). Over the course of working with the company, Challis's mother Lisa noted her extreme disappointment with the NHS. "When we finally went private," Challis's mother explained in a press release on an official Dorset Orthopaedic site, "we looked at the difference in the limbs. It just shows you what money can buy, so we've been very lucky" (qtd. in "Toddler's Best").

Although some entities like Dorset Orthopaedic in the UK were more skilled during the PCT era at appearing nonprofit than others, even (or perhaps especially) when applying for NHS contracts, their focus remained, and remains, essentially profit, even when that focus is cloaked in a liberal or even vaguely progressive, language: "Dorset Orthopaedic's financial strategy focuses on generating enough profit to reinvest into new innovations and paying staff a fair wage" ("Company Overview"). One UK physician told me that even calling an entity like Dorset Orthopaedic a "public-private partnership" would be, at least at the time Challis received her prostheses, a US-influenced misnomer obscuring a focus on profit (since 2010, with the Tories leading the British government, this focus on profit and competition in health care has become more apparent on both sides of the Atlantic). Comically, or tragicomically, to fill out this image's saturation by corporate interests, for the Össur corporation that designs the Flex-Run Cheetah blade, the inspirational phrase "Life Without Limitations" is literally trademarked.

The 2009 photo went spectacularly viral during the London 2012 Olympics and was widely disseminated globally via Facebook, Twitter, and other social media applications. As the image was shared, it usually had cancer survivor and former Olympic figure skater Scott Hamilton's quotation plastered on top of it: "The only disability in life is a bad attitude." The direct contexts from which the resurfaced photo and quotation came were likely not known to the vast majority of people passing it on: the photo with Hamilton's words on it initially reemerged on a fitness tumblr encouraging exercise and weight loss (and thus, in many ways, encouraging normalcy and a narrow sense of health erroneously linked to thinness).[4] Hamilton's words, moreover, in their original context, were tied to evangelical Christianity: he articulated the sentiment that the only disability is a bad attitude as part of his religious testimony for the "I Am Second" campaign (Hamilton, "I Am Second"). For evangelicals, the believer is "second," of course, to Jesus, and Hamilton dutifully positioned Jesus as always first in his life.

The fact that these words were both spoken initially by a deeply religious figure (who has also sometimes been charged with being openly homophobic) *and* used to market dieting and weight loss was lost in the frenzied sharing of the image in August 2012.[5] Indeed, as the image and quotation circulated in a range of languages—for example/por ejemplo, "la única discapacidad es una mala actitud"—Pistorius himself was at times wrongfully credited with the statement. Which is not to say that correct attribution is necessary to disentangle the Pistorius of 2012 from such sentimental soundbites; it's entirely plausible that Pistorius at the time *would have* articulated such thoughts, if not these exact words. In an interview in August 2012, for instance, he explicitly emphasized his hope that the memories that people would take away from the London 2012 Paralympics would be "inspirational." "The world is going to see the most successful Paralympic Games ever," he insisted. "Everyone here will be absolutely speechless when they see what these athletes can do, and they will be concentrating only on the phenomenal sport" (O. Brown). Ticket sales for the Paralympics reached £45 million, while sponsorship of both the Olympics and Paralympics (sold as a package for the first time and, across the country and the world, generating advertising that included Paralympians) reached £80 million (Topping). "Great Britain," Pistorius said, "is at the forefront in terms of education on disability. . . . I believe that's the only way to remove a lot of the stigmas, and to get over this being a taboo subject. . . . My experience is that disability here is regarded in a really progressive way" (O. Brown). With sentiments that would ironically not be unusual on the first day of an Introduction to Disability Studies class, Pistorius concluded, "People have not looked at it as a problem, but more as a challenge to change wider perceptions" (O. Brown).

Even though on the surface it suggested disability only existed as a "bad attitude," I contend that the Pistorius-Challis meme, alongside the far more extensive, unprecedented coverage of the Paralympics, made visible and global for a time a particular and circumscribed disability identity—albeit one labeled "superhuman" by advertising that, Liz Crow writes, quickly became "a Paralympic mantra" ("Summer of 2012" 63). Paralympic advertising invited the public to "Meet the Superhumans," seemingly spotlighting, to return to Marx, "in the fantastic reality of heaven . . . a supernatural being" ("Contribution" 53) [Figure 1.2]. Marx, however, of course issues a "call to abandon" such spiritual "illusions" (54), and to attend instead to the material conditions that produce such illusions, and the Meet the Superhumans campaign was in many ways simply neoliberal in its quotidian spectacularization of difference. Like the Pistorius photo and meme, the Paralympics advertising offered spectacular disability identities but foreclosed or *obscured* what I would call, drawing on Floyd and Kateřina Kolářová, a crip or queer/crip horizon (Floyd 195; Kolářová 270). My central points here are that the Pistorius-Challis photo was particularly useful as a smokescreen at the moment of its reemergence and that the photo functioned harmoniously in tandem with other representations. There was, again, nothing new about the photo's sentimental, inspirational message or about the contained disability identity that served as the vehicle for that message. The multifaceted disability critiques *and multivalent disability identities* that emerged in the wake of the Pistorius-Challis meme, however, indicated that many activists intuited that such messages were being *used* in new ways to direct attention away from what was happening to disability communities, *not* in the fantastic reality of heaven, but on the ground.

Figure 1.2. "Meet the Superhumans," Paralympics advertisement.

Philippa Willitts, writing in the UK's *Independent* on August 1, 2012, labeled the Pistorius-Challis photograph and internet meme "inspiration porn" and—perhaps more memorably—"cripspiration." A month prior to Willitts's piece, the comedienne and disability activist Stella Young apparently coined the term "inspiration porn" when she published a piece in Australia likewise critiquing the photograph. "I don't know Scott Hamilton personally," she wrote, "but that guy is really starting to burn my crumpets." Young explained, "Let me be clear about the intent of this inspiration porn; it's there so that non-disabled people can put their worries into perspective. . . . It's there so that non-disabled people can look at us and think 'well, it could be worse . . . I could be that person.'" "Inspiration porn" quickly gained a wide, even global, circulation in disability writing critical of such images, as did, to a lesser extent, "cripspiration."[6]

In August 2012, what cripspiration and the "overcoming narrative" that invariably accompanies it more specifically obscured was the complicated political critique of the Tory-Liberal Democrat coalition put forward in protests by disabled activists. The 2012 protests were specifically aimed at "work capability assessments" in Britain, contracted by the Department for Work and Pensions (DWP) and carried out at the time by the private French IT company Atos, proud sponsor of the Paralympics. Atos's contracted assessments declared a wide range of disabled people in Britain "fit to work" and thus ineligible for disability benefits that would allow them to live independently, access attendant services, or utilize assisted transport. Atos exited its contract with the government in early 2014; work that is fundamentally the same continues as of this writing, however, led by another private company, US-based Maximus. Thanks to Atos and other players in the conservative coalition's austerity plan leading up to the Olympics, £18 billion were cut from the welfare budget in 2010. At the time, an additional £11 billion per year was scheduled to be cut from budgets leading up to 2012 and beyond (Vale). When Atos's contract was implemented, it cost British taxpayers £110 million; Atos's assessment process, moreover, left more than half of those subject to scrutiny "destitute"—that is, without benefits *and* unemployed (J. Ferguson). One whistle-blowing former Atos nurse, Joyce Drummond, believes that the private corporation had been given a "target"—get two-thirds of people *on* incapacity benefits *off* of them (J. Ferguson).

Insisting that the 2012 Paralympics would be "incredible," David Cameron himself, lighting the Olympic flame in Trafalgar Square, spotlighted the "example of overcoming the difficulties you've been handed, pushing yourself to the limits, going way beyond the expectations others have set for you." Unsurprisingly, Cameron called the Paralympic example "truly inspiring" (qtd. in "London 2012"). Whatever Cameron said about the success of the London Paralympic Games, however, Owen Jones wrote at the time, "he leads a government that is systematically attacking the rights of the sick and disabled. Their financial support is being confiscated; their ability to lead independent lives attacked; they are subjected to humiliating tests; they are demonised as 'scroungers' and drains on the public purse; and abuse towards them is soaring" ("David Cameron"). For these reasons, at what they called the "Atos Closing Ceremonies" on August 31, 2012 (timed to coincide with the Paralympics and serving as the culmination to a week of protests), a broad coalition of activists mobilized by DPAC and by UK Uncut gathered at the corporate headquarters in Triton Square London (as they did across the country) to demand that the multinational be shut down and more immediately, that their lucrative contracts with the government be terminated. Their posters and banners proclaimed "Atos Don't Give a Toss" and attempted to quantify the numbers of lives lost due to work capability assessments that resulted in the termination of benefits. Activists insisted during the Atos Closing Ceremonies and other protests that ten thousand people had died after being found fit to work by Atos [Figure 1.3].

Activists looked toward a crip horizon, toward a world where disabled lives would be genuinely valued rather than tossed away and where the debilitating logic of privatization concentrating wealth in the hands of a few (a logic that arguably subtended Atos's contract and now subtends Maximus's) would be unthinkable. That crip horizon was foreclosed in August 2012 by an austerity of representation: the global circulation of inspiration porn or cripspiration. The inspirational Pistorius photo and meme, however, were *themselves* obscured by innumerable other photos of Pistorius, as the spectacle of inspiration in 2012 was replaced in turn by the horrible inverse spectacle of Pistorius's killing of Steenkamp and the ensuing trial. Photos of Pistorius from 2013 represented the athlete in the South African courtroom facing murder charges for the death of

Figure 1.3. Atos closing ceremonies, August 2012, London.

Figure 1.4. Oscar Pistorius in court.

Steenkamp, often with his head in his hands [Figure 1.4]. During the extended trial, moreover, both photos and videos circulated of Pistorius sobbing or trembling with anxiety (a condition ultimately labeled a potential anxiety "disorder," and for which he would later be, by court order, examined by a psychiatrist). The most extreme court representations showed Pistorius vomiting as images of the blood-stained bathroom and the body of Steenkamp were displayed by the prosecuting attorney; debates raged, as these images were broadcast globally, as to whether the world was seeing an excessive and perhaps planned *performance* (a performance ironically, or perhaps even cynically, mobilizing a currently less charmed disability, anxiety disorder). Eventually, the first court accepted the argument that Pistorius and his lawyers had sustained throughout the trial and sentencing: that, in his secured home in the gated Silver Woods Country Estate, Pistorius was frightened of noises in the bathroom and shot Steenkamp *believing* that she was an intruder.

It should be clear already that Pistorius's fall from grace following his murder of Steenkamp did little to dislodge the ways in which his image makes it difficult to perceive more complex issues, in the UK or in South

Africa, connected to the violence of neoliberalism or to the lived inter-sections of gender, race, class, and—indeed—disability. Both the 2012 and post-2012 representations function in two-dimensional ways that spectacularize and make representative (for good or, conversely, for evil) a disabled individual: as Michael Smith writes, reporting both on the aftermath of Steenkamp's murder and on a range of activist and artistic responses to violence against women in South Africa, "the ensuing court drama focused largely on his trauma, his story and his impending jail sentence, often neglecting the broken and dead female body at the cen-tre of it all." The etymology of *neglect* centers on that which is not chosen or picked up (*OED*); the austerity of representation that I am excavating from 2012 and 2013 made it possible for viewers or readers to pick up or choose only *his* spectacle, *his* trauma, and *his* story, even as *hers*, and the stories of multiple (broken) others, were far more urgent.

I return to his story and how it functions in relation to the globaliza-tion of disability in crip times at the end of the next section. My larger intent, however, as I move toward the final section of this chapter and toward the activisms I survey in the next, is to pivot away from Pis-torius and from individualism and toward other global or globalizing faces of disability that were not as visible as his widely disseminated image, whether pre- or post-2013, but that worked *tactically* through and around image and spectacle to materialize other possibilities.

Beyond Neoliberal Modes of Regulation: *The Reification of Desire* and Other Pornographic Possibilities

In the final chapter of *The Reification of Desire*, "Notes on a Queer Hori-zon: David Wojnarowicz and the Violence of Neoliberalism," Floyd surveys the work of the late queer writer and artist Wojnarowicz, who died of complications due to AIDS in 1992 and who had lived on the streets for part of his youth, before he produced his most well-known work. The state had officially codified HIV/AIDS as a disability two years earlier in the Americans with Disabilities Act, but Wojnarowicz never lived to benefit from that state recognition and indeed, while he was alive, never stopped directing intense criticism at state institutions. The state in turn continued an official censure of Wojnarowicz's life and work, even years after his death. In 2011, an unfinished thirteen-minute film of Wojnarowicz's, *A Fire in My Belly* (1986), was removed from an exhibition celebrating gay art (and identity) at the Smithsonian National Portrait Gallery, *Hide/Seek: Difference and Desire in American Portraiture*. *A Fire in My Belly* is an enigmatic film that includes a collage of images from the United States and Mexico and defies easy interpretation. Street scenes and Catholic imagery are woven together with some self-portraiture; most notably, *A Fire in My Belly* includes the now-iconic image of Wojnarowicz sewing his mouth shut (an act that of course would foreclose the possibility of speech). This image was also later used in 1989 as part of Rosa von Praunheim's AIDS activist film *Silence = Death*.

In 2011, Republican Congressmen Eric Cantor and John Boehner, who had recently become Speaker of the House of Representatives, demanded the film's removal from *Hide/Seek* on the grounds that it was offensive to their constituents' religious sensibilities. Unsurprisingly, no evidence was provided of actual constituents of Cantor's or Boehner's who had, during their Washington, D.C., vacations, wandered away from the Air and Space Museum or Spy Museum to visit (perhaps inadvertently) the Portrait Gallery and *Hide/Seek* in Chinatown, D.C., but the demand for removal of Wojnarowicz's film was made nonetheless, and for a relatively minor offense. The film includes, for a few brief seconds, images of ants crawling over a crucifix on the ground. Because of ants on a crucifix, *A Fire in My Belly* was deemed offensive by Cantor and Boehner and was literally cast out from a state-sanctioned gay exhibit in 2011. The image of Wojnarowicz's mouth stitched shut, however, makes clear that, at the level of content, the film has also *metaphorically* marked censure, silencing, regulation, or negation since it was first compiled in 1986.[7]

Wojnarowicz himself had written in *Close to the Knives: A Memoir of Disintegration*, "What some people call 'pornography' is simply a rich historical record of sexual diversity that has been made invisible in this world for centuries by organized religions" (148). Cantor's and Boehner's outrage against the dead artist, citing religious sensibilities, bears out Wojnarowicz's point. Attempting to discern a queer horizon that Wojnarowicz's work makes visible as against such regulation and against the capitalist spectacle that was swirling around Wojnarowicz at the time the bulk of his work was produced, however, Floyd considers a very different series of photographs from the early days of neoliberalism that some, or perhaps many, might *also* read as "pornographic" or virtually pornographic [Figure 1.5]: the famous gigantic Calvin Klein underwear ads that have appeared frequently in Times Square in New York City since the early 1980s. The first and most famous example of these ads is of Brazilian athlete Tom Hintnaus, a former Olympic pole vaulter, who appeared on the Times Square billboard in 1982. Bruce Weber's

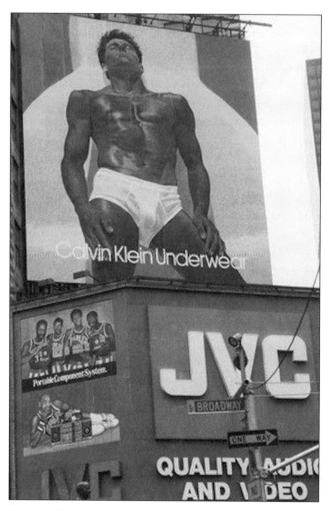

Figure 1.5. Tom Hintnaus, Times Square Calvin Klein ad by Bruce Weber, 1982.

photograph of Hintnaus in white briefs on Santorini, in the Greek islands, was declared to be among the "10 Pictures That Changed America" by *American Photographer* magazine (Wilson). These Times Square photos in general can be understood as marking one form of dispossession (and "pornography"); the critically queer work of Wojnarowicz, another. The argument that I will move toward in this section is that even as inspiration pornography likewise marks one form of dispossession, demonstrated already by its potential to take attention away from disabled activism during the London Olympics and Paralympics (taking away in the process disabled activists' capacity to define *themselves*), other, more generative, forms of dispossession (and forms of what Floyd theorizes as pornography), taking us out of ourselves and making action with others possible, have been put forward by a range of emergent disabled/crip subjects.[8]

Despite the fact that many would read the Calvin Klein images as virtually pornographic, Floyd implies that they are more properly, adequately, or comprehensively understood through the theoretical lens of *identity*, not *pornography*: "such ads began to reach gay audiences through the mainstream media by way of a marketing strategy called 'window advertising': appealing to gay consumers in ways that are sexual but not too sexual, ways intended to avoid alienating straight consumers" (201). This observation about substantialized gay consumers with legible gay identities is, for me, a key point, and one that I would also make about the cripspirational August 2012 Pistorius meme (it substantializes and makes legible a limited type of disability identity), even though, as I have made clear, that meme has been explicitly critiqued by disability thinkers as a type of pornography. Queer horizons, however, or crip/queer horizons, are best understood, I would contend, not so much through the lens of identity, but rather through that of pornography, which Floyd's theorization situates as "a basis for the constitution of queer sociality" (203). An expansive queer sociality was the primary condition of possibility for Wojnarowicz's work.

To make these theses about identity and pornography clear, it's important to provide an overview of Floyd's basic arguments in *The Reification of Desire*. Over the course of his study, Floyd is concerned with excavating the ways in which social formations are subject to various *modes of regulation* during two major periods in the early and late twentieth century: the era of Fordism or mass production (reaching to the early 1970s) and the era that Stuart Hall and others have termed (from *New Times* onward) post-Fordism (our own, current, neoliberal moment). "A mode of regulation," Floyd explains, "is a complex ensemble combining official political structures, practices, and policies with a network of broadly defined social norms and habits, an ensemble that ensures consent, at the level of everyday practical life, to the reproduction of the conditions of accumulation" (34). Fordism, in Floyd's analysis, on a *macroeconomic level* was centered on mass production that was simultaneously a *homogeneous* (and homogenizing) production. The era of Fordism privileged capital accumulation over the *long term*, and to achieve this goal, allowed for or put in place government checks on capital's "most socially destructive tendencies" (196). Put differently, however weak it was, a welfare state was constructed that kept capitalism's propensity toward destructiveness in check (and certainly this welfare state was even weaker in the United States that is Floyd's immediate topic than it was in the UK). This mode of regulation, for Floyd, required from the population a relative normativity or homogeneity in order to function efficiently: "macrosocial forms of regulation," he suggests, "have to be supplemented with microsocial forms of normativity and discipline" (35).

Floyd's conclusion about the *microlevel,* however, or the level of daily life, is necessarily double-edged (or dialectical); those microsocial forms of normativity inevitably generate resistance. Fordism as a way of life, put differently, may have implicitly required enforcement of social norms (Floyd terms it an "enforced uniformity"), but that very uniformity allowed for the germination of a radical "queer sociality" that would articulate and materialize collective refusals of the demand for homogeneity (173, 198). Told by homogenizing social and economic systems to be *either* the same *or* be understood as degraded, perverse, and pathologized, Floyd claims that gay and lesbian communities embraced new, gay ways of being-in-common that were *implicitly* critical of this particular mode of regulation (simply by drawing out its contradictions, its demand to consume in order to realize or possess a valid identity, but nonetheless to *be the same* in and through that consumption) and often, and increasingly, *explicitly* critical of the larger political system (important strands of gay liberation in the late 1960s and early 1970s, as is well-known, were anticapitalist, antiwar, anti-imperialist, antiracist, and antisexist).[9] This radical queer sociality was *not*, in other words, just in opposition to microlevel control (the demand to be the same), but also in opposition to the bigger picture, or the broader totality. Floyd terms this sociality as "pornographic," given its collective celebration of alternative ways for bodies to mingle and connect and share (including sexually but not only sexually) (203). It is in this sociality that Floyd discerns a queer horizon: potentiality, possibility, and—most importantly—an *aspiration toward understanding the social and economic in their totality*. I will discuss *aspiration* as a keyword more directly and dialectically in chapter 4. For now, in my reading a radical *crip* sociality likewise emerges in innumerable locations at this same historical moment, with similar kinds of *disabled* refusals to be degraded, pathologized, or made perverse and similar developments of alternative *disabled* ways of being-in-common together.

To flip things, for Floyd the era of post-Fordism or neoliberalism is characterized on the *macroeconomic level* by "flexible production" aimed at proliferating identifiable targets (target markets were in existence under Fordism but were more muted, and were certainly not "dominant" in Raymond Williams's sense). Post-Fordism privileges capital accumulation over the short term, and through massive programs of privatization has facilitated the rapid redistribution of wealth upward. This mode of regulation no longer uses the state to contain (but rather, arguably, to facilitate) capital's most destructive tendencies. Naomi Klein, as I suggested in the Introduction, actually calls this mode of accumulation "disaster capitalism," as "natural" and human-made disasters often provided the excuse for pushing through privatization and other neoliberal "reforms." If an imagined (and in many ways imaginary) stability was a component of Fordism, it has not been a necessary component of post-Fordism, which more openly (and structurally) thrives on instability. To this point, Klein reads the global rise of privatized security systems (and gated communities, such as the one in which Pistorius and Steenkamp lived) through this new form of capitalization on and through destruction and disaster: "It's easy to imagine a future in which a growing number of cities have their frail and neglected infrastructures knocked out by disasters and then are left to rot, their core services never repaired or rehabilitated. The well-off, meanwhile, will withdraw into gated communities, their needs met by privatized providers" (525). Throughout *The Shock Doctrine*, Klein demonstrates how "the business of providing 'security'" in the midst of perceived instability, in multiple locations including South Africa, has contributed to the massive, short-term accumulation of capital for the few at the expense of the many (552).

On a *microlevel*, post-Fordism is not so reliant on normativity and homogeneity. Floyd thus puts forward two significant conclusions. First, drawing on the work of Harvey, Floyd posits that the microlevel strategy for post-Fordism can be described not as normalization or enforced uniformity but as *dispossession* (Floyd 207). Not making it in this new social and economic system doesn't necessarily mean one is made to conform with or consent to social norms; it means that, whether you are "normal" or "freaky," you are simply and similarly dispossessed, displaced, shut out—literally made homeless, as parts of Floyd's analysis of Wojnarowicz suggest, or interred/made into a refugee, in various parts of Klein's analysis. Harvey, beginning his own analysis of "accumulation by dispossession" with a discussion of Rosa Luxemburg, of course makes clear that something that should be understood as "dispossession" has been a (or even the) structural component of capitalism from its origins (*New* 137). Harvey's study, nonetheless, is still called *The New Imperialism*, suggesting that he intends to spotlight important ("new") differences between generalized capitalist dispossession and what is happening in our own moment. Floyd quotes Harvey's insight that "the U.S. has given up on hegemony through consent and resorts more and more to domination by coercion" (Harvey 201; qtd. in Floyd 207). I interpret Floyd as using Harvey's insights to suggest that global capital has increasingly "given up" on some earlier forms of normalization or enforced uniformity, installing in place of those forms of control an accelerated (and essentially militarized) commitment to dispossession that does not always and everywhere require Fordist uniformity of behavior and identity.

Second, the architects of neoliberalism have strategically secured this new mode of regulation through a foreclosure or *containment of radical queer sociality and the identities that emerged from it*; indeed, Floyd suggests even more forcefully that "an ultimately global horizon of speculative capital threatens to eviscerate" queer sociality (204). Whatever Wojnarowicz's intent (and *Fire in the Belly* is a very cryptic film throughout), the images of the artist stitching his mouth shut are easy to read as part and parcel of a new mode of regulation that contains or domesticates radical sociality. This is why, in contrast, the Calvin Klein underwear ads were not exactly "pornographic" for Floyd. Even if they didn't explicitly present as "openly gay," the ads mark a capitalist recognition of queer sociality and a marketing to *some* of those whose identities emerge from it.[10] Ironically but perhaps poetically, Calvin Klein's first "openly gay" billboard in New York City, on the corner of Houston and Lafayette Streets, appeared during revisions of this book, in August 2015. The ad features two young white men, one sporting a leather jacket on top of the other, in jeans and a sweater. The young man on top has his arms around the neck of the second man, and the two potentially appear as though they are about to kiss. I'm tempted to flip Floyd and suggest that this is twenty-first century "window advertising" (even as it is a logical outcome of the processes he traces): "appealing to [antihomophobic straight] consumers in ways that are sexual but not too sexual, ways intended to avoid alienating [gay] consumers." Despite the "difference" the advertisers want to be legible, the 1982 and 2015 Calvin Klein ads are actually quite similar. Regardless of whether they are "straight" or "gay," they have for more than thirty years contained (and capitalized upon) more radical and queer forms of being-in-common.

The inventive pornography and difference of queer sociality, in other words, could disappear into the identities of neoliberalism. What Floyd terms "identity's glossy normalization" appears to value and integrate difference, but only by privatizing it, attempting to neutralize in the process the more radical forms of collective sociality that produced some identities or identifications as resistant to isolation and pathologization in the first place (203). New and celebrated identities are available to a few, but "a few" who are protected, securitized, gated (both locked into the system, but in many ways locked out of or inoculated from the world-transformative sociality that materialized those identities). Neoliberalism thereby takes possession of gay identity (not least by encouraging those with that identity to realize themselves *through* increasing their personal possessions) and forecloses upon the radical potentiality that gay identity at times signaled and signals.[11]

I draw three conclusions from Floyd as I adapt his arguments here for crip times (and *Crip Times*). First, radical forms of queer *and* crip sociality emerged simultaneously in the 1960s and 1970s with the advent of neoliberalism—these forms of sociality similarly resisted homogenization and normalization and argued for collective modes of existence, caring, and being-in-common. These forms of sociality were also radically embodied in far-reaching ways, including both new forms of engaging with others sexually and new forms of caring for others' bodily needs. In crip communities, and later with the rise of HIV/AIDS activism, these two forms of bodily engagement could at times come together—Corbett Joan O'Toole remembers how the occupation of San Francisco City Hall by disability activists for twenty-eight days in 1978, for example, generated precisely such care-based and sexual experimentation (activists in San Francisco were demanding that the administration of President Jimmy Carter enforce executive orders on disability rights that had been crafted but not implemented over three presidential administrations) (54–74). O'Toole explains in detail how bodily needs (such as bathing) were collectively met during the occupation, but pointedly emphasizes that the monthlong takeover of city administrators' offices included a range of bodily interactions, including "sex in their hallways" (66). Second, neoliberal capital *identifies or targets* some who are caught up in that crip or queer sociality and then *uses* their identities to mask capital's predations. Third, neoliberal capital essentially relocates, displaces, dispossesses, or disappears the rest. This move was quite literal with the Times Square ad—as gay consumers and travelers in a redeveloped Times Square gazed up at such ads, queer communities or collectivities were being dispossessed and displaced, gentrified out of existence. As Floyd puts it, "What lies behind this sheen of interchangeable identities and airbrushed bodies is a horizon of genuinely collective queer movement, as well as the distinctively neoliberal prospect of its disappearance" (202). This move was similarly quite literal from a crip perspective in the UK in August 2012 as disability identity at the most-watched Paralympics ever was spotlighted, globally broadcast, and turned into inspirational memes and advertisements about the Superhumans at the exact same time that disabled people on the ground in the UK were, in actual fact, being measured and assessed in ways that ensured they would be dispossessed of services, sustenance, and livelihood.[12]

Building on these theses from Floyd, I'm interested in the rest of this chapter (and in the next) in where, when, and how disabled people are moving beyond both literal austerity and neoliberal excess *and* the austerity of representation that a story such as Pistorius's, in 2012 and beyond, marks. I'm interested, put differently, in how crips move beyond not just what Cameron identifies in his photo op as "the expectations others have set for you," but beyond the class strategy of disability dispossession (in which Cameron's government was deeply implicated). Moving beyond the critique of *inspiration* porn, moreover, I'm interested in whether *other* forms of what we might call disability pornography, in an expansive understanding of Floyd's sense of the term, might be traced—a resistant, radical, *pornographic* crip sociality, as it were.

In South Africa from 2013 onward, Pistorius's story continued to exemplify processes that work to erase such forms of radical sociality and the connections and critical interventions they make possible. His story has been read, essentially, as a melodrama of identity (disabled role model turned evil disabled killer) rather than as a story taking place in a system that is (as Floyd makes so clear) inherently violent and that actually thrives on melodramas of identity. Indeed, thriving on such melodramas of identity, with their stock characters removed from a more politicized analysis, is arguably itself a form of neoliberal violence. "The focus on Oscar Pistorius as the fallen tragic hero," Sorcha Gunne writes in a book-length study of gendered violence in South Africa, "reinforces the cult of celebrity and . . . detracts from the structural nature of gendered violence" (xii). Pistorius—out and proud, openly disabled—was already incorporated into neoliberalism and securitized, due not directly to his disability but to his race, gender, and wealth. Given the "high priority" placed on security at the Silver Woods Country Estate, "the services of a specialist security consultant have been used to ensure the use of the latest technology"; this includes a "solid, electrified security wall with strict access control" ("Why Silver Woods"). The nearby Silver Lakes Golf estate had in fact been voted in 2009 "the most secure estate in South Africa," due to its nearly identical protection: twenty-four-hour security guards, electrified fences, and gates with controlled and perpetually staffed access ("Pistorius's Home"). Even though (or precisely because) the majority of physical violence occurs in nongated (and nonwhite) spaces elsewhere, and includes a high degree of state/police violence against black bodies, South Africa has one of the largest security industries in the world for white, monied, property owners

(Durington). Contemporary South Africa is in fact founded upon systems of privatization, securitization, dispossession, and identification (identification of the many who are supposed "threats" outside the gates and identification of the few who can be incorporated inside). "Disability" does not materialize in our moment in an environment apart from those systems, but the dominant, individualized modes in which Pistorius's story has always been disseminated makes it difficult to discern that fact.

Systemic violence, in South Africa, violence acted out *differentially* upon the bodies of women, and particularly women of color and queer women, was actually something that Reeva Steenkamp herself had spoken out against. Four days before her own murder, in fact, Steenkamp had tweeted, "I woke up in a happy safe home this morning. Not everyone did. Speak out against the rape of individuals in SA. RIP Anene Booysen #rape #crime #sayNO" (qtd. in Evans). Booysen was a black South African woman who had been gang-raped and disemboweled (her body had been cut open by her attackers) a week earlier, on February 2, 2013. She died in the hospital later that day. Booysen's murder was not explicitly positioned as a "corrective rape," a term that circulates in South Africa to describe the masculinist belief that rape will "correct" deviance (that is, lesbianism) in women. Rape in South Africa, disproportionately affecting black and lesbian women, may happen every 26–36 seconds, according to some estimates, although activists underscore that it is difficult to secure clear data (L. Peterson).[13] Additionally, the extent to which disabled women might be caught up in this gendered violence in South Africa remains very difficult to discern, given that—as one of the few available studies suggests—"disability remains a largely 'invisible' issue in South Africa and, as a result, there is a limited pool of research from which to draw" (Naidu et al.). The report, titled "On the Margins," makes clear that disability is also often an outcome of violence against women; several of the subjects interviewed in the report, for example, were blinded by abusive partners or fathers.

In the case of Steenkamp's murder, none of these dangers could come into focus: an austerity of representation helped to cement and globally disseminate what became the literal story in court. The story, again, that led to Pistorius's initial conviction for culpable homicide, was one about the threat to his own safety that Pistorius felt that evening. Despite the reports from neighbors who believe they heard a heated domestic argument, Pistorius claimed that there was no argument and that he shot Steenkamp four times because he believed she was a burglar. The cover story was thus about a threat to private space, property, and security (all in the masculinist space where the possession and use of firearms is entirely naturalized). A melodramatic story about private fears in private space, however, obscures the *systemic* violence acted out daily on South Africa's dispossessed.

Disability (Dis)Identification and Dispossession: This Is What Disability Looks Like

As I turn toward how things might be otherwise, I want to examine an explicit recent disability counteridentification with inspiration porn [Figure 1.6]. Or really, *dis*identification, in Muñoz's sense of the term "disidentification," since what I will examine here entails a working through and against inspiration porn, or really simultaneously working against but *with* pornography more generally.[14] In the wake of Paralympics spectacle, and in many ways in direct response to the global circulation of the August 2012 Pistorius/Challis image, self-described "badass lawyer-turned-sexologist" Bethany Stevens posted an image of herself and friend Robin Wilson-Beattie, along with Stevens's service dog Sully, as part of a "visual culture" campaign via Facebook (Wood). The black-and-white photo, by Stan Bowman, shows both women looking directly at the camera. Stevens—who is white—is seated in her wheelchair with her legs crossed (revealing her high femme shoes); Wilson-Beattie—who is black—stands behind her, her cane in one hand and a disability tattoo (the universal access symbol merged with a heart) clearly visible on the other arm. The tiny black dog, also looking at the camera, stands in front. "This Is What Disability Looks Like" is written across the top; "F*cking Awesome" across the bottom.

Although the cane, wheelchair, and service dog all have particular meanings that are generally flat, unitary, or objective as far as an ableist culture is concerned (that is, merely functionalist), this beautiful photo, to return to de Certeau on Charlie Chaplin's cane, "multiplies the possibilities" of each, enlivening them as signs of a crip/queer horizon—"in essence, *animating* them," as Mel Y. Chen might put it (37). The elements

Figure 1.6. Bethany Stevens and Robin Wilson-Beattie, This Is
What Disability Looks Like. Photo by Stan Bowman.

of the photo work in concert to exceed either functionalist meanings or
the meanings they would have in isolation to mark access to that crip/
queer horizon. The black-and-white composition of the Bowman photograph additionally marks access to horizons ironically *not* visible (or,
more properly, invisibilized) in the color photograph of Pistorius and
Challis. Although color photography generally allows for the possibility
of excess, given the ways in which it draws on the full spectrum of light
wavelengths that human eyes *might* perceive, the colors in the Pistorius/
Challis photo—white sunlight from a wall of windows in the background,

Challis's blonde hair and yellow sundress, Pistorius's white Nike tank top, the white lettering of the meme—actually collude to make clear how much the cripspirational photo and inspiration pornography in general both depend upon and buttress a univocal whiteness. In contrast, Bowman's photograph narrows or focuses the spectrum of light in ways that paradoxically unleash polyvocality and solidarity across difference: differences of disability, race, and desire are all legible in the black-and-white composition, and a range of queer ways of relating are invoked by the bold and black lettering of "F*cking Awesome."

After posting her own image with Wilson-Beattie, Stevens began to collect and promiscuously post images of others; the campaign quickly spread with dozens of disabled people participating and thousands of people viewing the images around the world. Stella Young, for example, participated from Australia with a similar tagline, "F*cking Irreverent." My own former partner Joseph Choueike (who is as much a central part of my own queer kinship network as when I first wrote about our life together in *Crip Theory*) participated with a smiling image tagged "Brazilian Beach Boy" [Figures 1.7–1.8]. He is posed with a statue of Neptune and wears only a hat and a skimpy bathing suit like those that were ubiquitous on the beaches of Ipanema in the Rio de Janeiro of his childhood. As these photos make clear, "disability" in the project sometimes included "visible" signs such as a wheelchair or cane, and sometimes not. Joseph is, for instance, an immigrant worker living in the United States who also has multiple sclerosis, but one has to either have that prior knowledge or, more commonly and effectively as far as the This Is What Disability Looks Like project might be concerned, to recognize simply that disability has countless valences that are not always apparent to one limited mode of perception, that is, vision.

Merri Lisa Johnson's contribution in fact explicitly included the word "Invisible," with a smiling Johnson standing beside a body of water on a sunny day, holding a dog. The picture, seemingly by accident, however, includes the word "cutting" on a fence behind Johnson, most likely referring to the availability of small cutters for rent nearby [Figure 1.9]. In Johnson's *Girl in Need of a Tourniquet: Memoir of a Borderline Personality*, however, she had actually written at length about a completely different kind of cutting, about what she describes as "the logic that structures every form of self-injury," including "eating disorders

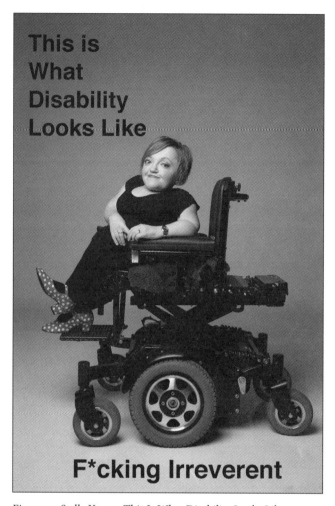

Figure 1.7. Stella Young, This Is What Disability Looks Like.

and cutting and alcoholism" (110). Johnson's portrait and her memoir of borderline personality both underscore that "invisibility" in relation to disability is less an essential quality and more a function of how an austerity of representation trains us to look. Cal Montgomery's widely circulated article, "A Hard Look at Invisible Disability," first published in the disability magazine *Ragged Edge* in 2001, makes a similar point. "In the disability community," Montgomery writes, "we speak as if some kinds of disability were visible, and others weren't. Let me suggest a different approach: think about the ways different kinds of disability have

Figure 1.8. Joseph Choueike, This Is What Disability Looks Like.

become more familiar, and more visible, to you as you've gotten to know more disabled people." The will to perceive disability more expansively that Montgomery and many other activists have invoked was one of the main conditions of possibility for This Is What Disability Looks Like, in 2012.[15]

As news about the project spread, Stevens reports on "how quickly it blew up," as it was taught in disability studies classrooms, profiled in feminist and disability news media, and displayed as part of a "mobile mural project" in Toronto, Ontario (qtd. in Wood). The most important aspects of the campaign, however, are not necessarily these measurable outcomes. Social media campaigns such as This Is What Disability

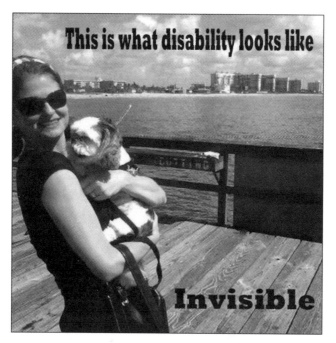

Figure 1.9. Merri Lisa Johnson, This Is What Disability Looks Like.

Looks Like capture, however fleetingly, an emergent affective politics that is particular to a moment in time. This particular campaign, in my reading, pinpointed a will to both register and resist the ways in which cripspiration was being used at a particular moment in the history of contemporary austerity. Cripspiration was working, in concert with other political and economic strategies, to constrain both actual disabled lives and what disability might mean or become. This Is What Disability Looks Like registered an affective discomfort with that constraint and a yearning for something else.

The primary components of This Is What Disability Looks Like are its sociality and potentiality. The campaign is tied to, but not exactly defined or restricted by, a certain identity politics. Disability as clearly delineated and two-dimensional object is soundly rejected, replaced by something that Stevens terms "real," but that can be interpreted as a realness of process rather than substance or essence; these images counter an austerity of representation that necessarily flattens dynamic, ever-evolving crip realities and relations. Critics of such rhetoric deploying what is supposedly "real," Lisa Duggan might argue, "focus on the identities, and overlook politics—which is a way not to take any of it seriously" (*Twilight* 86). To take the emergent politics of This Is What Disability Looks Like seriously means attending to the multiplicity that animates it, both on the side of those contributing images and on the side of those receiving them. How one apprehends the excessive images that are part of the campaign "depends on where you sit/ stand/wobble/lay/etc.," Stevens insists. "People are bloody hungry for images of disabled people that are glimpses of our real lives, not just flattened boring stereotypes of what we are supposed to be. . . . I am tired of images of disabled folks that are supposed to inspire or incite fear" (qtd. in Wood). Some have criticized the project (and by extension, the crip sexologist who spearheaded it) precisely for its excess; not insignificantly, criticisms of the project's excess have been directed toward its more "pornographic" elements. For some, Stevens says, it is "too queer, too sexually provocative, and too fabulous" (qtd. in Wood). Floyd argues, likewise, that certain forms of queer sociality invariably generate "a distinctively punitive reaction" (198). It is thus telling that criticisms of the crip potentiality (and proliferating forms of embodiment) on display in This Is What Disability Looks Like immediately label the project queer (and "too sexually provocative") in an attempt to dismiss or contain it.

The multiplicity and potentiality I am tracing are generated both by the collective mode of the project (making the "this" and "is" that "disability looks like" necessarily nonunitary and nonidentical) and by the mode in which the repeated "this is" necessarily and perpetually gestures toward ways of being-in-common that are *currently being invented*. "A subject," Badiou contends, "is the *local* status of a procedure, a configuration that exceeds the situation" ("Finally" 27). It is, likewise, for Bruno Besana interpreting Badiou, "something that exceeds the *bodies* that inhabit the situation, and the *language* that articulates the sense of their appearance" (40). The *subject of disability* emerging at this moment in translocal crip projects like This Is What Disability Looks Like, thus, is excessive precisely because available languages, even while *seeming* to be excessive (fear, inspiration), have been capable only of configuring disability as deadened object, and have been rigidly incapable of configuring it otherwise (as, that is, subjective in Badiou's sense). Again,

neoliberal excess (like pornographic excess understood more traditionally) proffers us an austerity of representation, but we intuit—or are
bloody hungry for—other crip/queer (pornographic) possibilities.

Simultaneously (and paradoxically) dwelling in the now while gesturing toward a disability yet to come, the assertion "this is what disability
looks like" signals potentiality *without* what Anna Mollow would term
the "rehabilitative futurism" of overcoming (and of course the Pistorius/
Challis meme I have been considering is both literally and figuratively a
rehabilitative image) ("Is Sex" 291). The clearest cognate for me for "this
is what disability looks likes" is the long-standing global activist chant,
"this is what democracy looks like." Although threading through a range
of world-transformative movements (from the Battle of Seattle in 1999
to reporting on the Arab Spring of 2011), "this is what democracy looks
like" has no *necessary* content even though its content is always *sufficient*
for both marking a "realness" of the multitude and gesturing elsewhere.
"This is what disability looks like" functions similarly and echoes the
earlier slogan.

The Calvin Klein underwear ads (appearing at a moment of gentrification and displacement in New York City) and the cripspirational
Pistorius meme (appearing more directly in an age of global austerity) covered over the literal dispossession disproportionately impacting
queer and crip bodies, dispossession marked by "experiences of uprootedness, occupation, destruction of homes and social bonds" emerging
from a "politics of economic precarity in the form of temporary, low-
paying, and insecure jobs, in combination with cuts to welfare provision
and expropriation of public education and health institutions" (Butler
and Athanasiou 11). The rallying cries "this is what democracy looks
like" or "this is what disability looks like," in contrast to these spectacular, individualized images, *generate* another kind of dispossession. What
we might understand as a critically crip dispossession insists on reaching toward new subjectivities opposed to the static identifications that
dominant discourses of neoliberalism both demand *and* use to still or fix
the pornographic excess generated by radical socialities. As Athanasiou
expresses it in her analysis of dispossession's critical possibilities, "rather
than a rehabilitation of the humanist subject in the form of liberal tolerance or assimilatory inclusion of ready-made identities, the political

potential of this critique, if there is any, would be to subvert those norms and open the human to radical rearticulations of humanness" (Butler and Athanasiou 34). Calvin Klein's famous underwear ads don't immediately read as calling for a caption like "This Is What Rehabilitation Looks Like." And yet, in a way, such an ironic caption is not inappropriate if we analyze them, like the inspirational Pistorius meme, as fixing gay and disabled identities for and in neoliberal capitalism and in the process, as foreclosing the resistant and inventive forms of sociality that crip times materialize.

Of course, the images from the This Is What Disability Looks Like project are not located in some magical space outside capitalism or the violence of neoliberalism; if these images aspire to be *inappropriate* (F*cking Awesome, F*cking Irreverent) there's nothing about them that is not *appropriable* like the sexualized images that were eventually translated into marketable fifty-story Times Square advertisements. My pleasure in imagining Stevens and Wilson-Beattie in the fifty-story-high place of the Calvin Klein ads, put differently, is kept in check by my awareness that such a moment of crip hypervisibility would necessarily be an ambivalent one, taming or short-circuiting what was most radical about their representational aspiration. Indeed, *any* moment of "visibility" within capitalism is infused with such dangers (not simply the fabulous moment of crip hypervisibility I am conjuring up). The tattoo in the photo, in fact, marks this ambivalence and danger effectively. In concert with the other elements of the photo, I read the universal access symbol (and heart) as something that shifts from being a merely indicative sign (here is the place where you, a minoritized figure, enter) to being an invitational, open-ended, and queer sign (here we might mark a place where you/we are embraced, celebrated, eroticized and where we haven't yet imagined all the things we might become together). I am aware, however, that the 3ELove Company founded by Stevie Hopkins (the brother of Annie Hopkins, who designed the symbol) in other contexts uses the design to market merchandise such as tote bags, friendship bracelets, and T-shirts ("Meaning of Symbol"). The fact that the symbol can be attached to that which is defiant and F*cking Awesome does not and cannot negate the possibility of its circulation elsewhere as a celebration of disabled entrepreneurship. Within neoliberal capitalism, the space between the inappropriate and the appropriable is *always* fully accessible. The familiar (and even at times a bit tedious) concession about potential appropriation that I am tracing in this paragraph, however, cannot in my mind mute the Gramscian optimism of the will and the critically crip dispossession reflected in the project.[16]

De Certeau argues that tactics "are procedures that gain validity in relation to the pertinence they lend to time—to the circumstances which the precise instant of an intervention transforms into a favorable situation, to the rapidity of the movements that change the organization of a space . . . to the possible intersections of durations and heterogeneous rhythms" (38). Crip tactics like those that can be traced in This Is What Disability Looks Like come forth in 2012 in response to the neoliberal spectacle centered in the UK, but can arguably still be read through the defiance that marked 2011, with which I began this book. My argument in this chapter has been that both critiques of inspiration porn and the differently "pornographic" crip tactics emerging in This Is What Disability Looks Like are a kind of intervention into austerity politics, as

Figure 1.10. "It's Not a Crisis, It's a Swindle," Puerta del Sol, Madrid.

disabled thinkers and activists responded to the rapidity with which the same old deadened images of disability were being put to new uses and obscuring critically disabled perspectives on crip times. In the chapter that follows, I examine some of the ways in which the heterogeneous rhythms of activism in a selection of locations might similarly be traced as varied and timely crip tactics and interventions that imaginatively provided access to crip/queer horizons.

What I would like to put forward in conclusion to this chapter is an imagined future for This Is What Disability Looks Like—and this is not exactly a prescription *for* the literal project because, as I will continue to detail in some of my examples in chapter 2, it was already legible *in* the literal project. Although disability was not obviously central to the varied resistance movements that emerged in and around 2011, it is nonetheless possible to desire an imaginative articulation or linking of "this is what disability looks like" to other global and globalizing cries that were heard at the time. I'm thinking in particular of another of the slogans of Los Indignados in Spain: "No es una crisis, es una estafa" [it's not a crisis, it's a swindle (or scandal)] [Figure 1.10]. Cripping the crises we are in arguably entails linking the lavish excess of "this is what dis-ability looks like" (the project itself, yes, but even more the simple poten-tiality and multivocality of the idea) to global resistance to an austerity politics and to the representational austerity of neoliberalized disability. Cripping these crises, moreover, entails calling out, in the process, the swindle or scandal to which disabled people have been subjected in this particularly dangerous moment.

2

Crip Resistance

Where in the world might crip resistance be located? What contours might such resistance take in an age of austerity? This chapter examines more closely crip tactics of resistance, analyzing a range of collective projects that speak back, in critically disabled ways, to a globalized politics of austerity and to the austerity of representation that subtends it. The modes of counterrepresentation or counterpublicity such tactics proffer have often been positioned by critical theorists, especially queer theorists, as "worldmaking."[1] Kevin Floyd turns in particular to the work of Lauren Berlant and Michael Warner to consider the "improvisational" nature of the critically queer "worldmaking" they theorize: the idea of a queer "'world,'" they write, "like 'public,' differs from community or group because it necessarily includes more people than can be identified, more spaces than can be mapped beyond a few reference points, modes of feeling that can be learned rather than experienced as a birthright. The queer world is a space of entrances, exits, unsystematized lines of acquaintance, projected horizons, typifying examples, alternate routes, blockages, incommensurate geographies" (558; qtd. in Floyd 209). As I indicated in the previous chapter, Bethany Stevens noted that the activist project This Is What Disability Looks Like was deemed "too queer, too sexually provocative, and too fabulous" by some critics. Overt sexualization and queerness, however, are not the only reasons that the campaign was worldmaking in Berlant and Warner's sense. The spatial metaphors Berlant and Warner turn toward to define the queer world (entrances, exits, projected horizons, alternate routes, blockages, incommensurate geographies) quite literally define the disabled world, as do the "unsystematized lines of acquaintance" that construct what Corbett Joan O'Toole (and many others) would characterize as the embodied "interdependent support system" that allows for disability's always-contingent materialization in space (67). Put differently, the improvisational crip worldmaking of projects like This Is What

Disability Looks Like emerges from the stuff of daily living for disabled people navigating and remapping the world as it is, multiplying what Berlant and Warner term "typifying examples" of such improvisation. To adapt or crip the concept of worldmaking, "more people than can be identified" are engaged in the critically disabled project of navigating the ableism upon which neoliberalism relies and remapping the ableist spaces neoliberalism has constructed. The varied activisms this chapter will survey, moreover, generate crip modes of feeling that are learned and passed on rather than experienced as a birthright.

Chapter 2 continues the project of analyzing a crip sociality that can be understood as "pornographic" in Floyd's expansive sense of that term. The pornographic sociality Floyd theorizes calls forth "a world of inherently critical practices and knowledges"; in his analysis, a queer pornographic sociality is radical for many reasons, not least its refusal of the "very distinction between the sexual and social" (203). My intent has been to expand Floyd's concept for crip times to imagine a *disabled* sociality that likewise has historically refused the very distinction between the social and bodies engaged in *a range of intimate practices* that can certainly include sex (as O'Toole's and many other memoirs make very clear) but that can also include other embodied ways of being-in-common. To texture this pornographic imagination, this chapter turns toward activisms that literally are, as Berlant and Warner would have it, "geographically incommensurate." These activisms are, however, like the other creative practices I consider throughout *Crip Times*, nonetheless contiguous in that each locates embodiment at the center of an opposition to austerity.

After a section focused directly on crip/queer theories of *resistance* (the keyword that is at the center of chapter 2), I turn toward activisms I will read as crip in the United States, Chile, Spain, and Greece before circling back to the United Kingdom. The first crip tactic I examine is thus located in the virtual space of crip/queer theory; the remaining five tactics are located in geographic locations where activists have worked to centralize disability as against the ongoing globalization of austerity. I describe what is happening in these distinct geographic locations as social sculpture, craving disability, conscientious objection, social medical centers, and appropriation and theatricalization. As he explicitly theorizes resistance, Michel de Certeau turns toward "tricky and stubborn procedures that elude discipline without being outside the field in which it is exercised"; in that vein, de Certeau might describe the six crip tactics I put forward here as "swarming activity," "proliferating illegitimacy," or "surreptitious creativities that are merely concealed by the frantic mechanisms and discourses of the observational organization" of the state (96). The 2011 rallying cry with which I ended the last chapter—"No es una crisis, es una estafa" [it's not a crisis, it's a swindle (or scandal)]—undermines or delegitimizes neoliberal states (in all senses of that phrase) and underwrites each of the tactics I consider in the pages ahead.

Tactic 1: Queering Crip Resistance, Cripping Queer Resistance

This chapter examines disability in relation to a keyword drawn from the subtitle to this book: *resistance*. In this section, I consider how crip/queer theorists have attended to the theoretical vicissitudes of this keyword; I position their theorizing as itself a tactic of resistance. *Resistance* has arguably had an uneven history of late in critical cultural theory, perhaps especially in queer theory. For a time, a certain foundational strand of queer theory indebted to the work of philosopher Michel Foucault has emphasized a theory of necessary or inevitable resistance. "Where there is power, there is resistance," Foucault famously wrote. "And it is doubtless the strategic codification of those points of resistance that makes a revolution possible" (*History* 95, 96). As something called queer theory was congealing in the 1990s, David Halperin, in his book *Saint Foucault: Towards a Gay Hagiography*, was a key figure spelling out what Foucauldian (queer) resistance could mean. Detailing in particular the ways in which Foucault's work makes possible an understanding of power not as always and everywhere repressive but as productive, Halperin insisted that "*the aim of an oppositional politics is . . . not liberation but resistance*" (18). For Foucault, in Halperin's interpretation, dreams of "liberation" from "repression" posited or imagined spaces outside power and could not really grasp the insidious ways in which the very languages to which we are subjected (languages of "sexuality," for example) materialize and secure specific ways of being and knowing and block inventiveness and creativity. "Does the expression 'let us liberate our sexuality' have a meaning?" Foucault asks. "Isn't the problem rather to try to decide the practices of freedom through which we could determine what is sexual pleasure and what are our erotic, loving, passionate relationships with others?" (qtd. in Halperin 193–194). The queer sociality that is Floyd's topic would, in this understanding, not seek somehow to liberate an underlying essence or truth; it would, rather, inventively generate new (and resistant) forms of pleasure and relationality.

A focus on practices of freedom that generate inventive new forms of intimacy and indeed, "life" has likewise characterized disability studies work on *resistance*. The most foundational work in this vein, such as the essays collected in Shelley Tremain's important edited collection *Foucault and the Government of Disability*, often pinpoints the ways in which the supposed "truth" of disabled lives is constituted diagnostically through the workings of what Foucault terms juridical power. Fixed with a diagnosis, disabled subjects are then reductively understood through, and always and everywhere made to speak the truth of, their pathology: this pathology and only this pathology, juridical power might say, is what disability looks like. Again, however, even as various forms of authority, especially medical authority, appear to be always and only negative or repressive, such encounters necessarily generate excessive subjects speaking otherwise. Tremain writes that "individuals and *juridically constituted* groups of individuals have responded to subjecting practices, which are connected in increasingly intimate and immediate ways to 'life,' by formulating needs and imperatives of that same 'life' as the basis for political counterdemands, that is, by turning them around into focuses of resistance" (7, emphasis in the original). Resistant practices of freedom echo across, or are made imperative in, virtually all the most famous slogans of disability movements globally. If juridically constituted groups of disabled individuals are objectified by medical authority, pitied by nondisabled others in and through that objectification, and perhaps even encouraged and assisted (in increasing numbers of locations) to end their own lives, those constituted as such respond collectively with assertions like "nothing about us without us," "piss on pity," and "assisted living, not assisted dying." "This is what disability looks like" is here put forward as a resistant counterdemand, unfixing what would appear to be (in Tremain's words) "that same 'life.'"

The urgency of such counterdemands, particularly as they individually and collectively reanimate those subjectified as disabled, underscores Halperin's point that "such radicalism is not merely a radicalism for its own sake, a fashionable attachment to whatever may look new in the way of personal and political styles" (66). Nonetheless, as queer theory in particular has flourished in the two decades since *Saint Foucault*, achieving in the process a legible cachet and marketability in the academy and in academic publishing (which arguably thrives on that which "looks new" in relation to a range of intellectual and political styles), a certain congealing of *resistance*, that perhaps *could* be described as "radicalism for its own sake," is evident. A well-intentioned critique of the mainstream lgbt movement's incorporation into state and capital has as its flip side a longing for a somewhat innocent figure of "resistance."

In his study *Under Bright Lights: Gay Manila and the Global Scene*, Bobby Benedicto traces both sides of this conundrum in queer theory:

> Indeed, much of the work on what might be termed *queer complicities* has focused on how gay white men (or conflated figures of gayness and whiteness) are implicated in practices of exclusion and embedded in market capitalism. This is an important focus but I am wary of how it leads, directly or indirectly, to the conjuration of a list of abstracted, othered figures: the queer of color, the third-world queer, the disabled queer, the working-class queer, and the like that are invested with the potential for transgression by virtue of their exclusion and on whom faith is placed for a still radical politics. (13–14, emphasis in the original)

Benedicto's important project thus attempts to pull back from abstraction, particularly removing the "third-world queer" (a figure based in the Philippines, in Benedicto's anthropological study, but a figure who imagines himself as a citizen of a global gay network) from a space of innocence: "the third-world queer is not just the other but an other that makes his own others: 'He' is at the center of the city and at the margins of the world" (14). "His own others," in the Manila of *Under Bright Lights*, are often haunting, disabled figures, "as when gay men drive around at night to head to the clubs, but are suddenly caught in standstill traffic and come face-to-face with the vagrants on the road: the old blind men and women with their plastic cups stretched out and their walking sticks tapping lightly on the wheels" (11). This passage, of course, arguably participates in exactly what it is critiquing, as blind men and women are objectified, made into others, through Benedicto's staging of the scene; the very syntax of the passage performs what it purports to describe, as the colon points toward vagrants made into objects. Still, Benedicto's larger point remains: if any queer theoretical location has invoked or produced the third-world queer as the figure "on whom faith is placed for a still radical politics," such claims should always be subjected to scrutiny. *Under Bright Lights*, at its best, disallows any innocent investment in the third-world queer, and by extension any innocent investment in other abstracted figures.

Resistance as it has congealed in some queer theoretical texts, for Benedicto is thus not necessarily something to aim for: "I want to suspend the academic desire to spot difference and *resistance*, and to acknowledge that local *agency* also works in the service of modernist aspirations, that it can be mobilized to reproduce the center in the margins, is constrained by the force of material environments, and remains animated by narratives of progress and modernity" (17). It's worth pointing out, however, that *simply* spotting difference and resistance is already a compromise of Foucauldian resistance, as Halperin's study makes clear. That is because spotting, identifying, and putting faith in a figure endows that figure with a substance or essence that is untrue to the ways power works in a Foucauldian sense. Spotting difference and resistance suggests that there is nothing left to do once it is found; it can, essentially, only be admired. Foucault himself, however, consistently turned away from the fantasy of simply spotting or naming that which was supposedly or inherently good (and, of course, thereby liberatory) or bad. In a famous quotation that would become Tremain's epigraph for *Foucault and the Government of Disability*, he insists, "My point is not that everything is bad, but that everything is dangerous, which is not exactly the same as bad. If everything is dangerous, then we always have something to do" ("Geneaology" 256; qtd. in Tremain front matter). In Foucault's sense, since identifying/spotting the third-world queer would always be dangerous, acknowledging, as Benedicto does, "that local *agency* also works in the service of modernist aspirations," is actually itself a resistant act. Moreover, writing a thorough anthropological study of how that complicit agency *functions* (including how it might function in relation to haunting crip figures who emerge in the margins of the text) is part of the "something to do" that always remains. This is not at all to undercut Benedicto's aim of suspending the academic desire to spot difference and resistance; it is to point out that where that academic desire has conjured up innocent others over the past few decades it is not actually *resistant* in the ways that concept has been theorized by some commentators on Foucault such as Halperin or Tremain.

Nirmala Erevelles, like Benedicto, is cautious about the ways in which *resistance* in academic writing can become a mesmerizing but ineffective "transgression": "Poststructuralism's deconstructive potential along with its limitless possibilities for (re)imagining the transgressive body makes for seductive scholarship—a point not lost on disability studies scholars who have done radical work in retheorizing disability outside the constricting limits of dominant discourse" (12). Erevelles's *Disability and Difference in Global Contexts: Enabling a Transformative Body Politic*, however, sustains a deep commitment to *collective* resistance: "At the intersections of race, class, gender, sexuality, and disability, we will find that collective resistance is more fruitful than individualized forms of resistance" (120). *Disability and Difference in Global Contexts* is one of the defining texts in what might be understood as a "global turn" in disability studies; it is now indispensable for theorizing intersectionality in the field. As the subtitle suggests, "transformation" is prioritized by Erevelles over a ludic "transgression." The book also furthers urgent conversations that remain underdeveloped in disability studies, considering in particular the ways in which disability is often caused by the devastations of capitalism, imperialism, and war. Throughout *Disability and Difference in Global Contexts*, Erevelles reaches for what she terms "a common platform of resistance" (130), and rightfully critiques theorists, including transnational feminist theorists, who do not or cannot incorporate a materialist analysis of disability into their work.

Erevelles calls for a disability studies that consistently theorizes disability in relational, transnational contexts; her call particularly resonates for me, writing in and about a period when a compulsory common sense about austerity has been imposed (often forcefully) globally. As should be clear throughout *Crip Times*, I share both Erevelles's critique of hegemonic forms of capitalist globalization and her sense that collective resistance remains urgent. I also agree with the implication that

a poststructuralist theory imagining what she terms "limitless possibilities" would not be particularly resistant. Such a theory would also,
however, not be particularly poststructuralist, as a rigorous poststructuralist attention to the instabilities of signification should certainly not
translate into a world of limitless possibility but rather a world where
the intertwined discursive and material construction of limits should be
continually interrogated. In a slightly different context, Sara Ahmed reminds us that "the poststructuralist critique of language was that words
are far from trustworthy . . . the poststructuralist turn begins with a
suspicion of words as much as things" (34); the necessary suspicion
Ahmed writes about is completely lost if poststructuralism is resignified (or fixed) as agentic, individualistic, and limitless.[2] Erevelles's char-
acterization of poststructuralism as encouraging limitless possibility
would essentially, in Judith Butler's terms, "restore a figure of a choosing
subject," and ignore the ways in which the poststructuralist theory Erevelles derides actually *encourages* "collective disidentifications [which]
can facilitate a reconceptualization of which bodies matter, and which
bodies are yet to emerge as critical matters of concern" (Butler, *Bodies*
x, 4). There is a difference between poststructuralist theory more generally and an academic marketplace which can indeed encourage writing that simply spots difference and transgression. The existence of that
academic marketplace (about which both Benedicto and Erevelles are
rightly wary) should not obscure the fact that there is far more common
ground than her study acknowledges between a critical attention to textuality, discourse, and the slipperiness of signification and the Marxist
materialism and collective resistance that *Disability and Difference in
Global Contexts* puts forward.[3]

Arguing that "we shall need a literary imagination" to supplement
conventional forms of political resistance or revolution, Darieck Scott
advances, in *Extravagant Abjection: Blackness, Power, and Sexuality
in the African American Literary Imagination*, a reading of bodily and
mental distress in the work of Frantz Fanon that *both* affirms the need
for "a reservoir of resistance to the colonizer's acts of subjugation and
enslavement" *and* attempts to account for what is lost when the complex workings of language and textuality are discounted (94, 65). Scott's
analysis is not explicitly crip, and yet his attention to wounded bodies
and minds (the bodies and minds Fanon tended during the Algerian

revolution) has much to offer disability studies, especially in relation to *resistance*. Surveying the ways in which Fanon writes about his patients, Scott particularly attends to the ongoing metaphor of muscular tension. Fanon examines bodies that have been beaten down and broken by colonization and war and sees in those disabled bodies both the *need* for an active and ongoing resistance to colonization and the *potential* for that active resistance. Wounded, tense muscles, in Scott's reading of Fanon, are indicative and anticipatory: they *indicate* what colonialism and war have done and *anticipate* an active resistance, by those same bodies, to colonial domination. Fanon can in some ways be aligned with Erevelles here, since—as I have indicated—she too focuses, more than fifty years later, on how disability is often caused by colonialism and capitalism. Like Fanon, moreover, Erevelles looks beyond language and textuality toward forms of active resistance that would counter those systems.

Scott, however, while consistently acknowledging that "the need to continue this pursuit [of active resistance] is clear" (9), lingers over the *language* of abjection, blackness, and woundedness, discovering within it other forms of resistance. Paradoxically, Scott reanimates *resistance* in and through abjection. If Fanon moves quickly from literal and metaphorical broken bodies and tensed muscles to "the robust self-endorsement" that is ultimately a form of Black Power (9), Scott examines what is lost in a too hasty dismissal of the conviviality, in language, of abjection, blackness, and woundedness. Although it is not at all his intent, Scott excavates an ableism that is inherent to Fanon's theory and by extension any theory that would conjure away the twisted contours of the literary imagination. Fanon's postcolonial subject cannot locate value in woundedness and brokenness; resistance *only* emerges when that subject overcomes his linguistic relegation to abjection, blackness, and disability. Scott, however, pinpoints another form of resistance that is always in circulation around the resistance, power, and consciousness Fanon puts forward. The "fading scars," to turn toward the title of O'Toole's memoir, remain scars for Scott.

O'Toole's memoir might be understood as performing, in a different vein, what Scott theorizes, although she more explicitly combines Scott's literary imagination with the (disability) materialism of Erevelles. O'Toole writes, "My scars define me. I have often wanted to host a Scar Camp where I can celebrate and mourn my scars with other disabled people, where being scarred is the norm. . . . Where we sing and paint and write and perform our scar stories. . . . Scars remind me that the traumas of my past will always accompany me, faded though they may be" (46–47). Scott would likely argue that "Fanon does not value this form of resistance except as the sketchy lineaments of a figure yet to be fully realized." Yet this scarred, wounded figure—a figure that is literally disabled but never named as such by Scott—"possesses an intriguing quality: defeated, working within and saturated by the defeat that constitutes its foundation and the limits of its effectiveness, yet not defeated, in such a way that it exceeds the defeat and takes on a powerfulness that the defeat does not quash or necessarily succeed in assimilating" (70–71). Scott uses the phrase "extravagant abjection" to describe the resistance that is legible in brokenness, wounds, and scars (10). In the remainder of this chapter, I carry Scott's (and O'Toole's) theory of resistance to a selection of locations, articulating extravagant abjection to crip tactics that are pushing back against austerity.

Austerity arguably generates extravagant abjection, literally wounding bodies and minds and then metaphorically redoubling that woundedness by pointing to the faded scars and insisting that they *merit* austerity, as they have no value and supposedly generate no value. Crip/queer theorizing of *resistance*, I have implied here, is itself a crip tactic that opposes both such austere ways of thinking and austerity as an economic policy. In the rest of this chapter, turning toward what I identify as an excessive crip sociality in the United States, Chile, Spain, Greece, and the UK, I note the ways in which subjects in those locations collectively linger over scars, woundedness, and disability. In Scott's sense, they take on a powerfulness that defeat does not quash or necessarily succeed in assimilating. The deconstructive potential of language and a desire to find value in abjection are at work in each of the remaining tactics in this chapter, *alongside* or *in and through* the more recognizable or legible, active collective resistance that is needed to counter austerity.

Tactic 2: Crip Camp/Social Sculpture

Before Occupy was Occupy, before Los Indignados were indignant, activists on a traffic island in Berkeley, California, set up a (crip) camp called Arnieville to protest the massive cuts to disability benefits

Figure 2.1. Petra Kuppers and Neil Marcus in Arnieville, Berkeley, California.

by Republican Governor Arnold Schwarzenegger's administration [Figure 2.1]. Described by Petra Kuppers as "an activist camp and tent village erected by a coalition of disabled, poor, and homeless people," Arnieville was set up in the late spring and early summer of 2010 to insist, "Cuts kill, taxes save lives. Interdependence, not independence" ("Introduction" 15). Arguably not unlike the Scar Camp O'Toole envisions, where disabled bodies are the norm, Arnieville was located across from the Berkeley Bowl supermarket, and included a giant Schwarzenegger puppet with a raised hatchet. Kuppers describes it as in some senses a toxic space, given both the fumes of exhaust and the loud noise of the traffic. The situation in California was also simultaneously toxic in a more metaphorical sense for disabled people facing the raised hatchet, which is why activists occupied the traffic island and declared it Arnieville. Arnieville activists were specifically responding to cuts at the time that would eliminate personal attendant services to about 400,000 people in the state of California. During Schwarzenegger's eight-year term, however (2003–2011), his austerity agenda targeted many different services used by both disabled and old people (groups that of course overlap), cutting more than $500 million from the budget.

Austerity cuts in California's (and other US states') budget are already a class strategy, in that vulnerable subjects bear the brunt of the supposed "crisis," while the wealthy are protected through tax loopholes, easy access to privatized services, or financial investment that is out of reach for the poor. In 2010 (and indeed, currently), the state had both the highest number of ultrawealthy individuals and the most residents living in poverty (one in every four individuals, nearly a quarter of the population); the wealth continued to flow upward toward that class of ultrawealthy individuals as the global economic crisis intensified (Miles). By 2013, the number of individuals with a net worth of $30 million in California was 12,560 (New York, in second place, had 8,945 individuals classified as ultrawealthy) (Miles). Beyond drawing attention to that redistributive class strategy (relocating wealth upward), however, Kuppers argues that the crip camp erected at Arnieville itself navigated class differences in more quotidian ways in order to flourish for the brief time of its existence: "Arnieville has changed my perspective on the homeless folk that I see around my home spaces, and I now do know some of them by name" ("Introduction" 17).

I'm calling this second tactic "crip camp" in order to mark its anticipatory connection to encampments (in the Puerta del Sol in Madrid, on Wall Street in New York, and elsewhere) that were more visible in 2011, the following year, but that were less explicitly or obviously defined by disability (Occupy Wall Street was, in fact, at times critiqued for its inaccessibility).[4] Emphasizing the embodied relationality or radical sociality of the space, Kuppers herself calls Arnieville a "social sculpture" ("Introduction" 17). Above and beyond any direct impact that the encampment had on California policy (and she is "skeptical" about a measure of success that would simply gauge Arnieville's impact via changes in policy), Kuppers argues that there was "a politics of engagement and relationality, of embodied contact, of shared space and common ground" (16). Kuppers's metaphor of "common" ground and the literal ground claimed by activists in Berkeley again suggest that crip times need to be understood not only temporally (times of austerity, times of resistance), but spatially.

Kuppers is both a disability studies scholar and a performance artist, and she often works with audiences in participatory ways that encourage bodily engagement. "Social sculpture," then, for Kuppers, both in her own work as a performer and as it materialized at Arnieville, refers to what she calls "a social somatics: a therapy for the world, an unhinging of space and time, for a moment. In that unhinged time, in the long duration, after those of us who talk are talked out, we can take shared breaths, with the tinge of exhaust on our tongue" ("Social Somatics" 191). "Unhinged time," as Kuppers imagines it here, functions very much as "crip times," the concept, does for me throughout this book. *Unhinged* clearly circulates as a term for disability, particularly mental disability, as the word is used to signify those who are "mentally unbalanced, deranged" (*OED*). Just as I deploy "crip times" throughout, however, to signify both the harshness of the austere moment we inhabit and the potentiality legible in vibrant crip resistance to that moment, Kuppers's "unhinged time" cannot be fixed by the abject, negative valences of *unhinged*. "Unhinged time" for Kuppers, even in the midst of the literal toxicity with which she concludes this passage, generates new possibilities and livable temporalities as bodies come together in inventive new ways.

Continuing their protests under Jerry Brown's administration, the Arnieville group used the name CUIDO: Communities United in Defense of Olmstead, but also "care," or "I care," in Spanish. CUIDO officially contends that the ongoing cuts in California "threaten to institutionalize people with disabilities and seniors against their will, in violation of Olmstead, a Supreme Court ruling on the Americans with Disabilities Act stating that unnecessary segregation of individuals with disabilities in institutions constitutes discrimination based on disability" ("CUIDO"). CUIDO's activism has of necessity extended beyond the traffic island (just as, a year later, Occupy Wall Street's 2011 activism eventually extended beyond Zuccotti Park in Manhattan). There have been marches and demonstrations in various locations; under the heading of "CUIDO demanding our rights," the group participated in the This Is What Disability Looks Like campaign [Figure 2.2]. CUIDO's activism has, moreover, extended itself into a virtual realm and, in that extension, moves beyond any unitary focus on US legislation. Indeed, the stretchiness of CUIDO's name allows for a reading of "crip camp" less as a physical reality and more as a contingent and ongoing practice of resistance or freedom, to be erected wherever and however neces-

Figure 2.2. "CUIDO Demanding Our Rights," This Is What
Disability Looks Like.

sary: in Spanish, it is a first-person statement, but the group's name
actually gestures toward nonunitary, collective, inventive social practices.[5] Such shape-shifting, moreover, is a long-standing disability activist tactic. The acronym for the radical group ADAPT, for example,
has likewise meant different things in a few different times and places,
according to the urgencies activists were identifying at any given moment (Fleischer and Zames 82, 104–105).[6] Crip social sculptures are
adaptive performances and as such, are always simultaneously embodied and spectral, materializing in unique and creative ways in different
times and places.

Tactic 3: Craving Disability: Huelgas de Hambre

The Summer 2011 antiausterity protests in Madrid had a more specific counterpart during what, in the Southern Hemisphere, came to
be known as the Chilean Winter that same year. The Chilean student

movement that grabbed the attention of the world not long after the emergence of the Spanish #15M movement was not focused on general austerity policies (and in fact the Chilean economy was being touted by pundits for its vibrancy and "growth" at the time). Instead, the movement was focused on specific neoliberal policies connected to the system of education—a system that many perceived as the most significant remnant of Augusto Pinochet's dictatorship and the violent beginnings of neoliberalism in the country. Chilean higher education was among the most expensive and unequal in the hemisphere, and the government of right-wing President Sebastián Piñera was seeking to increase fees for university students. Faced with that increase, a student movement, initially led by the charismatic Camila Vallejo (a member of the Communist Youth of Chile and former president of the University of Chile Student Federation), demanded on the contrary, no es una crisis, es una estafa, and that education be free and accessible to all.

The movement to reform Chilean education at all levels had actually begun during the previous administration of center-Left President Michelle Bachelet in 2006, in what was termed the March of the Penguins (because of the uniform that secondary school students in Chile wear). The March of the Penguins, or Penguin Revolution, demanded free transportation to schools and an end to the subsidization of private secondary schools, which essentially codified the unequal system: rich students would attend subsidized private schools with rich students, while the poor and working-class students attended public schools in which the government had not adequately invested (public monies, in other words, were often redirected toward private and essentially exclusive education for the upper and upper middle classes). The ultimate demand of the March of the Penguins was quality education for all, and the 2011 protests, more directly focused on higher education, continued and extended this legacy. When I myself arrived in Santiago two years later, in advance of the spring elections that swept Piñera's party out of office and Bachelet herself back in (along with several leaders of the student movement who were elected to Parliament, including Vallejo), the ongoing demand was still in evidence everywhere, with graffiti calling for "Educación Gratis Ahora" [Free Education Now!] visible on walls all around the city [Figure 2.3].

Figure 2.3. "Free Education Now!" Graffiti in Santiago, Chile.
Photo by Author.

The Chilean student movement from 2011 on did not immediately present as a "disability" movement (and still would not be understood as such by the vast majority of people who pay attention to it). Yet images of disability haunted the movement's emergence onto the global scene, as several passionate students connected to the movement began a hunger strike that lasted for more than two months. The strike began on July 19, 2011 with nine students in the Buin neighborhood of metropolitan Santiago; nearly twenty students around the country joined them in the following few weeks. On August 15, three of the students from Buin took their strike to a higher level, refusing liquids as well as solid food (B. Peterson; Medwave).

Although it was never the main focus, in the margins of newspaper reporting on the ongoing protests in Santiago and across the country, crip images began to appear because of these hunger strikes. The students on hunger strike were attending the protests and marches in wheelchairs, often pushed by their comrades ("Huelga") [Figure 2.4]. Even more ubiquitous were representations of masks covering the mouths of the hunger strikers, thereby protecting their weakened immune systems (this protection would be particularly important in Santiago, which

Figure 2.4. Chilean hunger strikers march in Santiago, Chile.

since its founding by conquistadors in the sixteenth century, has sat in a valley that traps dust, pollution, and—in contemporary times—heavy smog). This imagery of wheelchairs and masks perhaps remained in the margins of globally disseminated imagery because more popular representations of the movement emphasized more consistently an arguably mythologized health and vigor. Yet the *huelgistas de hambre* enable us to apprehend the movement otherwise.

An official statement issued by the "Comisión Apoyo Huelgistas" [Commission for the Support of Hunger Strikers] included an image of four students in masks, identified as "Estudiantes en Huelga de Hambre" above the words (in block letters) "Ni Un Minúto Solos" [Not One Minute Alone] ("18 de Septiembre") [Figure 2.5]. A number of Chilean hip hop artists—Portavoz, Profeta Marginal, MC Erko, and Raza Humana—produced and disseminated a collaborative video with the same title, extending the significance of the words "Ni Un Minúto Solos." If in the students' photo, the words signified both solidarity with each other and a literal protection of each others' health (they would not, that is, be even a minute alone because care for each other's potentially declining health and ability required collective vigilance), in the video that solidarity with increasingly disabled hunger strikers reverberated outward along with the beat to the Chilean student movement as a whole, to Chilean artists supporting the students' demands, and (in some ways) to other global movements becoming visible at the time. In fact, at some protests, identical signs were in evidence in both Santiago and Madrid: I saw protestors wrapped in Chilean flags identifying themselves as "Chilean Indignados" in the Puerta del Sol in Madrid in August 2011, while signs appeared in Chile that same month that had also been used in

Figure 2.5. "Not One Minute Alone," Chilean hunger strikers.

Madrid, announcing (for example), "Si Jesús estuviera aquí . . ." [If Jesus were here], he would be marching too because he was poor.

In "Ni Un Minúto Solos," Portavoz's opening lyrics declare:

> La democracia es un fraude gigante
> Niños y apoderados dando una huelga de hambre
> Por una educación gratis donde su calidad
> No dependa de tu bolsillo, tu apellido o nido social.
> [Democracy is a giant fraud
> Children and their guardians are on a hunger strike
> For a free and quality education
> That does not depend upon the wealth in your pocket, your last
> name, or social class.]

The video opens with flashing numbers, indicating the number of days of the hunger strike, and then shows several students with masks seated together on the floor. The flashing numbers anticipate Portavoz's beat, and the video continues with a montage of images, including protests and political cartoons targeting Piñera. One image, for example, represents police advancing on a lone protestor holding a volume, with the caption "¡Tiene un libro! ¡Tiene un libro!" [He has a book! He has a book!]. The individual shots of hunger strikers represent them wearing their masks: Karla, fifty days without eating; Francisco, starving for education, etc.

Several things interest me about all this imagery from 2011 onward. Taking seriously the potentiality and open-endedness of the rallying cry I considered in the previous chapter, this too, inescapably, "is what disability looks like." And again, although somewhat uniquely, this too is a disability committed to calling out swindles and scandals. Second, these images are even more clearly offering up disability loosened from a certain kind of identity politics more legible and important (at least for some disability activists and theorists) in places like the United States. Third, and perhaps seductively, the activist passion and commitment in these images put forward, provocatively, a tactical and contingent, but nonetheless real, *desiring* or craving of disability, an embrace of it in the interests of, and indeed as the contingently representative face of, a larger activist movement. The 2011 hunger strikes did eventually end as Piñera was ousted, but for a time students collectively wrote the larger movement onto their bodies with the aim of generating conditions more favorable to their demands for free and accessible education. Piñera's loss was seen as an important step toward generating those conditions.

The representative face of the movement shifted momentously yet again in the Chilean autumn and winter of 2015. Although Bachelet's government gave some lip service to a free and accessible education for all, even suggesting initially that it would come as early as 2016, the student movement remained dissatisfied with both the pace of reform and with the possibility that their demands for an equally accessible education for all would be diluted (in ways that would essentially preserve and even sediment the deep class divide that characterized the system). As of this writing, student protests have continued in Santiago, Valparaíso, and elsewhere in Chile, and police repression of those protests has escalated; observing one such protest in June 2015, I found myself suddenly running with students as riot police and water cannons moved in without warning to shut it down [Figure 2.6]. What made this heightened repression even more shocking was that at the time, one

Figure 2.6. Police disperse student activists with water cannons, Santiago, Chile. Photo by Author.

student had just emerged from a coma in a hospital in Viña del Mar, near Valparaíso. On May 21, 2015 Rodrigo Avilés was participating in a protest in the coastal city of Valparaíso, when water cannons moved in to disperse the students. The police were caught on video pointing the cannon at very close range at Avilés as he moved with a group of activists down the sidewalk; he suffered a severe injury to the head when he was thrust to the pavement. The incident resulted in neurological damage to the right side of the brain, and the coma was initially induced to save Avilés's life. Over the course of the winter, Avilés underwent surgeries and began a long process of rehabilitation, details of which were widely available in the Chilean media. Outside the hospital, across the country, and across social media, the movement began to coalesce around Avilés's image and story. The video of the attack itself and other videos, including interviews with those who were witnesses to it, were widely disseminated.

Emerging from the induced coma at the end of May, Avilés remained in treatment and was released from the hospital on July 21. A photograph from that day came to represent the movement at that moment; it circulated more widely within Chile than any single photo-

Figure 2.7. "Never Surrender!" Rodrigo Avilés.

graph of Vallejo had circulated in 2011 (Núñez). A red scarf around his smiling, bearded face, Avilés is depicted standing in his hospital room, holding a Chilean flag across which the words "Rendirse Jamás!!" [Never Surrender] are written [Figure 2.7]. Again, this is what disability looks like, although—as I am contending—the student movement in Chile has (still) not been interpreted as a "disability" movement as such.[7] Avilés's image, however, unexpectedly supplementing the earlier images of *huelgistas de hambre* and even, for a time in 2015, becoming representative, is arguably as crip as any of the imagery to result directly from the diverse resistance movements that emerged globally in 2011.

Tactic 4: También Soy Inmigrante: Conscientious Objection

As I noted in my Introduction, since the government of Mariano Rajoy took power in Spain in late 2011, it has consistently executed one of the harshest austerity agendas in the Eurozone. Since 2014, both Rajoy's Partido Popular (PP) [People's Party] and the Partido Socialista Obrero Español (PSOE) [Spanish Socialist Workers' Party] have been challenged by Podemos [We Can], an antiausterity party opposed to this agenda (and, according to some analyses, a direct result of the #15M mobilization). Although the two-party "common sense" consensus on the need for an ongoing and punishing policy of austerity has been challenged by Podemos, it remains unclear if or how the party will affect the future of Spanish politics, especially after Rajoy was confirmed again as prime minister in 2016. As with the cuts in California or the fee increases in Chile, the policies of the PP have both targeted and congealed vulnerable bodies that become signs of excess that must be trimmed for the economic crisis to be alleviated. The PP has congealed such bodies by materializing groups that can be managed through marginalization, exclusion, or expulsion. Badiou might term these vulnerable bodies, which "are present in the world but absent from its meanings and decisions about its future, the *inexistent* of the world" (*Rebirth* 56). Change begins to take place, or becomes "real" for Badiou, "when an inexistent of the world starts to exist in the same world with maximum intensity" (*Rebirth* 52). The fourth crip tactic in an age of austerity that I will cite here explicitly welcomes the inexistent at a moment when the state refuses such a welcome and in fact criminalizes those who desire it.

As of September 1, 2012 (in a move that was announced earlier that summer), Rajoy and the Partido Popular pushed through a measure—the Rey Decreto Ley 16/2012 [by Royal Decree, Law 16 of 2012]—that denies medical treatment to undocumented immigrants in Spain. Had Joseph, as "Brazilian Beach Boy" from the This Is What Disability Project in the last chapter, been living in Spain at the time of the law's implementation, it would have directly impacted him (Joseph's own documented status as an immigrant worker in the United States was only vouchsafed in early 2014). The law says that immigrants must be denied treatment at public hospitals if they do not have Spanish residency cards (Govan). Hundreds of doctors across the country signed statements registering as objetores de conciencia [conscientious objectors] to the new law. Since Catalonia and the Basque region have autonomy that allows them to decide their own health care policies, they made clear that they would "continue to provide free basic care and medicines to those that need it, whatever their residency status" (Govan).

Again, an identity politics, while not necessarily irrelevant, is importantly not *sufficient* for comprehending the signs of disability in circulation around the neoliberal targeting and trimming of excess in Spain, as the vulnerable bodies that materialize in the wake of the Rey Decreto Ley 16/2012 may or may not identify as disabled. Identification, however, in a few different senses, is nonetheless central to the crip tactic of negation and affinity that erupted in opposition to the law. First, there was a medical refusal to participate in austerity—a conscientious objection to the *identification of* sick, injured, or disabled bodies and minds as excess that should be expelled. Second, however, and across difference, there was a simultaneous and necessary *identification with* those same bodies and minds. This *identification with* emerged because, even if differentially, health care workers and their allies recognized that all those living in Spain have been subject to austerity—or, put differently, have been rendered as objects by austerity. When Podemos emerged a year after the policies I mention here, it affirmed that mobilizations across Spain had brought into being ("we can") a first-person plural (arguably a subject in Badiou's sense) that had not necessarily existed hitherto. The conscientious objection I put forward here anticipated that process of crip subjectification, the materialization of an excessive "we" that austerity policies cannot fully negate.

In refusing the law, some activists specifically mobilized the category of "the human" as something that could be chosen. #yoelijoserhumano [I choose to be human], the campaign insisted, with images of mouths covered/silenced by adhesive bandages [Figure 2.8]. These mouths are not at all directly related to the film that I discussed in the last chapter, David Wojnarowicz's *A Fire in My Belly*, that includes imagery of the artist's mouth being stitched shut. The #yoelijoserhumano mouths are bandaged, but an affinity between the critically crip deployment of images of suture in Wojnarowicz's 1986 film and activist efforts in 2012 can certainly be noted. #yoelijoserhumano was a deceptively simplistic humanist announcement that actually refused compliance with both more dominant forms of humanism and rehabilitation, opening the human, to again use Athena Athanasiou's words, "to radical rearticulations of humanness" (Butler and Athanasiou 34). "I choose to be human" of course relies upon a recognizable humanist demarcation of who is included in the category of the human and (by implication, because they supposedly do *not* choose to be human) who is not; this demarcation of the human has long been critiqued by critical theorists. Yet the defiant bandaged assertion "I choose to be human," with what Badiou would term its "element of *prescriptive universality*" (*Rebirth* 59), suggests that "humanity" in this

Figure 2.8. I Choose to Be Human campaign.

crip performance lies neither in unified subjects nor a unified citizenry (both characteristics of traditional humanism), but rather in a *tactical identification* with the wounded inexistent, with those who are silenced and who would literally be expelled from the human as far as that category is comprehended by the contemporary Spanish state. The #yoelijoserhumano campaign puts forward, alongside the images of bandaged mouths (which, of course, in their anonymity may or may not have been the mouths of "actual" disabled human beings), facts that make it possible to imagine alternatives to austerity and that point toward a collective crip horizon: numbers, they argue, disprove any supposed "abuse" of the system by immigrants; studies suggest that new cases of HIV/AIDS will increase by 20 percent as a result of the exclusions; almost a million men and women *como tú* [like you, but the familiar form of you used with intimates, friends, comrades] will be deprived of the right to health because of this new law; etc.[8] From one perspective, images of the bandaged mouths of activists are stark and austere, but from another, they directly oppose the austerity of representation upon which the Spanish state depends.

Tactic 5: Altered States: Social Medical Centers

No actual austerity state has altered more over the course of writing *Crip Times* than Greece, a country heavily indebted to international finance and subject to some of the harshest austerity agendas in the Eurozone, relentlessly imposed by the "troika": the European Commission (EC), the European Central Bank (ECB), and the International Monetary Fund (IMF). From the beginning of the crisis in Greece, Germany—led by conservative Chancellor Angela Merkel and Finance Minister Wolfgang Schäuble of the Christian Democratic Union Party—was widely perceived as the most powerful country influencing the troika and insisting on austerity measures in Greece. The troika continues to demand "structural reform" in Greece in order to service one of the most debilitating debts in the world, with "reform" an entirely recognizable code word for more and deeper austerity: assistance to Greece, while it has been unable to pay its debt, has been contingent on cuts to the public sector (including the outright firing of public employees), raising the retirement age, trimming pensions, privatizing assets, and opening the country to more and more foreign investment. As in Spain, the dominant centrist parties that held power until 2015 complied with the demand for more austerity in, through, and across crisis. Alexis Tsipras of Syriza, the party that began to congeal as an antiausterity alternative in 2012, labeled these compliant parties—New Democracy, the Panhellenic Socialist Movement (PASOK), and the Democratic Left—the "domestic troika" after they won the 2012 elections and formed a coalition. The coalition in Greece held power for almost three years.

On January 25, 2015, however, new elections swept Syriza into power, making it the first antiausterity party to hold office on the continent. The charismatic Tsipras became prime minister and Yanis Varoufakis, his finance minister. Panagiotis Kouroumblis, a blind activist whom Tsipras appointed health minister, became the first (openly) disabled Greek politician to hold office (Smith and Traynor). Kouroumblis was a founding member of the World Blind Union and had worked with other disabled groups and with groups focused on care for old people ("Panaghiotis Kouroumblis"). Under austerity, an already poor system of care had deteriorated for many disabled people; at an overcrowded and understaffed center in Lechaina, in the south of Greece, for example, the BBC reported that autistic children and other children with disabilities had been locked in cages. The conditions were exposed around the time of the global economic crisis, and the Greek ombudsman for the rights of the child published a report identifying the conditions as "degrading," "illegal," and in "direct contradiction with the obligation for respect and protection of the human rights of the residents" (Hadjimatheou).

Some staff at centers like the one in Lechaina reported a desire for change, but under conditions of austerity there were virtually no resources to initiate change and workers at times went without pay for a year or more (Hadjimatheou). As is now immensely clear, neither Syriza's win nor any individual appointments (Kouroumblis's included) ended austerity in Greece or anywhere else; an appointment such as Kouroumblis's, however, largely left out of English-language reporting, was nonetheless symbolically important given the bleakness of the situation for many disabled people in the country. Still, there was quick and predictable (and, as became clear, justified) skepticism on the Left about the containment of mass movements and about the possibility of working within the confines of bourgeois electoral democracy (similar skepticism was voiced in Chile as Vallejo and other student leaders entered Parliament).

At the same time, across the continent, the reaction by the establishment to Syriza's initial victory was even more predictable (and swift). The *Economist*, in its lead story for January 31, 2015, conceded that Greece's debt was essentially unsupportable, but insisted (in ableist language linking "craziness" with anything that would oppose the consensus around austerity) that what was needed was to "get Mr. Tsipras to junk his crazy socialism and to stick to structural reforms in exchange for debt forgiveness" ("Greece and the Euro's Future"). With yet more dismissive language (essentially comparing any position that would oppose the consensus around austerity to perverse desires), the article suggested that "Mr. Tsipras could vent his leftist urges by breaking up Greece's cosy protected oligopolies and tackling corruption," but that antiausterity measures would "all undo Greece's hard-won gains in competitiveness" ("Greece and the Euro's Future"). And indeed, as I suggested, Merkel's Germany and its allies showed absolutely no signs of compromise in relation to "structural reforms."

The *Economist* story from January 2015, however, is interesting on a crip level that exceeds both its predictable and manifest content and Syriza's utter incapacity, as the year continued, to effect change. The magazine's cover, gesturing toward this lead article, represents the Venus de Milo against a blue sky. Both arms of the actual statue are of course missing; disability artists and scholars have in fact long pointed out that this paragon of feminine beauty is ironically known to us only as disabled, even if an ableist art history or art education invisibilizes this rather basic fact. Mary Duffy is an armless contemporary performance artist who in fact appears as the Venus de Milo and, through her performance, deconstructs iconic Western notions of beauty, exposing the assumptions and erasures upon which such iconic notions depend.[9] The *Economist* cover, however, retains the amputation of the right arm and manipulates the photo on the left side so that the Venus de Milo has an extended left arm pointing a pistol roughly in the direction of the statue's gaze [Figure 2.9]. "Go ahead, Angela, make my day," reads the headline above the Venus's head; a smaller subheadline in the lower right corner adds, "Greece's challenge to Germany—and the euro." The suffering of Greece and the impact of austerity upon it are thus represented by a

Figure 2.9. Cover of the *Economist*, January 29, 2015.

disabled figure. Although this is an unintended or unconscious crip representation for the *Economist*, it is nonetheless right there on the surface of its cover, just as disability in general is right there on the surface of a global austerity politics even if it is continually unremarked. Resistance, moreover, in a strong reading of this image, is represented as crip resistance (and there is of course no reason *not* to read the image in excess of the intentions of the magazine or the neoliberal apologia that is the lead story). A vulnerable, impaired body here stands in for all vulnerable bodies in Greece, and essentially says, from that situated crip perspective (a situated perspective from which the social totality might be better perceived), enough is enough. The words deployed (Go ahead, make my day) of course circulate widely in popular culture, but there is some irony that they were first articulated by the US actor and Republican politician Clint Eastwood, emphasizing rugged and renegade individualism in the early years of neoliberalism (as Dirty Harry in *Sudden Impact* in 1983). In contrast, the words are here resignified via an image that directly and militantly opposes the chief representative of neoliberalism in Europe.

Responses to Syriza's actual political strategies over the course of 2015, however, tragically went from guarded optimism to resignation and extreme pessimism, and even bewilderment. Tsipras and Varoufakis immediately announced their intention to raise the minimum wage, rehire workers who had been fired (most notably, cleaners who had engaged in antiausterity activism following their dismissal), halt the privatization of public assets, and collect tax assets from the wealthy. The plan was to remain true to the platform that had led to their election. While they did not immediately plan on defaulting on their debt or exiting the Eurozone, Tsipras and his allies did make clear that they would not service the debt through deeper cuts.

The reality of the situation in Greece quickly proved more complicated than this and Tsipras in particular is now generally perceived, on the Left, as having capitulated. By February 20, 2015, less than a month after the election, without external support from any other countries in (or out of) the Eurozone, Syriza was pressured into an extension of the existing loan agreement. The extension recognized all the existing debt and the same terms for repaying that debt. Most importantly, during the extension period the debt was to be serviced under ongoing "supervision," essentially indicating that the troika would continue to administer austerity in Greece. As Stathis Kouvelakis described it in *Jacobin* magazine, ironically turning to the imagery of restraint that—as I have described—was a literal fact of life for some disabled children in the country, European leaders needed "to bind the Syriza government hand and foot in order to demonstrate in practice that whatever the electoral result and the political profile of the government that might emerge, no reversal of austerity [was] feasible within the existing European framework" ("The Alternative"). What can be concluded at the level of strategy (in de Certeau's sense) is not particularly hopeful: the guardians of austerity in Greece and on the continent are far more empowered both to craft strategies and to block antiausterity alternatives. At the very least, Syriza's election in Greece marked a fracture in the establishment's consensus on austerity. As *Crip Times* goes to press, however, that fracture has not nourished a sustainable counterstrategy.

In late June 2015, in the face of ongoing intransigence and even hostility from Merkel and Schäuble, Tsipras called a national referendum: the Greek people would either accept or reject the ongoing austerity the troika was demanding. A new agreement linking assistance to Greece to even more "reform" was put forward by the troika, without any compromise on austerity. Tsipras took it to the Greek people, calling a national referendum, in a moment that many read as affording him the opportunity to gain much-needed national and international credibility in his confrontation with European leaders. OXI, the Greek word for No, circulated rapidly around the globe, indicating support for *rejection* of the bailout package, contingent on austerity, that was being offered. On July 5, 2015, the Greek people indeed voted overwhelmingly against the package. Varoufakis resigned the next day, not because of disagreement with the outcome, which was widely and emotionally perceived as a national rejection of austerity, but because of the pressures he had faced from European leaders during the previous six months' negotiations. By mid-July, Tsipras, in spite of the popular referendum and to the incredulity of many observers around the globe, agreed to implement the troika's demands. The antiausterity crusader had essentially become a spokesperson for the idea that "There Is No Alternative" to austerity.[10] Although his popularity quickly sank, Tsipras called for a new election in September, which Syriza again won, this time arguably with resignation on the part of voters, or pessimism about the possibility that change would come through the electoral process.

My intent in this chapter, however, is to survey varied crip tactics, recognizing that those tactics (and a global austerity politics in general) gesture toward the urgency of larger strategies, even as such strategies have to date disappointed almost as soon as they have materialized. The Greek tragedy of Syriza and of Tsipras makes clear at this point that neither could be some sort of great antiausterity hope, and what will happen as Syriza continues to hold power remains unclear. For my purposes here, I'm interested in noting the ways in which activists on the ground have organized and sustained social medical centers both before and during Tsipras's administration. Pensioners and other disabled protestors in Greece have engaged in various forms of traditional activism. In fact, most of the tactics that I'm surveying in this chapter arguably contain some forms of traditional activism (marches and protests, for example), although they simultaneously (as social sculpture in California, craving disability in Chile, or radical rearticulations of humanness in Spain) have gone beyond that. Social medical centers in Greece, I argue, function in similar visionary ways.

What interests me about Greek activists shaping social medical centers is their urgent commitment to thinking with *and* against or beyond the state simultaneously. Following huge antiausterity protests in 2011, more than forty social medical centers were opened around the country. Since reimbursements for medicine in Greece have been cut in half (the *Guardian* reports that "even patients with insurance are paying 70% more for their drugs"), the clinics use donated drugs and donated medical equipment (Henley). In metropolitan Athens alone, more than 30,000 patients per month are treated in 16 different social medical centers (Henley). The clinics are part of a much larger movement of citizen-run groups (similar on-the-ground efforts exist, for example, in relation to food distribution); this movement is crip in its attention to collective bodily needs and vulnerabilities and in its resistance to the ways in which austerity politics capitalizes upon those vulnerabilities. Social medical centers have flourished *from the ground up*, but for a time at least they were also "powered by Syriza," as Joana Ramiro notes (102). Solidarity 4 All was the name of the (Syriza-powered) umbrella group working on the ground with activist movements distributing free medicine and medical care to those unable to access such care under conditions of austerity.

Given the ways in which the neoliberal state has so clearly functioned to safeguard the interests of capital, in partnership with capital, there are innumerable reasons to retreat from state-based solutions to the problems generated by an austerity politics. Solidarity for all, most obviously, is not, in crip times, the driving motive behind *any* actually existing state. Queer theory, in this bleak context, even more than disability studies (especially as queer theory has taken global and materialist turns), has been deeply suspicious of the embodiment and comportment required of what Margot Canaday terms "the straight state" (1). Certain theorists—perhaps most notable here would be the recent writing of J. Jack Halberstam—encourage us to stop shaping appeals at the level of the state, asking (in the process of such appeals) for the state to somehow "recognize" us (*Gaga* 95–130). In general, the appeal for state recognition across the world since the 1990s by lgbt movements has been an appeal for marriage rights. Given the ways in which it has blocked an attention to broader issues of social justice, critiquing the centrality of marriage in the mainstream lgbt movement remains urgent, and the queer work questioning the desire for state recognition is compelling and important.

That work, however, presents something of a conundrum when we're cripping the crisis. In many ways, it's actually easy to refuse state recognition when we're talking about gay marriage. It's not so easy, however, when we're talking about ventilators, wheelchairs, or medicine that keeps someone alive; retirees in Greece losing access to the medicine they needed seem entirely justified, in that emergency moment, banging pots and pans and making angry charges aimed directly at the recalcitrant state.[11] One banner at the 2011 protests read, "They handed 200 billion to bankers but cut down on medicine, treatment, and benefits for the disabled." There's a refusal of the state—"look at what they did," essentially—in that assertion, but there's an undeniable, and emergency, need to grapple with the state too, since we're talking about treatment and benefits that are needed right now. These disabled activists also, for what it's worth, seem not at all reducible to radical queers in the United States or Canada or the UK refusing marriage and its concomitant state recognition. The crip tactic of social medical centers, however, generates a double move, constructing anarchist forms of local care while keeping in purview the need for larger state strategies and extrastate tactics for ending austerity. Such larger strategies did not, in 2015, materialize in any lasting way around Syriza, but Syriza's failures to sustain solidarity for all have not halted the ongoing generation of creative and collective modes of resistance on the ground.

Tactic 6: Appropriation and Theatricalization

I return to the UK, the austere location that remains at the center of *Crip Times*, to consider a final crip tactic, one that David Halperin had already previously identified as queer: appropriation and theatricalization (49).

As a queer tactic, for Halperin the appropriation and theatricalization of dominant discourses, discourses directly constructed by "the apparatus of homophobia," allows for resistance: "What opportunities does the discursive formation of sexuality create for discursive counterpractices?" (48). Halperin gives as an example the San Francisco *Bay Times* response to a June 1993 issue of *Newsweek*, which featured two smiling white lesbians alongside the headline "Lesbians: Coming Out Strong, What Are the Limits of Tolerance?" A few weeks later, the *Bay Times* (an lgbt San Francisco newspaper) published the cover of a fictional magazine titled *Dykeweek*, with a white man and woman embracing: "Heterosexuals: What Are the Limits of Tolerance?" (49–50). The *Dykeweek* appropriation and reversal included a "glossary" explaining terms such as "Wife: Traditionally the 'feminine' partner [in a heterosexual relationship] responsible for domestic tasks and child care" (qtd. in Halperin 51).

As a discursive counterpractice in crip times, "cripping" has likewise been frequently, wildly, and flamboyantly theatrical; according to disability and performance studies scholar Carrie Sandahl, "Both queering and cripping expose the arbitrary delineation between normal and defective and . . . both disarm with a wicked humor, including camp" (37). Following the London 2012 Olympics, in September 2012 the British performance artist Crip2Night explicitly appropriated and theatricalized the spectacle of the Paralympics, laying out the situation quite literally in black and white, with the assertion "120 medals, 304 athletes, infinite national pride" critically counterposed (via the word *cripocracy*) to "DLA [Disability Living Allowance] slashed by 20%, half a million lose benefits," and the question "national pride?" [Figure 2.10]. On the left side of the photo, in full color, the Union Jack covers virtually every inch of both Crip2Night and her wheelchair: she wears a Union Jack hat and funky sunglasses; Union Jack paper plates adorn the chair's wheels; and flags fly from both the back and the side (with "Team GB" proudly written across one). On the right side of the photo, in black and white, Crip2Night is dressed in black and wears black sunglasses; the flag and the wheels of her chair have been covered in black garbage bags. The This Is What Disability Looks Like project explicitly sought out and shared Crip2Night's image.

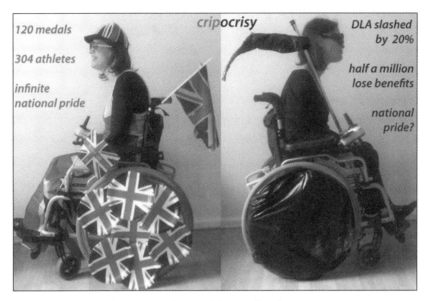

Figure 2.10. Crip2Night, This Is What Disability Looks Like.

This is of course just one photo or performance, and it is not one that received very wide circulation. It is arguably, however, representative of a discursive counterpractice very much alive in the UK, as artists, activists, and others have been appropriating, inhabiting, theatricalizing, and resignifying the very terms of extravagant abjection used to disqualify them: not only (quite clearly) crip, but also broken, malingerers, benefit scroungers, even (in one high-profile instance) scum. In the early days of the coalition, Kaliya Franklin, who blogs as both Bendy Girl and Benefit-Scrounging Scum, produced a photo that did receive a bit more circulation than Crip2Night's. It dates from March 2011, when the coalition government's initial Welfare Reform Bill was passing through Parliament; it is titled "Left Out in the Cold" [Figure 2.11]. The photo, produced for the Broken of Britain campaign, is a nude self-portrait on a desolate beach. It was shot on a cold January day at high tide on the shore in Hoylake, west of Liverpool. When we walked and wheeled along the shore on a warm day in July 2014, Franklin was quick to point out to me that, at the time of the shoot, there was snow on the ground and that she (and the photographer) were both wrapped up in multiple layers moments before the shot. In the photo, an empty wheelchair is on

Figure 2.11. Kaliya Franklin, "Left Out in the Cold," for the Broken of Britain Campaign.

the beach—not the power chair that Franklin usually uses, but a more austere version (a hospital chair that might, perhaps, be like those issued by the NHS). Franklin herself is on the ground alongside the wheelchair, her arms in front, perhaps reaching for the chair, and her gaze almost face down in the sand.

"Sick and disabled people are often left voiceless in society," Franklin says about the image, which she hopes provides a reflection on this voicelessness (qtd. in "Left Out"). This theatrical image (and performance) interests me for many reasons, including that the wheelchair again (as it did with the *huelgistas de hambre*) signifies "disability" but simultaneously and promiscuously gestures to other disabilities and impairments that are not so easily made visible. Indeed, Franklin's photo works with and against what Kelly Fritsch terms the "neoliberal circulation of affects" that usually can *only* comprehend "disability as wheelchair" (3). The wheelchair in "Left Out in the Cold," in contrast, beautifully represents both what it is and what it is not; Franklin uses her chair in the portrait to signify with *and as* all the others denigrated as benefit-scrounging scum, including those with mental health issues or "non-visible disabilities" (among those, to again gesture toward a campaign that has organized massive protests and marches around the cuts, "hardest hit" by austerity in Britain). The harsh testing of Atos often targeted not those with the most recognizable (or representative) disabilities, but those with disabilities that manifest themselves differentially or intermittently. An autistic person, or someone with chronic illness or learning difficulties may very much need incapacity benefits but may have impairments that vary from day to day. On the one day that Atos (or now Maximus) briefly evaluates many people, they are found "fit to work" (and ineligible for many benefits) based on how disability appears at that moment. They are left out in the cold, disappeared in a way, and "Left Out in the Cold" marks that active, motivated, disappearance—a vanishing engineered by the architects of austerity. When Cameron, in the campaign speech I mentioned in the Introduction, referred to a "Broken Britain," he intended to draw attention to individual and individualized failures. He of course wasn't explicitly talking about scum as he relegated thousands of people to brokenness and extravagant abjection, but that is clearly how many in the UK have received his words from 2010 onward. Broken of Britain, the campaign, and Franklin, as she participates in it, appropriate and theatricalize Cameron's denigrating rhetoric in the interests of collective resistance.

When I asked Franklin about her use of the most abject language for her blogging and cyber activism (Benefit-Scrounging Scum), she indicated that it was a conscious appropriation of the language used to disqualify (or, to rework Badiou, we might say to make inexistent) the most marginalized. It was a tactic in part inspired by a period spent living in the United States, where for a time she was part of various communities (including African American and lgbt communities) that have of course long resignified the very language used to disqualify them. "Left Out in the Cold," and appropriations like Franklin's, are perhaps more obviously or directly "pornographic" than the other tactics I have considered in this chapter; it would be hard to deny that such a beautiful and poignant nude image is intended to generate a hunger or desire that has complex but real affinities with images that more directly announce themselves as pornographic. It is not a commodified image, however, and does not generate the easy satisfaction of inspiration porn; it generates instead a queer, multifaceted hunger or desire, gesturing toward, to adapt Floyd on the potentiality of pornographic identifications, "the development of a range of [crip/]queer formations" (203). Since Franklin's identity as writer and activist germinated alongside African American and lgbt communities, we might say that "Left Out in the Cold" represents a longing for what Robin D. G. Kelley terms "freedom dreams" (6). The work of lgbt and feminist thought "encourages us to construct a politics rooted in desire," Kelley writes as he articulates that queer and feminist work to the radical black imagination in the twentieth century. Such work "interrogates what is 'normal' [and] shows us how the state and official culture polices our behavior" (6). Kelley is not explicitly talking about disability as he praises this politics rooted in desire that interrogates what is normal, just as Scott is not talking about disability as he theorizes the ways we might linger over woundedness and extravagant abjection. Both the language Kelley and Scott choose and the trans-Atlantic and embodied solidarity with other marginalized groups from which Franklin's own ethos emerges, however, suggests that freedom dreams are disabled too, just as they are always queer, feminist, and black.

"Left Out in the Cold" performed particular work in 2011; it was a pointed intervention at the time that a punishing bill was passing through Parliament. It has for me, however, come to represent well the urgency of cross-identifications and coalitions in the UK in the particular period of time (roughly, the Cameron years) that *Crip Times* analyzes. Clearly, "Left Out in the Cold" can have no direct connection to a photo that postdates it and that achieved worldwide attention three years later. Nonetheless, it uncannily presages for me the September 2015 photograph of Alan Kurdi, a three-year-old Syrian boy who died and whose body lay lifeless on a Turkish beach after the boat his family was in capsized in the Mediterranean Sea. Kurdi was part of a refugee family attempting to reach relatives in Canada. The family was not headed toward, nor was it planning to pass through, the UK. Refugees like Kurdi and his family, however, have been particularly targeted in dominant discourses, alongside disabled people, as unwelcome welfare scroungers in the UK. Anti-immigrant discourses were particularly pronounced in the months leading up to the Brexit vote and many immigrants have, essentially, been left out in the cold by the austerity agenda forged in the Cameron years. Following the Brexit vote, in a speech that was widely read as consolidating a nationalist discourse from which immigrants to the UK are excluded, Theresa May infamously said, "If you believe you are a citizen of the world, you are a citizen of nowhere" (qtd. in Bearak). It's not difficult, in such an anti-immigrant and ableist culture to read "Left Out in the Cold" backward through the tragic 2015 photo that postdates it. And it remains urgent, as we do so, to nurture the kinds of cross-identifications Franklin's photo and writing invite.

I will conclude with a quote from Lenin that can perhaps only be cripped or twisted out of context, given that Lenin is in many ways the premier architect of both active resistance and strategy, in de Certeau's sense, not the (crip) tactics and extravagant abjection I have been surveying in an effort to think beyond the dispossession generated by a global austerity politics. *Crip Times* is not a Leninist text. However, Lenin writes, "Whoever expects a pure social revolution will *never* live to see it. Such a person pays lip service to revolution without understanding what revolution is" (257–258, emphasis in the original). Lenin goes on to insist after this, that revolution in Europe "cannot be anything other than an outburst of mass struggle on the part of *all and sundry oppressed and discontented elements.* Inevitably, sections of the petty bourgeoisie and of the backward workers will participate in it—without such participation, mass struggle is impossible, without it no revolution is possible—and just as inevitably will they bring into the movement their prejudices, their reactionary fantasies, their weaknesses and errors" (258, my emphasis). My rewriting of Lenin is perhaps immediately clear in that, even as I am lingering in an expansive way over the value that might be perceived in and around "weakness," I am explicitly *not* seeing "reactionary fantasies," necessarily, in the snapshots of global crip activism I have put before readers in this chapter (or, for that matter, very clear representatives of "the petty bourgeoisie" or "backward workers"). I am, however, second, necessarily affirming and tracing in *Crip Times* revolution alongside and beyond a traditionally mobilized working class, revolution somehow *expansively* composed of scroungers, scum, wounded bodies, and "all and sundry oppressed and discontented elements." As I have noted before, along with many scholars in disability studies, we are fond of repeating the thesis that everyone will be disabled if they live long enough (*Crip Theory* 197–198). Perhaps, however, as I move through the remaining two chapters, a more speculative thesis might be appropriate for thinking through resistance in our time, especially in relation to a global politics of austerity. The excessive disabled resistance I have traced in this chapter perhaps points to a new, emergent, perhaps barely discernible truism, and that is that every revolution will be crip if it lives long enough.

3

Inhabitable Spaces

Crip Displacements and El Edificio de Enfrente

One of the most notorious legacies of the British coalition government's austerity agenda is an "under occupancy policy," introduced to much criticism in 2013.[1] This policy withdrew a significant portion of state subsidies from benefits recipients deemed to have "spare rooms" where they were living. Before it had even been implemented, critics had come to call the unpopular policy the "bedroom tax," following Lord Richard Best, a crossbench peer in the House of Lords, who coined the descriptor in late 2011, when the Welfare Reform Act of 2012 that included the policy was initially passing through Parliament (Best; C. Brown).[2] Since the bedroom tax essentially penalized "extra" space, it codified the idea that benefits recipients could, and really should, live with less— less space, or less money. In this way, more than any other policy, the bedroom tax *spatialized* austerity in the UK, tying it to actual, physical locations.

At the same time that the government was materializing austere spaces for its citizens at home, it was unsurprisingly staking out claims for itself in a range of global spaces, targeting locations where British *capital* might expand. As early as November 2010, for example, William Hague, the new secretary of state for foreign and commonwealth affairs, specifically set his sights on the space of Latin America: "History teaches us that Britain has a track record of underestimating Latin America and neglecting its opportunities. It is this neglect that the British government is determined to address" (qtd. in COHA). Although this chapter ultimately critiques the bedroom tax in the UK, one of my central contentions is that activists and artists in such "underestimated" locations have long attended to the ways in which "opportunity" and "neglect" function in uneven ways elsewhere. Their work provides critical tools for understanding the operations of austerity and the space-making practices of capitalism more generally.

I approach my analysis of the bedroom tax through the critical work of one such artist, Mexico City–based photographer Livia Radwanski, who has participated in a theoretically global and itinerant project, El Museo de los Desplazados [The Museum of the Displaced]. I argue that the literal production of austere spaces for living and the simultaneous production of expansive spaces for capital has been facilitated by what we might term an Anglo-imperial disability politics.[3] This chapter examines British expansion into a specific Latin American location, theorizing in the process the paradoxical role of disability and "access" in that neo-imperial expansion. Through a close reading of Radwanski's photography and an interrogation of how disability is or is not recognized as contemporary spaces are reconfigured by and for capital, I focus here on the shifting sociopolitical and socioeconomic landscapes of central Mexico City leading up to 2015, the year of the British general election as well as the year declared by the British and Mexican governments to be "the Year of Mexico in the UK and the UK in Mexico."

Chapter 3 examines disability through the keyword *displacement*. Building on the critiques of neoliberal incorporation and *dispossession* I put forward in chapter 1, here I consider how such critiques might attend to what I call *crip displacements*. In its psychoanalytic sense, displacement refers to the processes whereby one issue is avoided or repressed in and through a focus on or diversion to something else altogether—thus, a phobia or obsession might emerge because of an individual's inability to work through or resolve other issues. A graduate student unable to secure employment anywhere in the country and unable to alter on an individual level the larger structural position in which she is caught, for example, might displace concerns about that situation and her inability to resolve it onto a fear of flying. In a very different and at times more volitional sense, displacement can be comprehended as a tool of the powerful; class struggle and economic inequality—as *Crip Times* in many ways contends throughout—are often displaced onto identity concerns. For conservative politicians, the problem is thus never economic inequality, but problematic groups that can be identified and surveilled, such as people of color or immigrant workers; for certain well-meaning liberal politicians *and* academics, the "inclusion" of more and more substantive identity groups can direct attention away from class struggle and class analysis, even when that is not the explicit intent.

In a more literal sense, of course, displacement refers to processes whereby individuals and groups are uprooted or evicted, relocated from one location (usually where they had been living) to another. In its most basic sense, the phrase *crip displacements* should mark in this chapter the fact that such literal relocations need to be theorized through "una forma de política encarnada" [an embodied politics], to adapt the words of Míriam Arenas Conejo and Asun Pié Balaguer (227). Crip displacements, moreover, as I theorize them, are deeply imbricated with impairment. That imbrication of displacement and impairment is often not immediately evident, so *crip* again functions here as a modifier drawing out the ways in which disability's centrality to an inevitable component of neoliberal capitalism—in this case, displacement—might be overlooked or smoothed over. In a more metaphorical sense, then, the phrase *crip displacements* marks the kinds of critically crip interruptions Alison Kafer calls for when she urges us to think carefully about the complexity of bodies and minds "not only in sites marked as explicitly about disability" (9). Ultimately, the phrase *crip displacements* is multivalent; in what follows, I can of necessity present only a partial and introductory meditation on the violence of crip displacement in an age of austerity (and that necessary partiality is itself a crip displacement). In both the UK and Mexico, uprootedness, eviction, and relocation have been quotidian effects of a transnational neoliberal consensus. Drawing on the queer and crip utopianism of Kafer and José Esteban Muñoz, however, this chapter attempts to represent, or access, modes of resistance to that consensus.

Over the course of several years, Radwanski documented a literal displacement in Mexico City; she was subsequently included as one of the artistic/activist collaborators in El Museo de los Desplazados. During the years that she was engaged in this work, the British government was busily staking a claim to Mexico. In 2011, Deputy Prime Minister Nick Clegg noted that Mexico was an emergent economic power that would be the seventh largest economy in the world by 2050. Directly addressing the Senate in Mexico City during an official visit, Clegg stressed—in

Spanish, no less—how important it was for the UK to be part of that emergence:

> El Reino Unido desarrolla un extenso comercio practicamente en cada rincon del planeta. El comercio de Mexico supera al de Brasil y Argentina juntos. . . . Conforme a estas premisas, he acordado con el Presidente Calderon que trabajaremos intensamente con el objetivo de duplicar nuestro comercio bilateral de aqui a 2015. Deben saber que me acompaña en esta visita una delegacion comercial para conocer mejor nuestros mercados.
>
> [The UK trades extensively in almost every corner of the globe. Mexico's trade is now more than Brazil and Argentina combined. . . . So President Calderon and I have agreed to work towards doubling bilateral trade by 2015. I have brought a business delegation with me today to foster greater understanding in each others [*sic*] markets.] ("New politics")[4]

Notably, Clegg's speech gestured toward austerity back at home without naming it as such: "Nuestro gobierno ha puesto en marcha un programa integral de reforma. . . . Estamos trasladando facultades clave en la toma de decisiones en materia de salud, educacion y planeacion . . . desde el ejecutivo central a los gobiernos y comunidades locales" [My government is implementing a comprehensive programme of reform. . . . We are transferring key decision-making powers, on healthcare, education, planning . . . away from our central executive to local government and local communities] ("New politics"). Many back in the UK would have already understood English phrases such as "programme of reform" and "transferring key decision-making powers" as code words for the austerity agenda upon which the coalition government had embarked.

Interventions such as Clegg's helped to lay the groundwork for the initiative that would become the Year of Mexico in the UK and the UK in Mexico. Ostensibly a cultural initiative designed to promote better awareness of both countries' diversity and history, the Dual Year ultimately became an initiative targeting British investment and finance capital, "championing" Mexico for its "economic and commercial dynamism as an exceptional location for trade, investment and tourism" ("Dual Year"). "We are certain," the two governments announced in their press release for the Year of Mexico in the UK and the UK in Mexico, "that this Dual Year will motivate business, exchange and cooperation in various areas, greatly adding to what we have already achieved in our bilateral relation-ship" ("Dual Year"). This chapter both examines the ways in which the "free flow" of capital in this bilateral relationship was facilitated culturally and attends to the corporeal effects of a classed "dynamism" that, in both locations, arguably works through what Fiona Kumari Campbell terms the "contours of ableism" and opens up "exceptional locations" for only a few.

The next two sections of this chapter examine living spaces under threat in Mexico and the UK, respectively. I first introduce Radwanski's 2011 photographic project *Mérida90*. This section uses photographs of the exterior and interior of a particular living space photographed by Radwanski to meditate on how certain images are or are not made leg-ible as "disability" images. I then consider, in the following section, the policing of living spaces in the UK, positioning the bumpy implementa-tion of the bedroom tax there alongside the government's simultaneous efforts to export a vision of disability politics to a range of locations, including Mexico. The final two sections of the chapter push beyond displacement in the UK and Mexico by critiquing the visions of the fu-ture mandated by both states and looking instead toward what Kafer would identify as "accessible futures" (149). During the period when its economic relations with the UK were being celebrated, and when an Anglo-imperial disability politics allowing for the limited recognition of some individuals was congealing, Mexican officials famously refused to recognize a range of social movements, particularly student mobiliza-tions. I read that refusal to recognize them in the context of the Year of Mexico in the UK and the UK in Mexico; ultimately, however, in conclu-sion, I turn away from state- and capital-sanctioned futures. Radwanski's photographs, I argue, allow us to read a generative yearning into crip displacements in multiple and interconnected locations—a yearning for living spaces conceived otherwise, for inhabitable spaces and worlds.

El Riesgo de Colapso Inminente/The Risk of Imminent Collapse

I open this section with the image of a curb cut: an actual access ramp (or, perhaps more appropriately, an "access" ramp) in Mexico City [Figure 3.1]. This curb cut from a busy street to a sidewalk is from the opening to Calle Mérida, in the neighborhood known as Colonia Roma. It is at the north end of the neighborhood, where the street begins, just south of

Figure 3.1. Access ramp in Colonia Roma, Mexico City. Photo by Author.

Avenida Chapultepec. Access ramps not unlike this one are now in evidence throughout most of the central parts of the city. They are certainly in evidence in almost all the streets of Colonia Roma, and in fact the redesigned corners around the Plaza Luis Cabrera (a few blocks south of Avenida Chapultepec and west of Calle Mérida) include markers in the pavement that make clear that curb cuts can be read as "Nuestro México del Futuro" [Our Mexico for the Future] [Figure 3.2]. The curb cut at the corner of Mérida and Chapultepec is marked with a sign displaying the internationally recognized symbol for disability, a white stick figure in a wheelchair against a blue background. We supposedly know how to read this curb cut, as a cultural sign of and for disability, because of that internationally recognized symbol. This particular curb cut, however, is a rather *compromised* cultural sign of disability, which is why I pause over "access" here. There is certainly no guarantee that a wheelchair user could easily navigate this space at the corner of Calle Mérida and Avenida Chapultepec. Although the incline from street to sidewalk is not too steep (unlike many others in the Federal District), another sign, slightly twisted and faded, announces "Peligro Cables de Alta Tensión

Figure 3.2. "Our Mexico for the Future," Colonia Roma, Mexico City. Photo by Author.

Luz y Fuerza" [Danger: Cables of High Tension, Electricity, and Force], suggesting that a high-voltage shock (or worse) might await someone attempting to access the ramp.

Alongside the symbol that is explicitly designed to be apprehended immediately regardless of where we are, I want to place three crip images or three images to crip. The first image is a photograph showing a building near the final stages of demolition [Figure 3.3]. Beneath a mostly cloudy sky, and surrounded on three sides by walls (or perhaps a preserved façade), sits a pile of debris: red bricks, pieces of cement, wood, and dust. The other two images are photographs representing two haunting and empty bedrooms. They are, perhaps, not even immediately legible as "bedrooms," although it is clear that they are locations for sleeping or at least resting. The first [Figure 3.4] shows a simple blue sleeping bag on a wooden floor, with a worn yellow throw pillow, embroidered with three yellow flowers at the head. Crowded around the sleeping bag are a range of objects: shoes, books, blankets, perhaps a basket of laundry. The second [Figure 3.5] shows not a bed but a sofa alongside a cracked stone or plaster wall. Dingy shades indicate a window in the upper left corner, while the sofa—also faded and yellow, with one arm missing, perhaps indicating that this was once a sectional—occupies the center of the photograph. A colorful

Figure 3.3. View from the back of Mérida90 one year after the initial evacuation of the neighbors, July 12, 2011. Photo by Livia Radwanski.

Figure 3.4. Carlos Sr.'s room in Mérida90 which he shared with two children and five cats, July 10, 2010. Photo by Livia Radwanski.

Figure 3.5. The living room of Maricela, which she shared with two adolescent children before the evacuation of Mérida90, February 10, 2010. Photo by Livia Radwanski.

Spiderman quilt is thrown over the sofa and hangs off the end where there is no arm.

These photographs certainly do not immediately present themselves as disabled or crip images, not least because they do not directly represent human beings. Like the access ramps, however, these photographs do present images from a changing Mexico City, this time from the eventually largely demolished tenement "Edificio América," Calle Mérida, Number 90 [Figure 3.6]. Mérida90, a few blocks south of Avenida Chapultepec, is also in Colonia Roma, which is a rapidly gentrifying neighborhood west of the historic center. I would contend that illegible disability images (images that are difficult to categorize or comprehend in relation to the standard denotations of the signifier "disability") can in fact be quite worrisome; the reasons why such images are worrisome, and for whom, will be clearer as I move through a range of ways that disability is now recognized in and by Mexico and the UK. As I do so, however, I'll want to keep multiple senses of "recognition" in play: who or what is readily perceived as "disabled" in visual imagery? What visual codes allow for that perception and what codes generally forestall comprehending an image as "disabled"? What complex cultural

Figure 3.6. Entrance to Mérida90. Photo by Author.

work is performed as disability is recognized or made legible? How do standard modes of recognition ("I know what that is") preclude more expansive and perhaps resistant forms of re-cognition/rethinking? What might be gained from a crip analytic open to apprehending as "disabled" images that do not directly present as such?

Attentive to the challenges posed by disability and illegibility, I eventually return in this chapter not only to a thicker analysis of these particular, cryptic images but to more recognizable Mexican disability images. Put differently, I'll return later to what Roland Barthes would call (recognizable) texts of pleasure, even if this chapter and the next, detailing the artistic practices of Radwanski and (in chapter 4) Liz Crow, are ultimately about cripping a politics of recognition. For Barthes, a "text of pleasure" is quite familiar; it "contents, fills, grants euphoria." It "comes from culture and does not break with it, [and it] is linked to a *comfortable* practice of reading." What Barthes calls a "text of bliss," in contrast, "imposes a state of loss"; it "discomforts (perhaps to the point of a certain boredom), unsettles the reader's historical, cultural, psychological assumptions, the consistency of his tastes, values, memories." It "brings to a crisis his relations with language" (14). Although it would perhaps sound counterintuitive to call the politics I have been examining blissful in the more quotidian sense of the word, across the chapters of *Crip Times* a running contention has nonetheless been that a global austerity politics systematically imposes (upon all of us, although unevenly) states of discomfort and loss (and even, indeed, boredom) with which we currently have difficulty reckoning and for which we have inadequate languages. Those linguistic and material states of loss are in turn *populated* by figures whom we have difficulty recognizing. This chapter will contend that it is easier to displace, in all senses of the word, such figures. Recognizable texts of pleasure (including, in chapter 1, images in circulation around the 2012 Paralympic Games) put forward substantive (and even stock) characters who are more easily apprehended. In the process, texts of pleasure paper over all the difficulty of discomfort, loss, and boredom, or (more directly to my central topic) the difficulty of living with and through austerity.

The images from Mérida90 are part of Radwanski's project documenting (from 2009 to 2010) the changes in the neighborhood and the demolition of the tenement; they were published in book form, along with commentary, in 2011. Radwanski was born in São Paulo, Brazil, but passed much of her childhood in not only Brazil but also Argentina and Mexico. She has studied and worked in the United States, where she graduated from the Rhode Island School of Design in 2006, having focused in her studies on both film and photography. Her artistic collaborations have taken her to a range of locations, including Spain, Australia, and the UK. From October 2011 until February 2012, for instance, a short film of Radwanski's was part of *Infinitas Gracias*, an exhibition in London featuring the tradition of Mexican votive painting, which thematizes the "miracles" of everyday life. One of Radwanski's other published photobooks, *Unos Otros Méxicos* [Some Other Mexicos] received an honorable mention in the first Concurso Internacional de Fotolibro Iberoamericano [International Iberoamerican Photobook Competition] coordinated by RM Publishing, one of Latin America's most distinguished publishers for art books. As the title of her other photobook suggests, Radwanski's work as a photographer often focuses on those everyday lives and experiences that are neglected, forgotten, or discounted due to hegemonic social and economic relations. Her keen attention as a photographer to the ways in which uneven and unequal capitalist development has reshaped the contemporary landscape, and to the dignity of her subjects as they navigate the precarious economic situations into which such uneven development places them, has mainly centered on Mexico, although she has also pursued related projects in São Paulo, Lisbon, and Detroit.[5]

Radwanski returned from her studies in the United States to Mexico City in 2007, and from 2009 forward, resided alongside Mérida90, where she interviewed and befriended the people who lived there, eventually gaining the community's trust to be able to photograph them. Not long after her arrival in the neighborhood, a sign on the door of the tenement announced:

> *Inmueble propiedad del Instituto de Vivienda del Distrito Federal.*
> *Evacuado por riesgo de colapso inminente.*
> *Si usted continua ocupándolo, lo hará bajo su absoluta responsabilidad,*
>   *ya que ante un muy probable evento de siniestro, expone a su persona,*
>   *familia y bienes a sufrir daños severos.*
> [This building is property of the Department of Housing of the Federal
>   District.
> It is being evacuated because of the risk of imminent collapse.
> If you continue occupying it, it is completely under your own responsi-
>   bility; in the face of a probable accident, you are exposing yourself,
>   your family, and your belongings to the likelihood of suffering severe
>   damage or injury.] (Radwanski, *Mérida90* 12)

The building and neighborhood were significantly impacted by the earthquake that hit Mexico City in 1985, and by subsequent natural disasters, including floods and a sinking of the ground. "Natural," however, like "access" before it, again needs to be flagged as a word worth questioning, just as I flagged it in relation to Naomi Klein's theory of disaster capitalism in the Introduction. Most "natural" disasters in Mexico City, for centuries in fact, might as easily or justifiably be described as unnatural. Although an important location for the Aztecs, the indigenous population did not reside in some sections of what is now Mexico City, which was initially islands (regarded as sacred) surrounded by bodies of water. In the sixteenth century, the Spanish began the process of filling in the area around where the central city now sits and of constructing wells to extract water from deep within the earth. These actions have ensured that, five centuries later, especially as the city has grown into one of the largest in the world, there has been substantial sinkage throughout, as much as ten meters in some locations (Sample). The Palacio de Bellas Artes/the Palace of Fine Arts, in fact, has sunk almost four meters over the last century, so that what was the ground floor as the twentieth century began is now in the basement (T. Johnson).

Numerous families and individuals lived in or occupied Mérida90 at the time of Radwanski's project, and some families had lived there since the 1930s (although the building had not always been a tenement, it became one over the course of the century). By the end of the first decade of the twenty-first century, construction was booming in Colonia Roma, with hundreds of new buildings going up in tandem with the "preservation" of "historical districts." I pause over these terms as well simply because the determination of what counts as both preservation and historical districts is never innocent of the classed interests that drive shifts in the urban landscape. This was relatively clear to me in August 2014 observing construction of luxury apartments in Calle Chihuaha, one block north of the Plaza Luis Cabrera. Calle Chihuahua 120, a sign announced, would offer apartments with terraces, patios, high ceilings, two parking places, and a "Casa en Fachada Catalogada" [a house with a historically catalogued façade]. Nuestro México del Futuro, it seems, preserves the past for those who can afford to buy a piece of it. Such new construction alongside decrepit buildings that have been occupied by squatters or alongside makeshift shacks or tents ensures that class divisions are extremely legible in the architecture of Colonia Roma, as in other central neighborhoods such as Tepito, Juárez, and Doctores.

Radwanski's project documents the ways in which the people and location of Mérida90 were affected by this "desarrollo" (and in her description of the project Radwanski herself puts the word "development" *entre comillas*—that is, in quotation marks—in order to mark it as a word and process that her photographs will interrogate) (*Mérida90* 12). When Mérida90 was demolished, promises were made that the families living there could return, and indeed they worked with legal assistance to access that possibility of return. There were various means for accessing that possibility, including—most importantly—an expropriation law that essentially says that a new edifice needs to be constructed and offered to families within five years if their living space is expropriated by the government. At the time of her photographic project, Radwanski herself was cautiously optimistic about the future for the displaced families from Mérida90, given the existence of the expropriation law and the legal assistance. It was, however, a very tense moment for the residents, as there were no clear guarantees that they would be able to return to the same building after the expropriation law expired. Over the course of the writing of this chapter, the residents of Mérida90 were dispersed throughout the city and the region, waiting for their home to be reconstructed. Almost six years after their displacement and as a result of the ensuing struggle, many of the residents were finally able to return to Colonia Roma and to a reconstructed Edificio América, in the spring of 2015.

I want to pause briefly over this return before reflecting more on Radwanski's images of rubble and emptiness. The editors of the new quarterly *Salvage* insist in their opening issue, which they (poetically) title "Amid This Stony Rubbish," that "hope must be abandoned before it can be salvaged" ("Perspectives" 3). Hope is "too weak a formulation" for what they term "salvage-Marxism," which rigorously attends to the bleakness of contemporary neoliberal capitalism and a global austerity politics, to the immense and structural power held by those who benefit from and implement those systems, and to the lack of viable strategies on the Left for constructing real alternatives (15). A salvage-Marxism would sustain a necessary pessimism in and around Mérida90: amid literally stony rubbish, the quotidian miracle that is the return of the displaced families to Colonia Roma can generate an almost accidental optimism, yet larger processes of displacement, dispossession, and austerity have only accelerated during and beyond the Year of the UK in Mexico and Mexico in the UK. The editors of *Salvage* turn away from a naïve hope in their inaugural issue, published in 2015, and to what they describe as "utter yearning, for something familiar yet undiscovered" (15). In their attempt to theorize salvage-Marxism, the editors turn to C. S. Lewis to describe the affect they are scavenging for, noting his "'inconsolable longing in the heart for we know not what,' 'an unsatisfied desire which is itself more desirable than any other satisfaction'" (15). Such inconsolable longing and unsatisfied desire, I contend, is akin to the queer and crip longing I weave into this section and chapter as I continue. Lewis, the editors of *Salvage* suggest, called that affect joy, "a joy he insisted be 'sharply distinguished both from happiness and from Pleasure,' and 'might almost equally well be called a particular kind of . . . grief. But then it is a kind we want'" (15). The editors argue in conclusion that "to earn its—real—pessimism, salvage-Marxism is always-already surprised by joy" (15). Lewis wasn't talking about Barthesian pleasure as he reflected on the differences between what he himself termed "Pleasure" and what could be a painful, self-shattering joy, although both Lewis and Barthes are essentially pointing toward, and looking critically at, pleasures that consolidate and reassure and opposing those reassuring pleasures to something more difficult to name (bliss, yearning, inconsolability, we know not what). The return of families to Mérida90 is of course a real success that, in crip times, should not be discounted. The families in their "success," however, were surprised by joy that is still a kind of grief for readers of *Mérida90* and for antigentrification activists more generally, if that joy is comprehended, as it should be, as inescapably caught up in larger, ongoing, and transnational processes of displacement.

During the years that the families in Edificio América were displaced, gentrification continued apace in Colonia Roma and on the street. It is now necessary to pay for parking nights and weekends throughout the neighborhood, and in particular in the streets alongside Mérida90. An architect working in Colonia Roma suggested cynically to me that the new requirement would be a "gold mine" for developers. Diagonally in one direction from Mérida90 is the Federal District's only American Apparel store; the revolving sign in front confirms for consumers in Spanish (on one side) that the clothing was made "sin explotación" [without exploitation] and in English (on the other side) that it was made "without sweatshop labor." In May 2014, when I asked the clerk working inside how long the store had been there, he said that it had arrived from Polanco (one of Mexico City's most exclusive and expensive neighborhoods) about four years prior, which would have been around the time of the demolition of Mérida90. Diagonally in the opposite direction is an upscale sandwich restaurant and bar called Belmondo's that those who don't use wheelchairs can access by stepping down into the bar and dining area. A sign outside assures consumers that "En este establecimiento no se discrimina por motivos de raza, religión, orientación sexual, condición física, o socioeconomic ni por ningún otro motivo" [This establishment does not discriminate on the basis of race, religion, sexual orientation, physical or socioeconomic condition, or on any other basis]. The sign marks an earnest and clearly well-intended policy (a law, in fact) in effect throughout the Federal District, although only select establishments display it (especially, I would argue, establishments that want to appear gay-friendly). "No existe consume minimo, ni la modalidad de barra libre," this particular sign wryly continues [There is no minimum required purchase here, but it's also not an open bar]. The maître d' informed me that the restaurant had opened in March 2012. Although I am certainly noting an irony in the disjuncture between a stated desire to not discriminate against disabled people and a space that is not clearly wheelchair-accessible, I would nonetheless underscore the earnest hipness of the space; my observation of the staff and patrons of Belmondo's over the course of a few evenings suggests that indeed they would not want to discriminate against any recognized minority group. On the contrary, my sense is that they *themselves* want to be recognized as moving through circles composed of friends with a diverse range of identities.

Radwanski's photographic project was eventually displayed in the Museo de Arte Moderno [Museum of Modern Art] in Chapultepec Park in Mexico City, where I first encountered it in July 2013. There, it was one component of El Museo de los Desplazados, as part of the transnational artists' collective Left Hand Rotation's project "Gentrificación no es un nombre de señora" [Gentrification is not a lady's name], in which the role of culture in the process of gentrification is analyzed. Many of the initial installations for El Museo de los Desplazados (there have been about 75) were in Spain and Portugal, where it began in 2010. As of this writing in 2016, the project has involved artists and communities in Mexico, Canada, Brazil, Chile, Colombia, Peru, Ecuador, China, Germany, Bulgaria, Hungary, Greece, Turkey, the United Kingdom, and the United States.

Radwanski's image of rubble, in particular, might be easily read as, to adapt Kafer's words, a "sign of the future no one wants" (46). Kafer yearns for crip signs and crip futures, however, and her work in *Feminist, Queer, Crip* with Muñozian queer longing fuels that yearning. Photography plays an important role for Muñoz in his own book *Cruising Utopia: The Then and There of Queer Futurity*, where he often reads *queerness* into haunting spaces absent of actual bodies. Muñoz reads the photography of Kevin McCarty as queer, for example, even if (and in many ways, precisely because) it is not directly representational of human beings (100–113). Muñoz is not alone in contemporary queer theory with this approach to photography; J. Jack Halberstam, in *The Queer Art of Failure*, similarly reads queerness into the photography of Spanish artists Helena Cabello and Ana Carceller even though (and again precisely because) there are no human beings in the pieces under consideration (110). For Muñoz, McCarty's vacant photographs exemplify the central thesis of *Cruising Utopia*—the idea that "queerness is not yet here . . . [and] we are not yet queer" (1). If the present, with all of its uncertainty, hopelessness, and violence, can and should be described as a "quagmire . . . that lets us feel that this world is not enough, that indeed something is missing," Muñoz positions queerness as "a structured and educated mode of desiring," indicating other possibilities (and I myself use "indicate" here both in the sense of pointing toward and in a more embodied sense whereby a felt symptom—a fever, anxiety, physical pain—*indicates* necessary courses of action). Queerness, as Muñoz theorizes it, is "an ideality that can be distilled from the past and used to imagine a future" (1). Queerness is thus indissociable from both the quagmire we are in and from times, places, and modes of being yet to come. Indeed, we might in fact say that important strains of queer theory from the moment Muñoz began to theorize queer of color critique in the mid-1990s (and as these quotes from *Cruising Utopia* should make clear) have put forward a sort of salvage-Marxism *avant la lettre*.[6] As Muñoz himself in fact explicitly insists in the closing comment of his collaborative meditation with Lisa Duggan, "Hope and Hopelessness":

> When we started this writing project it seemed like most folks assumed that we would be writing about "hope vs. hopelessness" or at the very least "hope or hopelessness." But as this collaborative project progressed it became clear to us that the most important word in our title was the conjunction "and." . . . We write for and from an "and" in the hopes to better describe actually existing and potential queer worlds that thrive, with, through and because of the negative. (Duggan and Muñoz 281)

Muñoz brought this queer mode of desiring for and from an "and" to all of the objects and sites he examined near the end of his career, before his untimely passing in late 2013.

In *Cruising Utopia*, one example that Muñoz considers from McCarty's work represents an empty stage in the Silver Lake Lounge, a predominantly Latino gay club in Los Angeles. There is a dark rug on the stage, and the curtain glimmers silver-black in the background. The main source of illumination for the photograph is the word "SALVATION," which appears in arched lights above the performance space. "The bright shining ideality of salvation," Muñoz writes, "hangs over a space that is dark and not very promising except that the concept literally is writ large on top of the picture—in this visual study is embedded the nature of a utopian performativity within subaltern spaces" (109). Essentially looking at an empty, almost-forgettable space but reaching elsewhere for a queer "then and there," Muñoz's reading in *Cruising Utopia* of these enigmatic McCarty photographs (and in some ways, Muñoz's entire theoretical project) allows us to hear aspirational echoes of "we are not yet here, we are not yet queer, get used to it." I will argue that similar, crip, echoes linger in the air of the bedrooms Radwanski photographs and bounce off the crumbling walls in risk of imminent collapse.

Mexico City for Everyone; or, Under Occupancy

I examine more of Radwanski's images of Mérida90 later in this chapter, including photographs that do include some of the former (and now, again current) residents of the building. With Radwanski's haunting, vacant images in the background, however, I first want to think more carefully about bedrooms in our moment, *pero no esos dormitorios mexicanos*, not those Mexican bedrooms. In this section, I open with a consideration of British bedrooms to generate the key points that I carry back to Mexico City as the section concludes. In March and April of 2013, the British press was in fact filled with stories about bedrooms. In its April/May 2013 edition, to pick one example, the Left British magazine *Red Pepper*, like many other online and print periodicals, reported scathingly about the bedroom tax [Figure 3.7]. The *Red Pepper* cover image, designed by Matt Littler, depicts a bulls-eye or target over a generic two-story single-family dwelling and arguably calls

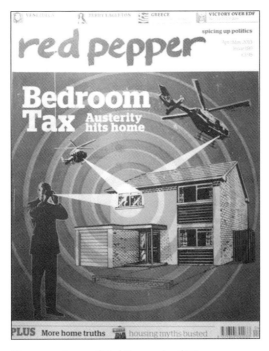

Figure 3.7. Cover of *Red Pepper*, April/May 2013.

up themes of surveillance and securitization and of arrest, detainment, or incarceration (themes that variously appear throughout *Crip Times*). The single-family dwelling is surrounded, in the image, by helicopters and by a generic authority figure with binoculars. Shining bright lights emanate both from the figure and the helicopters, all pointing directly into one room, presumably a bedroom, in the top floor of the building.

Many impacted by the new policy indeed immediately felt that they were under siege, and in less than a year a study commissioned by the government itself could quantify evictions that had resulted from it (P. Butler). Officially, the public was not directly "taxed"; the bedroom tax mandated a reduction of benefits, and Tory politicians in general avoided the language in more popular circulation in relation to the policy, continuing to call it "the under occupancy penalty." The policy was implemented beginning April 1, 2013, as just one new piece in the sweeping austerity measures put forward by the coalition government upon taking office in 2010. Perhaps more than any other austerity measure in the UK, however, it exposed fractures in the coalition (which, at the time the bedroom tax was implemented, most British voters believed would not hold through the 2015 elections; this prediction proved to be true). These fractures in the coalition sometimes materialized around the differing ways poverty was perceived, represented, or rationalized by the minority party in the coalition, the Liberal Democrats, and by the majority party, the Tories. Notably, for example (in terms of exposed fractures), the conservative mayor of London, Boris Johnson, pronounced in late 2013 that people were poor because of a low IQ. Many quickly dismissed Johnson's outrageous announcement for implying that poverty was ever "deserved"; the statement also depends upon contours of ableism as it conjures up the specter of someone scoring low on a standardized intelligence assessment test in order to naturalize the uneven distribution of resources. Clegg (the leader of the Liberal Democrats at the time) responded by saying that Johnson—and by extension, the Tories in general—were treating people like dogs (Mason, "Boris"; Mason and Watt). In relation to the bedroom tax in particular, there was pronounced disagreement at the time of its implementation, with some Liberal Democrats denouncing Tory support for the under occupancy penalty and proposing instead what was termed a "mansion tax" that would target families and individuals in higher income brackets (Mason, "Liberal Democrat"). Certain local councils largely dominated by the Labour Party—especially in the north, the west, or across Scotland—explicitly resisted the policy and put in place local protections for claimants to counteract it (Carrell).

Essentially, the bedroom tax mandated that benefits paid to claimants be reduced if they were found to have what was deemed "too much," or "excess," living space in the property they were renting. If social housing tenants of working age had so-called "spare bedrooms," the housing benefit they received was reduced. If tenants had one "spare room," for example, they lost 14 percent of their housing benefit; if they had two, they lost 25 percent. This steep reduction explains why the under occupancy penalty was *experienced* as a tax by those affected. *Red Pepper* reported that "On average those affected . . . lose £14 a week in housing benefit. . . . Of the 660,000 people affected by the tax, two-thirds of households include a person with disabilities. The tax will disproportionately hit the north, where the old industrial towns traditionally built bigger houses and there has been little demand for one- or two-bedroom dwellings" (Koksal 23). On this point, it's worth noting that there is no little irony when thinking and talking about the "Global North" in relation to England itself, since most of the capital and neoliberal spectacle is actually located in the south and not in often more-impoverished areas of the north (one recent comparison looked at the United States and suggested that, if the UK were a state, it would be the second poorest, but would rank at the bottom without the wealth of London and the southeast) (Schwarz). Indeed, in relation to issues of affordable housing, potential displacement or eviction, and homelessness, a catch phrase like "the United Kingdom in Mexico and Mexico in the United Kingdom" resonates far beyond what the UK government ever intended. If such a catch phrase is reimagined or resignified as gesturing more generally toward the idea of the Global North in the Global South and vice versa, and the vast economic inequalities that mark the distance between those imagined locations, it captures the ways in which the class divisions of transnational neoliberal capitalism that can be mapped globally have long been built into the very landscape or architecture in both locations. Margaret Thatcher herself noted in a 1994 speech delivered in Mexico, that "all of the fashionable discussions about 'North-South' dialogue" that emerged during the period when she assumed power in the UK "were damagingly, even dangerously wrong. It was in any case untrue that the world was divided into a homogenously 'rich' north and a homogenously poor 'south': there were so many exceptions that the rule just did not hold" ("Speech in Mexico"). Of course, what Thatcher means to exemplify here is very much contrary to my own intentions; more than twenty years before the Dual Year, Thatcher seeks to encourage emulation of "the British example" and to praise "Mexican miracles" such as "curbing the power of trade unions" and "pressing ahead with privatization" ("Speech in Mexico"). The ubiquity of state-sanctioned displacements in both locations, however (not unconnected to privatization and union-busting) ironically indicate that indeed it is inadequate to speak of poverty in particular as something that can be simplistically located elsewhere.

By the end of 2013, Prime Minister David Cameron was, to an extent, in damage control mode in relation to the bedroom tax, arguing that disabled people were exempt from the policy. Eighteen prominent disability organizations drafted a letter that December insisting that

Cameron's backtracking was misleading (Lyons). Two exemptions appeared to be in place, one for families with disabled children who—for whatever reason—could not share bedrooms with siblings and one for families who frequently needed someone not living with them to be present for overnight care. Roughly matching the *Red Pepper* figures, the disability organizations noted in their letter that 400,000 disabled people would be hit negatively by the tax. Of course, the organizations' arguments with the prime minister over numbers were not intended merely to clarify what the exact figure was; instead, their point was that—regardless of a few exemptions—the new and drastic austerity measure (like the other cuts) was devastating the lives of disabled people and their families across Britain.

On the surface, of course, Global South in the Global North notwithstanding, this bleak housing situation has little or nothing to do with housing in Mexico City. My interest in this section and chapter, however, is in placing the bedroom tax in a larger, globalizing British disability context that might allow for comprehending crip displacements in the UK alongside displacements elsewhere. The transnational scope of El Museo de los Desplazados already affirms the value of considering displacements in disparate locations in relation to each other; my more specific aim here is to spotlight the workings of an Anglo-imperial disability politics that makes such a consideration even more viable, or urgent. Moving back to Mexico City, then, I'm interested in what the British government was doing in 2013 across the Atlantic in the days leading up to the implementation of the bedroom tax.[7] Somewhat unbelievably, even if—as I will make clear—the cultural logic of neoliberalism was obviously at work, the British government was in fact busily *exporting* its disability vision to its Mexican partners.

The UK was busy exporting, however, a more *recognizable* disability vision: on Friday, March 22, 2013, British Ambassador Judith Macgregor presided over an event called "Mexico City for Everyone: The Accessibility Legacy of London 2012." The embassy proudly displayed images on its website commemorating the event, including one with an elderly woman using a walker crossing the street with clearly delineated crosswalks and most importantly, new curb cuts allowing for access from the street to the sidewalk. The street shot is an image of the intersection outside the British Embassy on a sunny day. The Union Jack is prominent in the background, and a marker on the pavement indicates that the intersection has been "donado por [donated by] GREAT [all caps in English] Britain." When I visited the intersection in August 2014, the lettering was still visible in the pavement, although the intersection was already somewhat cracked and in disrepair. In relation to the March 2013 event, "Mexico City for Everyone" is the English translation the embassy uses on its website; the much longer Spanish-language description of the event uses both "Ciudad de México para tod@s" [Mexico City for Everyone] *and* (more prominently) "*Ciudades* para tod@s" [Cities for Everyone] (my emphasis), gesturing toward universal design in its move out from the specificity of Ciudad de México para tod@s and implying in the process of that expansive gesture that this British export can work anywhere and everywhere.

The four corners redesigned outside the British Embassy were part of an important larger initiative (not solely British) that redesigned thousands of other intersections in Mexico City. Indeed, in Colonia Roma the very similar markers in the redesigned corners around the Plaza Luis Cabrera suggest its renovation was part of the same, largely private or charitable, initiative. Curb cuts, however, are apparently only one element in a city for everyone and only one part of what Britain might have to offer the world as it moves toward that imagined city. At the March 2013 event, Julie Fleck, director of accessibility strategizing for the London 2012 Olympics and Paralympics, gave a talk called "Accessible London: Achieving an Inclusive Environment." The British embassy's photo of Fleck positions her in front of a slide that was part of the talk; the slide includes four images of the London Aquatics Centre in Queen Elizabeth Olympics Park. The London Aquatics Centre was designed by architect Zaha Hadid and is now the post-Olympic training ground for one openly gay star of the London 2012 Olympics, Tom Daley. The Centre is not just gay-friendly, however; it is "designed for swimmers of all abilities, from absolute beginners to Olympic and Paralympic champions" (London Aquatics). Corporate or individual memberships can now be purchased, or daily passes starting at £10.

There is no sign at the London Aquatics Centre like the sign at Belmondo's in Colonia Roma across from Mérida90. No one, in other words, wryly suggests that there is no minimum purchase price but it's still not an open pool. But the effect is the same, as a celebrated openness to swimmers of all abilities covers over the fact that the space is broadly inaccessible. The daily pass price is out of reach for many Londoners, and certainly for Londoners who have had their housing subsidy cut by *more* than £10. Or even more literally, Londoners who have been evicted: in the area immediately adjacent to the Olympic Village, there has been vibrant housing activism and some occupation of vacant buildings. Residents were evicted from a cluster of buildings called Carpenters Estate and two thousand homes were left empty as the Newham Council, where the available housing is located, hoped to sell the land to private developers. At an action near Carpenters Estate that I witnessed in February 2015, activists covered the street with banners reading, "Social Housing, Not Social Cleansing," and "London for EVERYONE Not Just the Rich" [Figure 3.8].[8]

Figure 3.8. "Social Housing, Not Social Cleansing," London, March 2015. Photo by Author.

The activist dream of "London for everyone" is more than a little ironic, given Fleck's "Accessible London" talk. Fleck gave versions of the presentation not just in Mexico City but also in other international venues; it appears to be based on a plan published in July 2011 that was made available online by the mayor of London as part of the Greater London Authority's official website ("Accessible London"). According to that plan, achieving an inclusive environment requires not only accessible streets, but also improved access to goods and services, new fully accessible hotel rooms, and a somewhat vague commitment to "tackling inequality." The plan also requires "Housing Design" in which "all new dwellings have adequately sized rooms, convenient and efficient room layouts" that "meet the needs of Londoners over their lifetime, and address social inclusion" ("Accessible London"). The latter aspiration, for London, is certainly both laudable and urgent; in 2014, the Leonard Chesire Disability charity determined that five million people in the country were in need of living space that was more accommodating to a range of disabilities. Their study noted the high number of disabled people washing in their kitchens and sleeping in their living rooms; these problems were generally caused by the absence of lifts, ramps, grab rails, or wide doors (Doward; Leonard Cheshire).

Such studies, alongside activist resistance to the warehousing of housing for speculation and private development, make clear that an "Accessible London" remained illusory in April 2013. Nonetheless, a British disability politics was ready for packaging and shipment abroad. Put differently, "Accessible London" was in circulation as a commodity in Mexico City even as the ongoing labor of fighting for a truly accessible London was invisibilized. Several Mexican dignitaries and celebrities were in attendance outside the embassy with Ambassador Macgregor and Fleck for the ribbon-cutting ceremony and photo opportunity, a public relations event also essentially donated by (donado por) GREAT Britain. The group included Fidel Perez, executive director of the Program for People with Disabilities in the Federal District, and Gustavo Sánchez Martínez, a Paralympic swimmer intimately familiar with the London Aquatics Centre, since he won two gold medals, one silver, and one bronze there during the 2012 Games.

Inevitably, however, the sunny booster narrative put forward by the British embassy in Mexico City obscured what we might understand as the climate change around disability back on the other side of the Atlantic; undoubtedly, even if "Housing Design" was part of Fleck's presentation, no mention was made (in English or Spanish) on March 22 of the taxed UK bedrooms or of the fact that the weekend of March 22 saw marches and protests in Birmingham, Bournemouth, Brighton, Bristol, Edinburgh, Glasgow, Leeds, London, and Sheffield. Activists that weekend were protesting the coalition's austerity plans in general and specifically workfare, which had been put in place by the Department for Work and Pensions and which meant that unemployed people could be forced into six months of compulsory unpaid charity work as part of the Community Action Programme. On December 3, 2012 (International Disabled People's Day), the DWP had introduced such compulsory unpaid work for disabled and sick claimants.

For Sánchez Martínez himself, the March 22 ribbon-cutting ceremony wasn't the first time that his London successes had brought him into contact with politicians in Mexico City. At an awards ceremony a few months after the London 2012 Paralympic Games and the day before the DWP in the UK introduced compulsory unpaid work for sick and disabled claimants, Sánchez Martínez received the Premio Nacional de Deportes [National Prize for Sport]. The December 2 awards ceremony was held by the newly elected Mexican president, Enrique Peña Nieto, at his official residency, Los Pinos. Los Pinos is *also* in Chapultepec Park, where one could, as I said, visit El Museo de los Desplazados. Although the exhibition with Radwanski's photographs didn't open until May 2013 and Peña Nieto's ceremony for Sánchez Martínez was in December 2012, in a sense displacement and dispossession were almost literally in the shadow of incorporation. Sánchez Martínez as out and proud disabled person and athlete, in other words, was recognized by the state in essentially the same geographical location where the artists' collective Left Hand Rotation would later interrogate a range of state-sponsored projects of eviction and displacement (included alongside Radwanski's work in the Museo de Arte Moderno were exhibits focused on processes of gentrification in São Paulo and Rotterdam). In contrast to incorporation, which is about targeting—even spotlighting—certain individuals or groups for recognition, displacement is always implicated in an inability or even a willed refusal to recognize.

My intent here is to examine how *layered* that willed refusal to recognize can be, and how it paradoxically works in tandem with (indeed, depends upon) the construction of "Mexico City for Everyone," a happy aspiration that—like the sign outside Belmondo's—explicitly and in seemingly innocent language insists that it *is* recognizing, well, everyone. "Mexico City for Everyone," however, is actually a speculation: like the forced under occupancy at Carpenters Estate it basically lodges a bet that by keeping certain people out, a different class of people (and of course, capital) can be seduced in. "Under occupancy," as a theoretical concept, is useful for interrogating the seeming innocence of "Mexico City for Everyone" and for examining the various layers of displacement masked by happy aspirations: who is missing in this snapshot of Accessible London/Accessible Mexico City, and where did they go? In Mexico City itself, especially in areas like Colonia Roma targeted for "development," whose space is expropriated and by whom? Put differently, who might be prohibited from occupying the space of "Mexico City for Everyone" and why? Does Nuestro México del Futuro come with spare bedrooms and safe, affordable housing? Furthermore, how does the laudable British vision of a city for everyone function transnationally, as the state continually (re)positions itself locally and globally in relation to disability in our moment? With such questions in the background, I linger, in the section that follows, over some of the unique ways recognition and misrecognition (and under occupancy) have been in evidence in Mexico since 2012, before returning to the Mexican-British partnership celebrated and photographed on March 22, 2013. In the final section of this chapter, I return to Mérida90 and more analysis of the critical photographic work of Radwanski.

Wider Relations: El Momento de México y Operaciones Más Amplias

The tension between recognition and misrecognition has been particularly thick around President Peña Nieto.[9] Peña Nieto's recognition of Paralympian Sánchez Martínez's achievements was in fact the first official act of his presidency. Others, however, have been wary of recognizing Peña Nieto's candidacy and presidency *themselves* as legitimate. In May 2012 a Mexican student movement emerged and was made famous by a hashtag on Twitter: #YoSoy132 (I am Number 132). On May 11, 2012, Peña Nieto, then-presidential candidate for the Partido Revolucionario Institucional (PRI), spoke to a group of students at the Ibero-American University in Mexico City. He was questioned by some of the students about civil unrest and charges of police brutality that occurred in San Salvador Atenco in 2006, when—as governor of the state of Mexico—Peña Nieto called in police to shut down a protest by local flower vendors and their supporters. The protestors had barricaded the highway leading from Atenco into a local market where the vendors had been prohibited from selling their wares. Peña Nieto called in the police to break up the protest; in the ensuing clash, two protestors were killed and many women were sexually assaulted (Berehulak). Peña Nieto defended his 2006 actions as governor, but the Ibero students were not satisfied. They sharply critiqued his campaign in particular and state violence in general, and later uploaded a video of their confrontation with the candidate to YouTube.

When the major Mexican news outlets covered the events at Ibero, they reported, contrary to the facts, that the vocal critics of Peña Nieto were not actually enrolled students of the university. Legitimate students were, in other words, unrecognized and delegitimized by dominant media. In response, 131 students published another video on YouTube identifying themselves with their Ibero-American University identification cards. The video was circulated across the city, country, and world, eliciting the hashtag #YoSoy132. The statement "I am 132" indicated support for the students as well as for a burgeoning movement against police brutality, corruption, and institutionalized political power. Although in 2012 the PRI had been out of power for more than a decade, it was still perceived by the students, along with its primary rival (the Partido Acción Nacional, or PAN, which had held power since 2000), as both entrenched and corrupt. Perhaps most importantly, #YoSoy132 marked collective resistance to the ways in which the dominant media had colluded with political power structures that are—in the view of the students and their supporters—undemocratic and brutal. #YoSoy132 imagined other worlds and other representations. It also called for recognition that was necessarily both individual and transindividual. "I am" the hashtag shouted, demanding recognition and condemning willful *misrecognition*. But "I am" simultaneously and paradoxically meant "we are." Like other Latin American uprisings around the same time—students in Chile from 2011 on demanding free and accessible education for everyone, or protestors across Brazil in 2013 calling for hospitals and schools rather than multimillion dollar stadiums—the Mexican student movement insisted that "we" have another, collective, vision of openness, access, democratic inclusion, justice, and freedom.[10] Strategically, across Peña Nieto's increasingly unpopular presidency, the "we" conjured by the movement continued to demand recognition while refusing to recognize the legitimacy of the administration; indeed, a hashtag from 2014 proclaimed #MexicoNoTienePresidente [Mexico doesn't have a president]. When *Time* magazine put Peña Nieto on the cover of its February 13, 2014 international edition, with the headline "Saving Mexico," it intended to celebrate both his business-friendly policies and a supposed reduction of violence (especially violence associated with the narcotics trade). Innumerable parodies of the cover quickly circulated globally with the same image surrounded by photos of police brutality, silenced students, and wounded and bleeding activists alongside the question "Saving Mexico?" [Figure 3.9].

In 2012, the protests against Peña Nieto and the dominant media continued throughout the year, right up to the weekend of his inauguration and occupation of Los Pinos and his awarding of the Premio Nacional de Deportes to Sánchez Martínez. While students and other activists protested outside Chapultepec Park and were countered at times quite violently by the police, inside the park, in Los Pinos, Peña Nieto declared, "Este es el momento de México y vamos a hacerlo realidad. Quiero una nación sana, y fuerte, y ustedes, los deportistas son el mejor ejemplo a seguir" ("Entregan") [This is Mexico's moment and we are going to make it reality. I want a nation healthy and strong and you, the athletes, are the best example to follow]. Julie Avril Minich, in an important study of disability in "Greater Mexico" largely focused on Chicano/a cultural production, notes that contemporary states regularly put forward the "image of the nation as a whole, nondisabled body whose health must be protected from external pollutants . . . including those with disabilities and diseases" (2). Even as Peña Nieto decidedly invokes that trope of the healthy nation, however, he demonstrates that *certain* disabled bodies can actually be flexibly included in it: Mexico's moment on December 2, 2012 was a moment of disabled recognition and incorporation. At the

ENRIQUE PEÑA NIETO
EL PRESIDENTE DE
LA IGNORANCIA,
CORRUPCIÓN.Y EL ODIO

SAVING
MEXICO?

by @vickoohh

Figure 3.9. Activist parody of *Time* magazine cover, February 2014.

same time, the "health of the nation" is still implicitly positioned here as a form of protection from those on the outside or those who will go unrecognized; the "best example to follow" suggests that "we" could conceivably choose to follow other leaders. On December 2, 2012 Peña Nieto tried to rhetorically define or fix Mexico's moment; nonetheless, that moment was inevitably haunted by what had come before and what the students had called out: corruption, state violence, and the willful misrecognition of embodied citizens and activists.

Of course, as I've already implied with my comments about the spatiality of Los Pinos and Chapultepec Park, the haunting and vacant Mexican bedrooms of Radwanski's photos and the under occupancy that they highlight in a city that is ostensibly for everyone, are discernible in the shadow of the president's accolades for Paralympian Sánchez Martínez. My larger point in this section, however, is that those bedrooms are also in the shadow of the British goodwill event and in larger patterns of transnational exchange between the two states. As openness and accessibility are exported and imported, *so too are the forms of displacement and dispossession that are masked by them.* Cripping a politics of recognition entails grappling with those processes and noting a sharp distinction between access and neoliberal access. I suspect that Marx would see *neoliberal* accessibility as "a very queer thing, abounding in metaphysical subtleties and theological niceties" (*Capital* 319). If, like the fetishized commodities Marx is discussing, neoliberal openness and accessibility could "themselves speak, they would say: Our use-value may be a thing that interests men. It is no part of us as objects. . . . Our natural intercourse as commodities proves it. In the eyes of each other, we are nothing but exchange values" (328). Attending to this imagined speech entails recognizing/re-cognizing the relations between (disabled) human beings that are transformed into relations between things in the current geopolitical moment.[11]

Widening such relations between things was precisely the goal of the bilateral partnership of 2015. As the UK prepared for a state visit from Peña Nieto in March of that year, the UK government was reporting double-digit growth in trade between the two countries since 2012, growth which Clegg had envisioned in his 2011 speech to the Mexican Senate ("UK and Mexico Celebrate"). Sir Vince Cable, David Cameron's secretary of state for business, innovation and skills noted that Mexico remains "an important growth market for our exports and British firms can also use Mexico as a base for wider operations throughout Latin America" ("UK and Mexico Celebrate"). Queen Elizabeth II herself recognized Peña Nieto at a state dinner during his visit, emphasizing the two countries' identities as "natural partners" (Perring).[12] Peña Nieto in turn again emphasized identity, along with national unity, in his remarks at the dinner, addressing Elizabeth directly: "Usted, su Majestad, ha sido fuente de identidad y unidad para su pueblo. Su figura ha sido clave para reafirmar a su nación como una potencia global. Los mexicanos tenemos un especial sentimiento de afecto y gratitud hacia la Reina Isabel II" [You, your Majesty, have been a source of identity and unity for your people. You as a figure have been key in reaffirming your nation as a global power. We, the Mexican people, have a special feeling of emotion and gratitude toward Queen Elizabeth II] ("Cena de Estado"). Meanwhile, again unrecognized by Peña Nieto, protestors outside the banquet hall decried in English and Spanish the very lack of liberty, democracy, and human rights that the president was lauding in his speech ("Peña Nieto es recibido").[13]

At one point on the British government's website, "2015: The Year of Mexico in the UK and the UK in Mexico" is "mistranslated" into Spanish: "El año del Reino Unido en México y del Reino Unido en México" [the Year of the UK in Mexico and the UK in Mexico] ("2015"). "El intercambio desigual funciona como siempre" [The unequal exchange functions like always], Eduardo Galeano might say (269). The mistranslation (or, more likely, typographical error or oversight) is a comical exposure of what the photo opportunity with disabled dignitaries outside the embassy could not exactly capture at first glance: transnational investment *and more* transnational investment, with fewer barriers, not necessarily for disabled people but precisely for that investment, are what should be seen as really at stake with celebrations of openness and accessibility in and around 2015. Indeed, a mere two years after the celebration at the British embassy, Radwanski herself documented the training of other Mexican Paralympians, some of whom were living in the Olympic training center since access in other parts of Mexico City remains so limited. The trade in neoliberal accessibility is not necessarily impeded by such disabled stories. What really matters, in the end, is the doubling of bilateral trade and the concomitant consolidation of capital in both capitals. The UK government has gone so far as to cite its "success" in locations like Mexico as proof that austerity works. The economic "growth" that an increase of free trade marks, however, never speaks to and for those who have been displaced ("Supporting Business").

My argument is that these processes of displacement and dispossession cannot exist without disability, even as *attending* to these processes, these crip displacements, requires that we "read and write disability differently," to borrow and rework a phrase from Tanya Titchkosky (*Reading* 9). The larger project of El Museo de los Desplazados uses a photograph from Gijón in the north of Spain on its main page in a way that perhaps makes such reading and writing differently easy [Figure 3.10]. The photograph—not one of Radwanski's—represents four old women seated on a bench in

Figure 3.10. Museo de los Desplazados, Gijón, Spain.

front of a sterile, brown, industrial-looking wall. A few of the women are wearing dark glasses; one has a modest black shawl over her shoulders. There are stark windows, perhaps the windows to a factory, above the women's heads in the upper third of the photograph. One of the women holds a newspaper; three of them are holding canes. A caption does not identify where this photograph was taken; it is thus used as a placeholder for all the projects included in "Gentrificación no es un nombre de se-ñora." When I say that the photograph makes it easy to read and write disability differently, I mean that the women's age, their canes, and per-haps their sunglasses simultaneously make "disability" legible and—by virtue of its positioning as the "representative" photograph for El Museo de los Desplazados—connect disability to the larger themes of displace-ment that are central to the global artistic project. In my Conclusion, however, I return to other haunting and perhaps more enigmatic crip im-ages from Mérida90 in order to texture my arguments about recognition, access, and wider relations in ciudades para tod@s.

México Se Mueve/Mexico Moves: The Then and There of Crip Futurity[14]

One of the PRI's slogans, which Peña Nieto has used as a brand of sorts in an attempt to forge a legacy, is "México Se Mueve" [Mexico Moves]. It was not immediately obvious when Peña Nieto was elected in 2012 that his legacy would be deep and fresh austerity cuts, but by early 2016, the Mexican finance minister and the head of Mexico's central bank announced a cut in public services equivalent to 7.3 billion US dollars. Sounding very much like their counterparts in the UK, the officials explained that this was "not a popular but necessary measure" in difficult economic times ("Mexican Government"). Peña Nieto made clear in his 2015 state of the nation address that the austerity measures would be a key component of the 2016 budget ("Mexican President Delivers"). México se mueve, however: not long after the new year actually began, Peña Nieto took the inaugural flight on a deluxe aircraft valued at 430 million US dollars, as he attended the World Economic Forum in Davos, Switzerland. *Telesur* reported that the debt associated with the aircraft would be paid for by using public funds through 2027 ("Mexican President Flaunts").

Ironically, one of the most notable moments when "México se mueve" had circulated as a slogan was in Fall 2014, as plans for a new airport for Mexico City were unveiled. British architect Lord Norman Foster, the son-in-law of Mexican billionaire Carlos Slim, was chosen to manage the project, which was estimated to have a price tag of £5.5 billion, and which would quadruple the number of passengers flying through Mexico City to 120 million annually by the middle of the twenty-first century (Magrath). The airport will reach from the Federal District to the state of Mexico, where Peña Nieto was governor, potentially crossing Atenco in the process. The government has claimed that no land will be expropriated, but those who live in Atenco remain quite skeptical. Farmers and others who worried they would be affected by the plan again mobilized against Peña Nieto in Atenco, to mark their opposition to displacement and to vocalize their demand that they *not* be moved ("Los machetes"). There is concern as well that the airport's design uses the dry bed of the Texcoco Lake east of Mexico City—a spot that environmental activists want to restore, not least as one way of addressing the chronic flooding and sinkage that plagues the city as a whole. Alberto Kalach, a Mexico City–born architect, put forward an alternative, environmentally sensitive design that would restore Texcoco lake, but developers chose Foster instead (Bose). The UK's second largest trading partner in Latin America se mueve, but deep, classed contradictions remain between who has the ability to move in Mexico and who must repeatedly be moved out of the way.

The crip images with which I will conclude also highlight contradictions around movement, stasis, and displacement. As I suggested earlier, crip echoes linger in the empty bedrooms and around the seemingly mute objects from Radwanski's photographs of Mérida90. Indeed, after attending to the voices of powerful figures in both the UK and Mexico, particularly to the ways in which their voices drown out, or render inaudible and unrecognizable, other stories, we might conclude that the domestic objects, clutter, debris, and rocks in the Radwanski photos I have examined so far are not somehow inherently silent but rather muted. As neoliberal capitalism and an Anglo-imperial disability politics transforms relations between human beings into relations between things, it hears and amplifies only particular things/commodities—such as neoliberal access—speaking in the ways Marx imagined, even as other objects and stories are silenced. The pile of rocks in the first photograph with which I opened my consideration of Mérida90, for instance, might in fact speak otherwise. "Rocks," Jeffrey Jerome Cohen writes in a somewhat different context, "possess much of what is supposed to set humans apart. They are neither inert nor mute, but like all life are forever flowing, forever filled with stories" (62). In contrast to fetishized commodities, the rocks that Cohen imagines speaking in some way do not block a consideration of relations between human beings; they in fact facilitate a consideration of the *operaciones más amplias/* wider relations (including economic and ecological relations) through which human stories are articulated.

As I conclude with a consideration of some of the human beings whose stories were in fact lived out within the concrete walls of Mérida90 (walls that were eventually reduced to the rubble Radwanski captures on film), my intention is to keep in motion a crip wonder around them that cannot so quickly be incorporated or so easily congeal into recognition of the sort Sánchez Martínez received, for a moment, from the state. A "politics of wonder," Titchkosky writes in an extended consideration of the imaginative limits of "access" in our moment, means "pausing in the face of what already *is*" and transforming "the assumed clarity of what is already said and done into a place of questions where doubt can open on to new horizons of possibility" (*Question* x). There is a displacement here, certainly, as Titchkosky specifically relocates what is clear to "a place of questions." This is, however, crip displacement in another, critically disabled and politicized sense. I wonder, in Titchkosky's sense, whether these final images, representing displacement, might not simultaneously and paradoxically open onto another place, another world, beyond displacement.

Some of the images I examine now will also allow for a return, in passing, to the other two Radwanski photographs with which I opened—the photographs, that is, of bedrooms. Like those bedroom images, none of the images with which I will conclude this chapter, even as they call for pausing in the face of what already *is*, are immediately legible as "disabled." I begin with a photo of a sixteen-year-old boy named Carlitos, caught—as Radwanski's notes inform us—"durante un momento de contemplación" [in a moment of contemplation] (91) [Figure 3.11]. Carlitos is seated in a bedroom, an unlit cigarette in one hand and a lighter in the other. His thumb is poised (perhaps distractedly, perhaps expectantly) to ignite the lighter. The bed is made with a simple blue bedspread with blue and purple embroidery (barely visible), and there is a thin pillow (also covered by the spread) at the head. The concrete wall behind Carlitos is a few different shades of blue, gray, and white; a

Figure 3.11. Carlitos in a moment of contemplation, November 26, 2009. Photo by Livia Radwanski.

thin, yellow curtain with a floral design (perhaps affording some privacy for this bedroom) hangs behind his right shoulder. Carlitos wears a necklace and a red and black striped hoody that partially covers his head. The hoody is open to reveal a *Trainspotting* T-shirt. Carlitos's gaze is directed slightly away from the camera; the expression on his face is neither happy nor sad, but thoughtful.

This is an in-between image, of course. Moments of contemplation arguably always come between what has happened and what might or will happen: Carlitos is living between childhood and adulthood ("tropezando al madurar"/stumbling to maturity, Radwanski's notes tell us [91]); all of those photographed and interviewed in Mérida90 are between this place and somewhere else. To turn back to and rework Muñoz, we do not yet know; we are not yet here (or there); we are not yet crip. Carlitos is "aflijido por su dependencia al alcohol" [afflicted by his dependency on alcohol] (91), but I do not introduce this "fact" in the preceding paragraph because I want to place this photo in the larger interpretive framework of wonder and of crip displacements. I'm not reading this photo, in other words, only through what would in some cultural locations be a potentially recognizable identity marker (say, "addict") but rather, through a moment of crip contemplation that would perhaps always render identification more elusive and uncertain.

The photo does not necessarily capture pain, although Carlitos's family has in fact experienced a great deal of pain. Indeed, the blue sleeping bag in the second Radwanski photo I introduced in this chapter was laid out on the hard wood floor so that Carlos, Sr., Carlitos's father, could at times sleep there. Carlos, Sr., lives with chronic back pain and used the hard wood of the floor to maintain his back in one position throughout the night, thereby managing the pain. Carlitos's expression of thoughtfulness in this photo is not obviously connected to concerns about impairment (pain, addiction, anxiety) as it structures family and community life. An expansive crip analytic, however, allows for the in-between image, along with the image of the blue sleeping bag, to be read through and across all the textured complexity of psychic and embodied life.

The *Trainspotting* T-shirt ironically carries us back to the north of the UK, to the depressed area around Edinburgh captured in Danny Boyle's 1996 film. Virtually all my concerns in this chapter are uncannily captured in the shirt: the Global South in the Global North and vice versa; disability in, as, and perhaps against, a globalizing British context; displacement; and incorporation. *Trainspotting* is not, to my knowledge, regularly positioned as a "disability" film, despite the fact that one of the main characters is a heroin addict literally nicknamed "Sick Boy." It is, however, a film about addiction, depression, and HIV/AIDS and about a community of *desplazados*, some of whom are at times incarcerated and all of whom are at times surveilled or pursued by the police. Incredibly perhaps (given the issues I have considered in this chapter), the two main areas of economic activity in the film are connected to housing (the main character, Mark Renton, tries to sober up, moves to London, and takes a job as a "letting agent"—that is, a broker between landlords and tenants) and to the underground and illegal drug economy that, in fact, some across the north of the UK did turn to after Margaret Thatcher's attack on working-class communities and the subsequent collapse of stable, industrial, working-class jobs.

Moreover, the thematics *within* the film are as caught up in issues of displacement and incorporation as Danny Boyle's story *outside* the film. Boyle's critically acclaimed film about outsiders went on to become both the top-grossing British film of 1996 (at that time, the top-grossing British film ever) and a major British export. For the purposes of *Crip Times*, it's important to note that Boyle's incorporation into the processes of cultural production was by 2012 so pronounced that he was tapped to produce nothing less than the opening ceremonies for the London Olympic Games. As part of a spectacle designed to depict British history in sweeping overviews of color, light, music, and dance, "We Love Our NHS" was at one moment broadcast around the world in thousands of bright lights. The coalition government, meanwhile, was at that moment targeting as many aspects of the National Health Service for privatization as possible. Carlitos's moment of contemplation predates Boyle's spectacle, but the T-shirt nonetheless captures well the class struggle in both locations, as well as the tension between the many who remain outsiders and the few who are recognized for their achievement and incorporated into the system.[15]

I noted that in some cultural locations, "addict" might be a potentially recognizable identity marker, although a consideration of "addiction" in relation to disability culture or disability studies remains rare in almost any location. In Mexico, substance use is not generally understood as a disability issue or an issue of public health (or, put differently, the government and public health system are perceived as having completely failed in relation to the treatment of alcoholism or addiction). As in many locations, it is still largely comprehended more in and through individual choice or behavior. Private "rehabilitation centers" called *anexos* exist and have been widely debated in Mexico; it is not uncommon for them to be compared to prisons. Approximately 50 percent of *anexos* operate illegally, without being registered (Téllez). For a fee, family members can have someone admitted to an *anexo* for one to three months, and Radwanski informed me that the threat of incarceration in them has worked as a mechanism of fear for some men in Mérida90 struggling with substance use, including Carlitos or Eleazar [Figure 3.12], who lived in the attic apartment and who explained to Radwanski when she photographed him that "lo que más extrañará al mudarse será la libertad que ahí disfrutaba" [what he would miss most about the move from Mérida90 would be the liberty that he enjoyed there] (Radwanski, *Mérida90* 92). With substance use as the ostensible reason, Eleazar had been admitted in the past to an *anexo* against his will, and would thereby have a clear sense of what a loss of liberty felt

Figure 3.12. Eleazar in his kitchen, Mérida90. Photo by Livia Radwanski.

like. Crip theory has begun to theorize the intersections of disability studies and incarceration studies, most notably with the publication of the important anthology *Disability, Incarcerated* (Ben-Moshe, Chapman, and Carey). Given wide reports of "labores domésticas, castigos y abusos sexuales" [domestic labor, punishments, and sexual abuse] in *anexos* (Téllez), it is clear that such locations for the containment and control of bodily, mental, and behavioral difference are indeed ripe for such an intersectional crip analysis.

Another of Radwanski's photographs represents a woman named Remedios and her daughter Ludmila in a moment of tender and gendered sociality in a room filled with Disney images of childhood and femininity that again mark both an aspiration and a reinscription or perhaps localization of a globalized mediascape [Figure 3.13]. Remedios is getting Ludmila ready for Christmas; she is standing and tending to her daughter's hair and face, while Ludmila is seated. Ludmila wears a pink shirt and holds a fluffy stuffed animal with a pink bow around its neck on her lap; behind her is a nightstand or shelf with more colorful objects, including a small selection of beauty products. Pink stickers

Figure 3.13. Remedios and her daughter Ludmila on Christmas Eve, December 24, 2009. Photo by Livia Radwanski.

adorn the mirror behind the nightstand. The top half of the wall behind Remedios and Ludmila is painted green and the bottom half a
light orange; a poster on the top half includes a selection of six Disney
princesses.

Remedios herself wears a blue sweater and her hair is tied back in a
bun. A light blue mask covers her mouth as she tends to her daughter.
Radwanski's notes on this photograph do not speak to Remedios's mask,
although such protective masks are often crucial for those with environmental illness or sensitivity living in humid locations—and the humidity, sinkage, and occasional floods in Mérida90 would have allowed for
mold and mildew to grow easily in the cracked walls and ceilings. There
is, perhaps, an ironic poetics in the fact that the third photo I introduced at the beginning of this chapter represents a "bedroom" with a
Spiderman quilt, given the powers that Peter Parker/Spiderman acquires
after a toxic bite from a spider.[16] Radwanski's notes for that photo do
indeed gesture toward the family's concerns about humidity and about
a very different and threatening kind of toxicity in the crumbling walls
(90). When I visited Mérida90 with Radwanski in October 2015 and met
some of the families that had returned there earlier in the year, Radwanski's first questions to Israel, the young man who had been sleeping on
the couch with the Spiderman quilt, were whether his individual respira-
tory health had improved and whether the renovations had addressed
ongoing problems connected to mold and mildew in the older structure.

The occasional or long-term use of a protective mask for environmental sensitivity does not directly indicate that Remedios, or anyone,
might resist the forces of displacement. However, Remedios was in
fact one of the community leaders who worked most tirelessly with
the lawyer to navigate the expropriation law and to understand the
families' options in the face of the municipal government's actions.[17]
Protective masks such as the one worn by Remedios in this photo have
actually long been widespread not just in Colonia Roma but in Mexico
City more generally, a metropolis known for its pollution. "Make-sicko
Seedy," Carlos Fuentes parodically names it in his 1989 novel *Cristobal
Nonatal* [Christopher Unborn], where the narrator imagines his child
breathing, "The pulverized shit of three million human beings who
have no latrines./The pulverized excrement of ten million animals that
defecate wherever they happen to be./Eleven thousand tons per day of

chemical waste./The mortal breath of three million motors endlessly vomiting puffs of pure poison, black halitosis, buses, taxis, trucks, and private cars, all contributing their flatulence to the extinction of trees, lungs, throats, and eyes." The duality of the Spanish word "contaminación" captures better, I'd say, what Stacy Alaimo might call the transcorporeal (and crip) resonances of what we in English call "pollution" (2).[18] With the larger history of Edificio América in mind, we would be justified in reading crip resonances even in this specific photo: Remedios's awareness of the dangers literally built into the crumbling edifice surely in part spurred her more general work on behalf of the Mérida90 community.

In "El Edificio de Enfrente" [The Building across the Way], talking about Mérida90, Antonio Zirión insists that there is a correspondence between spaces and physical forms and between social forms and the behaviors of subjects who inhabit such spaces (76–77). Zirión is not putting forward an explicit crip argument, but I am reworking his point into one as I wonder about the bodies, minds, and behaviors in Mérida90 and about "disability" in a globalizing context where, even as "access" is increasingly visible all around us (from the London Aquatics Centre to Colonia Roma), eviction and displacement have accelerated. One more photograph, the last I will consider from Mérida90, represents fifteen-year-old Manolo before the altar of the Virgin of Guadalupe on the day Mérida90 was closed for demolition [Figure 3.14]. The viewer only sees Manolo's back, as he stands in front of the empty altar. He wears a blue and red striped football jersey with the name "Ronaldinho" on it and a big number 10—Ronaldo de Assis Moreira, better known as "Ronaldinho," is a Brazilian soccer star who was FIFA World Player of the year in 2004 and 2005. The wall in the background of the photograph is chipped and peeling; a tangle of wires on the wall and ceiling lead to a cluster of electrical meters that are visible in the far right corner. Boards leaning up against the altar suggest that something is in the process of being dismantled, or perhaps packed. Like other homemade sites honoring the Virgin of Guadalupe, the one before which Manolo stands contains colorful papers, artificial flowers, and various trinkets, although in this image the Virgin of Guadalupe herself has already been removed and is thus not part of this particular makeshift altar. A garland of many colors is, nonetheless, still draped across the top.

Figure 3.14. Manolo at the empy altar to the Virgin of Guadalupe, July 17, 2010. Manolo himself was killed when he was hit by a cash transport truck in July 2014. Photo by Livia Radwanski.

The photograph represents another moment of contemplation, another in-between moment. As a discreet object capturing a moment in time, it obviously could not, at the time that it was taken, provide details about the future of Manolo or his community, but it is nonetheless before disability, in at least two senses. First, it is before disability in the spatial sense—in front of or in the presence of disability, given the varied bodies, minds, and behaviors around Manolo in Mérida90, Colonia Roma, and Mexico City. Second, it is before disability in the temporal sense—preceding the disability and illness that will, with certainty, be present in this community's, or any community's, future. The photograph captures bleakness and precarity in the face of impending dispossession and displacement but also necessarily, I would argue, Kafer- and Muñoz-like, yearning and aspiration. "The here and now is a prison house," Muñoz writes. "We must strive, in the face of the here and now's totalizing rendering of reality, to think and feel a *then and there*" (1). Muñoz's then and there is queer, although he does explicitly invite readers to imagine that "then and there," later in his book, through what he calls "crip time": "we have been cast out of straight time's rhythm," he argues, "and we have made worlds in our temporal and spatial configurations" (182).

The beautiful photograph of Manolo, perhaps more than any other included in Radwanski's larger project, captures well the moment of being cast out, displaced, or disappeared by the processes of gentrification or development. And five years after it was taken, when some of the families were able to return to the renovated building, it can certainly still be read as representing a particular kind of aspiration—to salvage again the words of C. S. Lewis, it can represent an "inconsolable longing in the heart for we know not what." Following the community's return in 2015, however, the photo now must be read as carrying, tragically, another kind of inconsolable longing. In October that year, Manolo stepped out onto a busy street in Colonia Roma and was struck and killed by an armored cash transport truck, carrying money from one side of Mexico City to another. Members of the community held a memorial service for him and continue on, in Mérida90, without him. He remains an absent presence there, with his photo before the altar of the Virgin of Guadalupe now marking a human precarity in excess of anything Radwanski intended when she took the photograph.

I build on the complex valences of *aspiration*, my final keyword in this project, in the following chapter. My first main point in the current chapter, and indeed in *Crip Times* in general, is that we need to read beyond the cultural signs of disability that are identified and made useful for neoliberalism. Cripping development or gentrification in particular, entails reading beyond the cultural signs of disability we think we know and recognizing displacement and dispossession in the shadow of incorporation. My second main point is that displacements are always crip displacements, in several senses. Even if and as "disability" is sometimes and in some locations given pride of place, unruly bodies are moved elsewhere, evicted, relocated. To return to the current code words of the British government, those "unruly bodies" are scroungers, shirkers, malingerers, and we might add here (with the aspiration for accessible housing in both the UK and Mexico in mind) squatters. Such literal displacement of unruly bodies, or bodies inconvenient to and for processes of neoliberal development, not only ensnares already disabled bodies or minds, but inescapably produces *more* disability and illness. And this production of more disability and illness is a straightforward fact about precarity; I do not put it forward here as a simplistic or ableist lament about more disability in the world, but rather as a recognition that we need more ways of talking about precarity and embodiment in global disability movements.

Finally, however, and perhaps paradoxically, crip displacements generate unpredictability and precarity *and* a generative longing. In Kevin Floyd's words (to pull again from his discussion of homelessness and HIV/AIDS), we might say that they articulate "both the impossibility of any absolute, timeless social integration, and the absolute historical importance of refusing capital's enforcement of social disintegration" (224). Douglas C. Baynton has famously said that "disability is everywhere in history, once you begin looking for it" (52). Rewriting his assertion here, and in *Crip Times* more broadly, I'm suggesting that once you know how to look for it, the aspiration generated by crip displacements is arguably everywhere in contemporary history, from the residents of Mérida90 working the expropriation law to secure their right to life and dignity in the place they have known as home, to El Museo de los Desplazados more generally, to global disability gatherings such as the Cripping Development or Cripping Neoliberalism conferences I discussed in the Introduction, to cross-border crip networking resisting austerity, to the material and geopolitical turns both queer and disability theory have been taking for more than a decade, to scroungers/shirkers/malingerers fighting back in the UK or in Mexico. We may not yet have arrived at El Edificio de Enfrente, the building just across the way, but it is imaginable, discernible, and accessible.

4

Crip Figures

Disability, Austerity, and Aspiration

On the surface, the keyword *aspiration* could appear to be at the very least neutrally descriptive of a straightforward desire or yearning. At its best, the concept is in fact quite positive, as the queer, Muñozian aspiration or striving "to think and feel a *then and there*," with which I ended the previous chapter, demonstrates. Aspiration has basically been codified, however, in the era of neoliberal capitalism, as an individualist, libertarian concept oriented around personal achievement and merit. This sense of aspiration is in many ways now compulsory; it secures consent to the dominant economic and political order, effectively dividing people from each other and short-circuiting any kind of class analysis. The term's neoliberal codification is legible in virtually all locations affected by austerity; Prime Minister Mariano Rajoy, of Spain's conservative Partido Popular, for instance, has spoken about "nuestra gran aspiración nacional" [our great national aspiration] as he justifies maintaining the harsh and deep spending cuts his government has implemented ("Paro"). These neoliberal valences of aspiration are exceptionally, and even tragicomically, pronounced in the UK.

This chapter considers some key moments in the contemporary history of aspiration, attending in particular to able-bodied rhetoric that Margaret Thatcher was employing in the 1970s in her initial efforts to chip away at the postwar consensus. Unsurprisingly, the rhetoric of Thatcherism has not been previously read as "able-bodied"; providing notes toward such a reading is one of the main projects of this chapter. The so-called "postwar consensus" had both Labour and Conservative governments in the UK defending, for a time, a relatively strong welfare state, the nationalization of prominent industries (the National Health Service, most importantly, but also postal services, transportation services, and so forth), and at the very least a mixed economy that included government intervention in and regulation of the economy, supposedly in the interests of the collective good. This postwar consensus is at times satirically called Butskellism, a word coined by the *Economist* in 1954. The coinage combined the names of the Tories' R. A. Butler, chancellor of the exchequer from 1951 to 1955, and the Labour Party's Hugh Gaitskell, chancellor of the exchequer from 1950 to 1951 and shadow chancellor during Butler's term. The *Economist* suggested that a "Mr Butskell" must have devised Butler's policies since they were so close to the policies of the official opposition (Boxer 38).

The Thatcherite ideas of aspiration that germinated from the 1970s forward *in opposition* to this collectivist consensus had become hegemonic by the end of the century. Before Jeremy Corbyn in 2015, the most prominent Labour spokesperson espousing a collectivist consciousness was Tony Benn; following Labour's defeat in general elections during the 1980s, Thatcherite ideas of aspiration were articulated not just by Tories but by prominent New Labour politicians during and after Tony Blair's rise to power in 1997. Aspiration is now part of a new consensus that journalist Peter Oborne and others dubbed "Blameronism" to indicate how much continuity in fact existed between the philosophy of Tony Blair's New Labour party and that of David Cameron's Tories (and, whether it is Oborne's intent or not, the comical word effectively demonstrates that "blame" for this devastating new consensus should be borne by the leadership of both parties) ("This Infatuation"). Those unable to be part of the Blameronist "Aspiration Society," or those deliberately positioning themselves in opposition to it, have been figured as disabled for more than four decades. My analysis here traces the beginnings of such a figuration in Thatcher's own rhetoric. A central contention of this chapter is that this figuration of disability has been one of the key discursive building blocks of neoliberalism.

I ultimately center, however, on very different figures, as I analyze a 2015 performance piece by Bristol, UK-based artist Liz Crow. Crow's performance piece is titled *Figures*; over the course of twelve days in March and April 2015, she sculpted 650 distinct objects from river mud, each approximately 13 cm tall [Figure 4.1]. These 650 sculptures were intended to represent 650 distinct stories from across the UK, many of them disabled stories. The stories recounted the specific ways in which people's lives had been harshly impacted or cut short by austerity in the

Figure 4.1. Liz Crow sculpts one of her figures. Photo by Matthew Fessey/Roaring Girl Productions.

UK. Crow is a self-described artist-activist writer-director; her official Twitter description explains that she works in "film, sound, performance, text and crip culture." She is the founder and creative director of Roaring Girl Productions, which has been working in all these mediums since 1999. Drawing again on the queer Marxist theory of Kevin Floyd, I offer here a close reading of Crow's performance that opposes it to the performance of various players in the ongoing dramas of Thatcherism and Blameronism. Put simply, this chapter lays out a tale of two aspirations and two figurations—one, neoliberal; the other, critically crip.

Crow literally generated objects through *Figures*, and I examine that process closely in what follows. Thatcher repeatedly objectified disabled people as well, in far more recognizable and two-dimensional ways. In a 1977 speech to the Greater London Young Conservatives, for example, critiquing the postwar consensus and predictably arguing that "welfare can be abused," Thatcher nonetheless insisted that "we do not neglect our responsibility to help people back onto their feet and to look after the handicapped." The subjective "we" recognizes and objectifies "the handicapped," and through that ability to recognize and objectify sustains a patronizing responsibility to "look after" them. Thatcher's grammatical construction, with "the handicapped" literally positioned as objects of a prepositional phrase, of course precludes the possibility that disabled people themselves might aspire to subjective positions; they are always and only objects of care or charity.

This easy objectification, however, is not the only appearance of disability in this particular address to the charitable young Conservatives of Greater London. Trumpeting the importance of both "choice in a free society" and "responsibility on the part of the individual" earlier in her speech, Thatcher notes that such choice should never be taken away "by the state, the party or the union" and that there is "no hard and fast line between economic and other forms of personal responsibility." When "the right and duty to choose" is taken away from an individual, Thatcher explains, "his moral faculties . . . atrophy, and he becomes a moral cripple in the same way as we should lose the faculty of walking, reading, seeing, if we were prevented from using them over the years." Thatcher turns to her metaphor to illustrate efficiently her trademark commitment to economic "freedom" and a noninterventionist state. The easily identifiable irony, however, of looking lovingly at "the handicapped" not long after she has invited her audience to gaze at the horrifying specter of a cripple who cannot walk, read, or see is apparently quite lost on her.

Extending the irony forty years later, I could identify Crow herself as a moral crip, if such a descriptor was meant to contingently and playfully mark both her location in crip culture and her passionate commitment to politically engaged, activist art. In the next section, I briefly introduce the 2015 performance piece that is at the center of this chapter. The section sketches Crow's basic plan for the piece, placing *Figures* in the context of *Crip Times* and of Crow's earlier art and activism. The chapter then proceeds as follows: the next section returns to Thatcher's early speeches and considers the emergence of dominant forms of neoliberal aspiration by following the disabled thread legible in that rhetoric, as that thread helped stitch together the decades that followed. I then invert neoliberal aspiration and consider other valences that the keyword has had, or might have, by returning in the central section of the chapter to a thorough overview of the conception, execution, and reception of Crow's 2015 performance. In the final section, I consider how

Crow's public installation and performance might be situated against certain dominant understandings of "public" art that have essentially lubricated neoliberalism and materialized a public not unlike the limited "we" Thatcher imagined four decades earlier. In particular, I sketch the differences between Crow's *Figures* and another public installation from the same time period—an installation of 888,246 ceramic poppies that was put on display in November 2014 alongside the Tower of London to honor Britain's war dead. The installation was effusively praised by David Cameron and almost every other public figure in the country. I argue that Cameron used discourses about the unifying, virtually salvific, potential of "public art" to obscure the class dynamics of his policies and the effect those policies have on vulnerable or rejected bodies.[1] The work of Crow and other public artists and activists, however, aspires to figure otherwise (and change) the actual crip web of social relations we inhabit in an age of austerity.

Remains, Waste, Rubbish: Liz Crow's *Figures*

In chapter 3, one of the first images I considered from Livia Radwanski's photographs of Mérida90 was an image of debris: an immense pile of wood, bricks, dirt, and other objects from what had been part of Edificio América in Mexico City's Colonia Roma. It is, in many ways, an austere image of and for crip times, and it gestures toward processes of *dispossession* and *displacement* that are endemic to neoliberalism (and these are the processes—and keywords—that I have considered, alongside *resistance*, in previous chapters). The image's connection to a story of resilience—the aspiration and ultimately successful fight of the residents of Mérida90 to return to their homes—marks it as crip in other ways, since the story of Mérida90 is simultaneously a story about bodies collectively accessing spaces and, even if implicitly, resisting the forces that would restrict access: in this case, both the specific and ongoing gentrification of Colonia Roma and Mexico City and the more general redistribution of wealth and resources upward and elsewhere that has characterized neoliberal capitalism everywhere. I argued that the "access" that the British government commodifies and exports, in contrast, even as it allows for limited inclusion and photo opportunities, has the potential to work not against but in tandem with gentrification and the consolidation of wealth and resources in the hands of a few.

Debris is a useful term for approaching Crow's *Figures*. The etymology of *debris* positions it, in its multiple valences, moreover, as a word appropriate to crip times. As a noun, reaching back at least to the sixteenth century, the word comes from the French *débris*, meaning "remains, waste, rubbish" (Harper). The *OED* connects *debris*, in a specific geological sense, to "any accumulation of loose material arising from the waste of rocks; also to drifted accumulation of vegetable or animal matter"; it goes on to link the term to "any similar rubbish formed by destructive operations." *Debris* seems to derive from an Old French or late Latin verb (*debriser* or *brisare*, respectively), meaning "to break down or crush." It possibly has a Gaulish history, and the word's origins may be closer to the British Isles than they at first appear, given that the Old Irish word *brissim* signifies "I break" (Harper). "I break," of course, could potentially convey an active, destructive operation on an object ("I break his arm," for example) or, conversely in a more subjective sense, some type of personal, physical disintegration (in other words, "I am breaking").

As I pointed out in the Introduction to *Crip Times*, during his first campaign Cameron described a "Broken Britain" in a speech that captures well his emphasis on individual comportment and the supposed need for behavioral change rather than (of course) any attention to the structural inequalities endemic to the British class system (and to capitalism in general). The UK disability campaign "the Broken of Britain," I suggested, resignified the language of British brokenness to highlight the ways in which disabled people were being crushed by the coalition's austerity measures (and after 2015, by the Tories governing alone). Disabled people, under austerity, have been rhetorically figured by the establishment media and politicians across the political spectrum as excess, waste, rubbish, or debris that needs to be cleaned up or moved away; through this rhetorical figuration, they have been essentially positioned and treated as "drifted accumulation." Broken of Britain's resignification of Cameron's language connoted both a subjective disintegration *and* the sense that "I break" or "we are breaking" *because of* the destructive operations carried out by powerful others. Kaliya Franklin's photographic self-portrait "Left Out in the Cold," which I examined in chapter 2, could in fact be read as conjuring up that figuration of disabled people as akin to waste or drifted accumulation in an age of austerity, as she appears in the photo to be broken down or crushed, little more than debris washed up on a cold and desolate beach, not far from where the River Dee meets the Irish Sea.

The 650 sculptures that compose Crow's *Figures* could also be read in various ways as debris, or even—in some interpretations or from some perspectives, especially given their color and consistency—as literal human waste. The objects sculpted by Crow consisted entirely of dense, dried, brown river mud. Each figure had a thick, crude base, wide enough so that it could be positioned upright without falling over. About three-quarters of the way from the bottom of the base, a slight indentation all the way around the figure suggested a neck, and two almost-but-not-quite identical cavities in the bulbous part of the figure above this "neck" suggested eyes in a head. Each figure was carefully molded by Crow, although in their rough appearance they arguably seemed to hover, hauntingly, somewhere between the "natural" and the human-made. In the same way that clouds can appear to take the shape of humans or other animals, each figure could easily be, in isolation, a hardened piece of found debris that "accidentally" conjured up an abstract living being. Despite the rough, abstract beauty and artistry of Crow's sculpture (and I will return to how that abstraction and artistry function later), it is not unimaginable that a piece of clay or stone in the pile of debris in Radwanski's photograph would just happen to have, if uncannily, the same appearance or shape as one of Crow's figures.

In its mission statement, Roaring Girl Productions puts forward a vision that could describe well most of the cultural production I have considered throughout *Crip Times*: "We combine high quality creative work with practical activism" ("About"). Crow's work has appeared at locations such as the Tate Modern in London and the Kennedy Center for the Performing Arts in Washington, D.C. Before *Figures*, Crow was perhaps best known for the performance *Bedding Out*, which was conceived in 2012 as an initial response to the coalition's first round of benefits cuts. For that project, Crow had been commissioned, along with seven other disabled artists working on autonomous projects across the UK, by Disability Arts Online's "Diverse Perspectives" project. In *Bedding Out*, Crow appeared in a "public" arena in the "private" space of her own bed over a period of forty-eight hours, drawing attention to the varied and always partial way that disability presents itself (one may appear, for instance, "less disabled" at times in "public" than in "private"). As Roaring Girl Productions describes it, the performance was intended to demonstrate that "what many see as contradiction, or fraud, is simply the complexity of real life" ("Bedding"). Members of the public were invited to participate in conversations with Crow at her bedside, and those unable to participate in person could participate in other ways, as the performance piece was broadcast live, and continuously, over social media. When the cost-cutting Personal Independence Payment (PIP) for benefits recipients began to replace the Disability Living Allowance (DLA) in April 2013 (the same month in which the infamous bedroom tax was implemented), *Bedding Out* went on tour as part of an exhibition at the Salisbury Arts Centre titled "People Like You."

Another social media project or installation that ran from 2013 until 2015 was Crow's *In Actual Fact. In Actual Fact*, or #InActualFact, mobilized mass tweets intended to counter the ongoing campaign of misinformation emanating from Cameron's government and from the establishment press. A tweet might begin, for example, with "Public believe benefit fraud at least 27%," and go on to counter that belief with information on record: "DWP's [Department for Work and Pensions'] own statistics say 0.7%. #InActualFact" ("#InActualFact"). Or: "DLA to PIP: Gov to cut 20% claimants. 500K disabled people's independence on the line #InActualFact." Like *Bedding Out*, but perhaps even more obviously given its location in a virtual space defined by and dependent upon the ongoing sharing of information, *In Actual Fact* was invitational, calling on the public both to retweet the correctives put forward by the campaign itself and to create their own. Each tweet was verified through a source and the two-year project was ultimately archived online, the intention being that it could serve as a lasting database in opposition to "government and press propaganda about the cuts and benefit claimants [that] continues to skew public opinion toward division and hatred" (Crow, *In Actual*).

Figures itself is in Crow's own description "a mass-sculptural performance that makes visible the human cost of austerity and urges action against it." With an Awards for All UK grant and a grant from the Arts Council of England, Crow and her artistic team excavated river mud

Figure 4.2. Excavation of river mud for sculpting. Photo by
Matthew Fessey/Roaring Girl Productions.

from the banks of the River Avon at Shirehampton in February 2015
[Figure 4.2]. They traveled to London in late March, and in the afternoon of March 30 a performance piece choreographed by Crow commenced. On the chilly south bank of the Thames, on the foreshore at
the Oxo Tower Wharf at low tide (roughly corresponding to dawn and
twilight), Crow began sculpting, for about three hours a session, 650 clay
figures like the ones I described [Figure 4.3]. The sculpting would last
for almost two weeks. Each of the 650 figures was intended to represent
someone across the UK living life, as Crow describes it, deploying language also used by Mary O'Hara in *Austerity Bites*, at "the sharp end" of
austerity (O'Hara 1).

At the end of each session, the 30 or 35 figures Crow had completed
went on display in an exhibition space behind the Oxo Tower. At the
same time, the stories Crow had chosen to accompany the sculptures
were released online, directly through Roaring Girl Productions and
through a "We Are Figures" website, as well as other forms of social
media such as Twitter and Instagram. I return to these stories and to

Figure 4.3. Liz Crow sculpts on the banks of the
Thames. Photo by Author.

an analysis of the various components of Crow's performance later in
the chapter. Through the imagined perspectives and histories of those
left behind by austerity, I contend, *Figures* crips austerity and manifests
traces of a materialist history of *aspiration* opposed to the Thatcherite
aspiration I overview and historicize in the next section.

"And Some Taller than Others If They Have the Ability in Them to Do So": Cripping Thatcher's Aspiration

I begin my overview with a crip analysis of a key 1975 speech by Margaret Thatcher, delivered at the St. Regis Hotel in New York City, sketching
out the differences between her vision for the (neoliberal) future and
the collectivist postwar consensus: "Let Our Children Grow Tall." To my
knowledge, this speech has never been analyzed from a disability studies
perspective; again, Thatcher's rhetoric in general has never been read in

relation to the history of able-bodiedness. Although the vast majority of disability studies scholars and activists are sharp critics of the legacy of both Thatcher and Ronald Reagan, there has been very little direct crip analysis of what they said.[2]

Long before Cameron praised the ceramic poppies on display in front of the Tower of London, Thatcher turned to poppies to illustrate her philosophies. In her St. Regis Hotel speech, the poppies were American, and specifically Midwestern. I quote at length from Thatcher's speech both to convey its substance and to focus attention on one of the metaphors that is the vehicle for that substance:

> Now, what are the lessons then that we've learned from the last thirty years? First, that the pursuit of equality itself is a mirage. What's more desirable and more practicable than the pursuit of equality is the pursuit of equality of opportunity. And opportunity means nothing unless it includes the right to be unequal and the freedom to be different. One of the reasons that we value individuals is not because they're all the same, but because they're all different. I believe you have a saying in the Middle West: "Don't cut down the tall poppies. Let them rather grow tall." I would say, let our children grow tall and some taller than others if they have the ability in them to do so. Because we must build a society in which each citizen can develop his full potential, both for his own benefit and for the community as a whole, a society in which originality, skill, energy and thrift are rewards, in which we encourage rather than restrict the variety and richness of human nature. (Qtd. in Seymour, *Against* 51)

Richard Seymour rightly identifies this moment in Thatcher's rhetoric as a key display of "the meritocratic creed in all of its glamour and tawdriness" (*Against* 51–52). Such rhetoric had been consolidating across the political spectrum on both sides of the Atlantic for years before Thatcher's speech; in the United States, the meritocratic creed was more obviously racialized from its inception. Roderick A. Ferguson, for example, has carefully excavated the ways in which the 1963 Moynihan Report in the United States demonstrated that "citizens instantiate the ideal of liberty by competing in the political, educational, and economic spheres. Liberty preserves competition but does not imply equality of outcome" (*Aberrations* 120). In Ferguson's analysis, an emphasis on "equality of opportunity" not only domesticated more radical demands for racial and economic justice that would have required systemic change and a redistribution of power and resources, but also essentially provided an alibi (or a smokescreen) for the maintenance of "racial, gender, and class hierarchies": such inequalities, in other words, in the "just" society imagined in (or written into existence by) the Moynihan Report, "would be the outcome of competition, not power and domination" (*Aberrations* 120). Moynihan's and other authoritative reports both effaced the possibility of equality of outcome and vouchsafed white dominance.

The meritocratic creed has undoubtedly sedimented in racialized ways in the UK as well as the United States since the 1970s, and that racialization has surfaced at key moments, perhaps most obviously in the 2016 Brexit vote, where white resentment on the part of those voting to exit the European Union was often directly aimed at supposedly undeserving people of color and immigrants. Although that racialization is not yet explicit in Thatcher's famous 1975 speech, insidious moves similar to the ones Ferguson identifies are nonetheless at work in it. First, implicitly rejecting the ways in which the postwar consensus might be weighted more toward the dream of equality of outcome, Thatcher explicitly foregrounds the rhetoric of "equality of opportunity" (if you believe in equality of outcome, it is as though your eyes are not working as they are "supposed" to, as though—in other words—you are seeing a mirage). Second, however, Thatcher foregrounds "equality of opportunity" through a purported valuing of *difference* (and of "the variety and richness of human nature"). This is not the difference, however, that social movements were putting forward at the time (in the United States and to a lesser extent, but certainly noticeably in 1975, in Britain). Social movements at their most radical materialized "differences" of race, class, sexuality, gender, age, and ability as the source of what Audre Lorde described as "that raw and powerful connection from which our personal power is formed" (112). Difference understood as such, Lorde contended, gesturing toward equality of outcome, could allow us "to make common cause with those others identified as outside the structures in order to define and seek a world in which we all can flourish" (112). As neoliberalism congealed, however, and as Ferguson's analysis demonstrates, a very different understanding of difference materialized. The architects of neoliberalism would, moreover, increasingly work *with* and not against "difference." Even as Thatcher's rhetoric in her St. Regis Hotel speech is a rhetoric of meritocracy, it also exhibits (as the Moynihan Report before it did) the capacity to deploy and dilute languages of difference that had been or would soon be used to more liberationist ends elsewhere. In some ways, perhaps, examining Seymour's description of the speech, we could say that the liberationist potential of some of the language is what *partially* gives this excerpt its "glamour," while the absolute and manipulative short-circuiting of that potential gives it its "tawdriness."

Third, although by 1987 Thatcher would infamously insist that "there is no such thing as society" ("Interview"), in this early speech in New York City "society" exists but it is essentially made up of individual figures striving to develop their "full potential," even if that brings them more than it brings others around them. What, substantively, that striving would in fact *bring* people who have ability (in the form of objects, things, commodities, possessions) is crucial for understanding Thatcherite, and later, Blatcherite aspiration. Property ownership, most obviously, was to become a key sign that one was, in fact, aspirational.

Beyond the rejection of equality of outcome in and through the appropriation and domestication of "difference," however, it's important to interrogate the structuring, able-bodied metaphor that specifically allows Thatcher to conjure up what Lee Edelman would likely understand as "the 'innocent' Child performing its mandatory labor of social reproduction" (19). Edelman's psychoanalytic analysis of the figure of the Child is arguably ahistorical and universalizing, as though the "innocent Child" functioned in similar, future-oriented (and antiqueer) ways in all times and places. Thatcher's 1975 speech, in contrast, allows for a historically specific consideration of the functions of that figure within neoliberal capitalism. At first we are asked to imagine Midwestern poppies, but Thatcher changes the metaphor immediately, imagining "our children" growing up. The developmental directionality of growing *up*, as Kathryn Bond Stockton has demonstrated in *The Queer Child*, is itself a compulsory metaphor across the twentieth century, as we are never asked to endorse the idea of children growing "sideways" or in any other queer (and we can certainly add crip) manner or direction (4). "Let our children grow tall," Thatcher urges, but then emphasizes that some embodied characteristics in the neoliberal future will be more desirable than others: "and some taller than others if they have the ability in them to do so."

Tallness has a complicated place in disability history; it is undeniably the case that some exceptionally tall figures, alongside numerous short-statured people, faced an invasion of their privacy and explicit exploitation, particularly in the era of the freak show. Robert Bogdan in fact opens his famous study of US freak shows with the story of Jack Earle, a University of Texas student who attended a circus sideshow and was invited by the show's manager, Clyde Ingalls, to become a "giant" who would be displayed for the amusement of others and the profit of the sideshow managers (2–3). As Lennard J. Davis has pointed out, however, desirable traits in an age of normalization are not simply those that fall in the middle of a bell curve, with the extremes of the curve consistently representing abnormality or freakishness. During the historical period Davis surveys, high intelligence most obviously (as the emergence and valuation of IQ tests evidences), but also tallness, especially for men, came to be valued more at the expense of both the other extreme of the bell curve (that is, a low IQ or short stature) and the middle (typical or ordinary intelligence or height). The eugenicist Francis Galton in fact revised the bell curve, Davis points out, "to show the superiority of the desired trait (for example, high intelligence). He created what he called an 'ogive,' which is arranged in quartiles with an ascending curve that features the desired trait as 'higher' than the undesirable deviation" (*Enforcing* 33–34). To adapt Thatcher, we might say that Galton's ogive didn't cut the bell curve, but let it grow tall, privileging all those who fell on the ascending side of the spectrum.

The history of Earle and a few other individuals notwithstanding, the valuation of height in modernity has largely borne out Davis's analysis. By 1928, at the US Democratic National Convention, Will Durant could explicitly evoke tallness as the sign (or as an able-bodied *figuration*) that Franklin Delano Roosevelt had essentially *overcome* disability; Durant described FDR as "a figure tall and proud even in his suffering" (qtd. in Davis, *Enforcing* 96). In industrial societies, at this point, tallness is routinely and unthinkingly connected to other "positive" character traits: "intelligence, employability, and leadership," for example. "Additionally," a recent sociological study noted (drawing on numerous similar findings in a wide range of cultural contexts), "height is positively associated with various socioeconomic indicators of well-being such as wealth, income, education, happiness, and success" (Undurraga et al.). In the United States, studies have made explicit the fact that tall people in general (but especially tall men), earn more: those in the bottom quartile of height average between 9 and 15 percent less in income than their taller peers (Pinsker).[3] Given these associations, it is not surprising that Thatcher begins to articulate her theories of aspiration deploying an embodied metaphor like tallness. From a crip perspective, it is noteworthy that she is not simply describing neutral physiological characteristics of these beautiful, poppy-like figures who materialize "at the shrine of the sacred Child" (Edelman 19); she is, instead, explicitly praising these tall children for a supposed "ability" that others do not have.

Metaphors praising able-bodiedness are ubiquitous in contemporary culture and, once you know how to look for them, they are easy to detect in speeches like "Let Our Children Grow Tall." We are still, however (to say the least), not used to considering how compulsory able-bodiedness or able-mindedness structure the rhetoric of political economy. If anything, paradoxically, harsh critics of Thatcherism and Reaganism have turned to *disability* to account for the global atrocity that is neoliberal capitalism. Ask your friends what was wrong with Ronald Reagan's policies, especially in his second term, and I guarantee you that in short order *someone* will point to his dementia. In relation to Thatcher, this equation was basically codified in Phyllida Lloyd's film *The Iron Lady* (2011), which garnered Meryl Streep her third Academy Award. The film consists of narrative jumps between Thatcher's final years (when she herself was experiencing dementia and in need of significant assistance with the basic functions of daily living) and her younger years, when she emerged as the driving force behind the Tory consolidation of power over the 1970s and 1980s. The film arguably can be read as at times criticizing or at least questioning Thatcherism, even if it is in other ways a straightforward biopic or even hagiography. In terms of criticism, there are, for example, visual representations of out-of-work miners pounding angrily on the windows of the younger Thatcher's limousine. Streep's tepid critique following Thatcher's death, in a press release that largely focused in "awe" on the "different dream" Thatcher's leadership gave "women and girls around the world," in fact suggests that she herself sustained at least some awareness of the legacies of Thatcherism during her performance in *The Iron Lady*: Thatcher's "fiscal measures took a toll on the poor, and her hands-off approach to financial regulation led to great wealth for others" (qtd. in Child). Of course, a feminist call for female leadership is not wrong, but Streep's liberal feminism obscures here the gendered opposition between "the poor" (disproportionately female) and those with "great wealth" (overwhelmingly disproportionately male). The critique of an emergent Thatcherism in the film, moreover, is visually connected (through the narrative jumps and thus through a certain narrative logic) to Thatcher's (later) dementia, as though there was some sort of natural link between disability and bad policy that only becomes visible when we know the fuller (disabled) story. My analysis of "Let Our Children Grow Tall" is intended not only to question the ways in which disability routinely functions in our cultural narratives to explain something bad but also to introduce a new and opposite equation more attentive to the ways in which able-bodied supremacy and disabled oppression have actually operated discursively. Put differently, compulsory able-bodiedness, not disability, was one of the forces that allowed for the emergence of Thatcherism and that sustains austerity, and ability and ableism are structural components of its rhetoric.

In her speech to the Conservative Party Conference in Brighton in 1976, Thatcher spoke of the need to move beyond "what is known as 'the British sickness.'" This "sickness" was marked, apparently, by three main symptoms: a Labour government had "spent and spent again with unbridled extravagance"; it had codified an "increasing interference and direction in industry [that had] stopped it doing its job properly"; and, finally, it was exhibiting what Thatcher called "chronic schizophrenia." It is telling in many ways that Thatcher turns to the metaphor of schizophrenia to present her alternative, able-minded, vision for the future, not least because the commonsense notion of how to treat actual schizophrenia that was solidifying in the decade of the 1970s emphasized detainment and incarceration. Thatcher, in other words, does not turn to just any disability to disqualify Labour in this particular speech but rather to a disability increasingly perceived as dangerous and in need of extreme measures of control.[4] Invoking "chronic schizophrenia" was a pivotal rhetorical move in the 1976 speech that enabled Thatcher both to set a stage of undeniable crisis and to posit a congealing Thatcherism as the rational, sane alternative ("let us be clear in our thinking," she demands). Labour was "no longer able to act in the national interest," and remained "confused and divided" (Thatcher's understanding of schizophrenia) specifically over free enterprise. Free enterprise, in and for the Tories, in contrast, is figured as endangered but nonetheless robust and able-bodied ("in spite of everything, it has survived," uncontaminated by the British sickness). In contrast to the "frankly and unashamedly Marxist" program supposedly favored by the Labour Party, Thatcher then proceeded to list the key components of her political philosophy (exhibiting thereby the basic tenets of neoliberalism): cuts to government expenditure, the elimination of legislation that would in any way regulate industry, privatization as opposed to nationalization, and "positive, vital, driving, individual incentive."

Thatcher closes her manifesto of health, vigor, and clear-mindedness by linking it to the "aspirations" of working people: "what a distortion, what a travesty of the truth it is for the Socialists to call themselves the party of working people. Today we are all working people. Today it is the Conservatives and not the Socialists who represent the true interests and hopes and aspirations of the working people." Thatcher's "all," of course, can in no way comprehend anyone with chronic schizophrenia, or who has confused thinking, or who is sick or not feeling energetic or vital. Shortly after her election, indeed, she explicitly affirmed that Britain would no longer be "sick—morally, socially, and economically" ("Renewal"). With sick and disabled *figures* in the shadows, over the course of her subsequent election and decade as prime minister, in numerous other speeches and locations, aspiration as a keyword would be tied ever more firmly to everyone else, the (able-bodied) "all" working to uphold the neoliberal truisms Thatcher had laid out in Brighton.

After the Thatcher years, Labour too (in an effort to once again become relevant) began espousing a kind of individualistic aspiration very similar to that forged by their Tory predecessors, and likewise grounded in compulsory able-bodiedness and able-mindedness. Stressing increased consumption and property ownership (especially, again, the importance of home ownership already put forward by Thatcher) as the signs of a healthy middle class, Stewart Lansley writes, "a re-invented Labour Party wooed back . . . lost voters—a mix of aspirational white collar and skilled manual workers—to bring Tony Blair a landslide victory" (2). Indeed, Lansley points out, after Blair's victory it was the

Labour Party and not the Tories that explicitly put into circulation the idea of an "Aspiration Society"; the phrase was coined by Blair's Labour culture secretary James Purnell and identified, during Gordon Brown's campaign for prime minister, as "one of the party's central new goals" (Lansley 20). Although directly opposing, on the surface, Margaret Thatcher and (even more specifically) David Cameron as a "throwback to an earlier Tory tradition," Purnell and Labour's Jim Murphy, writing about the party's Aspiration Society in 2007, nonetheless make ample use of Thatcherisms. Even as they do advocate for a state that is more active than it had been for the previous two decades, this advocacy is in the interests of "individuals" and indeed, "difference": "But the old social democratic approach, which saw the State providing broadly the same service to everyone, will not be enough. . . . People today have different aspirations from each other. . . . [As] Tony Blair and Gordon Brown have made clear, we should aim for an enabling State, which gives power to individuals and communities, and trusts them to know how to use it." Writing thirty years after Thatcher herself posed the question, "what are the lessons . . . that we've learned from the last thirty years?" Purnell and Murphy unconsciously made clear that *her* lessons from the St. Regis Hotel had deeply sedimented across the political spectrum: equality of outcome should never be expected and only equality of opportunity facilitating, or rather *enabling*, individualist aspirations should be nurtured.

In the year before Ed Miliband's campaign challenging David Cameron, Blair himself cautioned the would-be prime minister, implying that Labour should maintain and even extend Tory policies on privatization: "The financial crisis . . . doesn't mean that people have fallen back in love with the State, it doesn't mean that the individualizing force of technology has retreated and it doesn't mean that the whole private sector is somehow contaminated" (qtd. in Holehouse). Contamination, sickness, and disability, it would seem, in what Kateřina Kolářová would call "the normatively progressive futurity of straight *and* abled time (or rehabilitation, shock therapies, and cure)" (259), are only available as metaphors to describe those who would critique or regulate private industry, private ownership, and individual aspiration. In such a political landscape, unsurprisingly, disability is never available as a more generative metaphor.

Following Miliband's loss and resignation as party leader in May 2015, numerous spokespeople affirmed the Blameronist continuities between New Labour and the Conservatives (with, ironically, Miliband increasingly "blamed" for the harsh loss and positioned as Old Labour). Culture minister for Labour Ben Bradshaw insisted that the next Labour leader should again "celebrate our entrepreneurs and wealth creators and not leave the impression they are part of the problem" (qtd. in Feeney). A former Labour home secretary, Alan Johnson, similarly argued that Labour had been unable to beat Cameron in 2015 because of Miliband's and others' reluctance to embrace the philosophies of "the aspirational Blair years": "The issue of aspiration in people's lives; we can no longer relate to them as the party of aspiration. And that was one of the big successes that won us three [previous] elections" (qtd. in Feeney). During the summer of 2015, after Miliband failed to defeat Cameron, the word *aspiration* was endlessly invoked and often ridiculed; its ubiquity is a quotidian testament to the neoliberal common sense that Thatcher hoped to implant forty years earlier as she imagined poppies growing tall.

In January 2016, Corbyn's shadow chancellor John McDonnell, along with another antiausterity spokesperson, Greece's former finance minister Yanis Varoufakis, announced a series of open seminars on economics—seminars that would, presumably, publicize alternatives to the economic consensus put forward by the Tories and other governing bodies in Europe and elsewhere standing by austerity politics. Cameron's chancellor George Osborne suggested that the plan for the seminars made clear that McDonnell and Varoufakis had "lost their marbles." Luciana Berger, in a newly created position as Corbyn's shadow mental health minister, immediately suggested in an open letter that Osborne's comments contributed to "stigma, prejudice and discrimination" against people with mental health issues or mental disabilities (Perraudin). I would certainly not dispute Berger's minoritized critique, which implies that the language we use has effects on specific and identifiable groups (indeed, such a minoritized critique is one condition of possibility for my own work here). In this section of my chapter, however, I have attempted to put forward a more universalized argument attending to the ways in which figurations of disability and contours of ableism have been structural components of neoliberalism and austerity politics from their inception. I would even suggest that my rhetorical analysis here implies that, in some ways, austerity and neoliberalism can *make no sense* without disability.[5]

As Owen Jones made clear even before the 2015 election, and as should be obvious from this overview, rhetorics of aspiration in neoliberal Britain were "part and parcel of [Margaret] Thatcher's determination to make us think of ourselves as individuals who looked after ourselves above all else. . . . Aspiration was no longer about people working together to improve their communities; it was being redefined as getting more for yourself as an individual, regardless of the social costs" (*Chavs* 61). In the UK in the 1980s and beyond, as neoliberalism took hold as a national and increasingly global common sense, Jones argues that Thatcherite aspiration generated "left-behinds" who "faced the consequences of official disapproval" (consequences that have included, over three decades, literal, ongoing, and now accelerated dispossession and displacement). It is to that group, specifically as it materialized in Crow's work, that I turn in the next section.

Bearing Witness to "Left-Behinds": Crow's Artistic Aspiration

Given Thatcher's Bristol speech on the "chronic schizophrenia" of her opponents, it's poetic that Liz Crow's *Figures* is both conceived in the diverse British city of Bristol and materially tied to that location, in the sense that the actual physical material for the project came from the region.[6] Again, clay for Crow's 650 figures was excavated on the banks of the River Avon near her home and transported in late March 2015 to the banks of the River Thames in London. The figures that emerge from Crow's performance have some affinities with the terracotta figures sculpted by the British artist Antony Gormley in his installation *Field*. Since 1991, *Field* has appeared in a number of instantiations; Gormley has sculpted thousands of figures for *Field* and his work has been displayed in multiple locations around the world. Crow herself suggests that both she and Gormley are strongly influenced by ancient sculptural forms; her contemporary performance is also indebted to a range of ancient creation myths from around the world, in which the human is created from (and thus part of) the earth.[7]

The very name of the Avon near Bristol (it is one of several rivers and tributaries in England, Scotland, and Wales with that name) conjures up ancient displacements and a colonial history: it is an anglicization of *afon*, the Welsh word for river (*afon* is still widely used in Wales).[8] Contemporary displacement is likewise an integral part of Crow's mass-sculptural performance piece; by bringing the clay for her figures to the Thames, Crow traces the contemporary migration of many people (perhaps especially during the years when Thatcherism decimated industry in other parts of the country) to London, to the metropole, in search of better lives. In both ancient and contemporary senses, Crow's 650 figures are thus in some ways always out of place.

Perhaps more promisingly or generatively, however, and in the translocal spirit of my subtitle to this book (*Disability, Globalization, and Resistance*), Crow's figures are also always *multiply* placed. The clay that the artist used in her performance doesn't, or can't, stay put; it is what Jane Bennett might term "vibrant matter." Clay is composed of alluvium, a material that a river has been moving along over great distances. The matter with which Crow worked, in other words, inescapably conveys (in the sense that it transports *and* communicates) motion. We might say that the matter for *Figures* won't settle, and it was thus an appropriate vehicle for the project: the medium of clay itself, in one sense, marks Crow's refusal as an artist to settle for the austerity and suffering of our moment. The journey Crow then embarked on with her clay from Bristol, and later beyond both London and Bristol, suggests furthermore that she won't or can't settle; she won't allow London and the Thames to become metonyms for the whole of the UK or placeholders that would leave the rest of the UK behind. Crow refused, perhaps especially, to allow "the City," the site of financial power in the capital and the country, to become such a metonym. The Oxo Tower Wharf on the south bank of the Thames, where Crow sculpted, is positioned in a clear line of sight toward the skyscrapers of "the City," on the opposite side of the river looking toward the north [Figure 4.4]. The performance of *Figures* thus commenced directly in the face of, and opposed to, the financial power of contemporary neoliberal capitalism.

The number Crow chose for her mass-sculptural performance piece—650—is of course not arbitrary; there are 650 constituencies in the UK, and thus 650 members of the House of Commons in Parliament. When I initially talked with Crow about the project in July 2014, she was hoping for a number that ultimately proved illusory: she intended to sculpt

Figure 4.4. City shot across the Thames. Photo by Matthew Fessey/Roaring Girl Productions.

figures representing the number of people who had died in the UK as a result of austerity. Our conversation, however, rapidly moved across the many challenges involved in pinpointing that number: how do you quantify those deaths? During the 2012 Olympic and Paralympic Games, some activists had worked with the number 10,000, suggesting that 10,000 people had died as a result of being deemed "fit to work" by Atos. But which deaths should be counted in that or any other number? Deaths by suicide, certainly, and the government's own research a year later in fact linked 590 suicides to work capability assessment (Pring, "'Damning' research"). Yet work capability assessment is only one component of the government's austerity agenda, and of course the reason for a suicide is not always clear. Numerous other suicides are undoubtedly connected to austerity in the UK, as are deaths as a result of stress-related illnesses, addiction, homelessness, an increased infant mortality rate, or deaths that were hastened because of a delay in accessing care or because a terminally ill patient was forced to seek employment. The figure that Crow aspired to in 2014 proved to be impossible to quantify, and she decided over time to sculpt the 650 figures that came to exist over the course of her performance. Incorporating stories of the living alongside stories of the dead, moreover, allowed Crow to avoid a certain distancing that might have resulted if only the dead were memorialized. Representative narratives of both the living and the dead would accompany each sculpture, Crow decided: a story would be attached to each figure—the story of someone from across the UK whose life (or death) was directly tied to the experience of austerity in the UK from 2010 to the present.

Crow is a wheelchair user, and the foreshore of the Thames at the Oxo Tower Wharf does not have a ramp. Thus, for each of the twenty sessions of sculpting, members of the artistic team (wearing bright yellow "We Are Figures" jackets) used equipment to transfer Crow from her chair to the ladder going down to the bank. She was then carried to the spot where she sculpted for the session, and when she was done, the whole process was repeated in reverse [Figure 4.5]. This of course generated a great deal of attention and curiosity among passersby, so other members of the artistic team (including myself, for a few days in April 2015) were charged with talking to the public during this time, giving them flyers and explaining what was going on. From the beginning, when Crow

Figure 4.5. Liz Crow transported to the sculpting site. Photo by Claudio Ahlers/ Roaring Girl Productions.

was seeking funding for *Figures* from the Arts Council of England and other venues, interaction with the public was intended to be part of her performance; the interaction with the public was to consist of conversations held by volunteers on the walkway above the foreshore both during the moments when Crow was carried back and forth and during the time that she sculpted. It was also to consist of conversations held by volunteers with visitors to the exhibition space as the figures began to accumulate. The exhibition space was wired with monitors displaying a constant streaming video of the Twitter and Instagram feeds, which provided some fodder for exhibition space conversations, even as the accumulating sculptures themselves generated the most immediate discussions.

The conversations with the public during the sessions were incredibly varied. The standard opening for my own explanation as passersby observed Crow being transported to the spot where she would work for each session or as the clay figures began to accrue around her, for instance, was something along the lines of "It's okay; she's an artist. It's a performance piece. She's sculpting 650 figures out of river mud to represent lives impacted by austerity. Each figure represents someone's story from across the country, and the stories go online as she completes each piece. You can see the figures in an exhibition space behind the tower." Some of the interactions were quickly dismissive ("she's wasting her time"); some were deeply engaged with local and national politics (reflecting on the politics of a given UK constituency, the history of Left activism in Britain, or on the ways that US-influenced ideas were endangering the NHS); some were even flirtatious (one sunny afternoon, I was working with China Blue Fish, another member of the team, who discretely wandered off to another section of the walkway when a smiling young man, for no apparent reason, returned two or three times to rebegin a conversation with me).

Every conversation was different depending upon the identity or social location of the people who stopped; for instance, a lot of Spanish-speaking people now live in London because of austerity in Spain (where, as I noted earlier in *Crip Times*, the unemployment rate is still close to 45 percent for young people).[9] With those conversations, I would switch to Spanish and attempt to shift the conversation to Spain: "Ella es artista, y cada estatua pequeña, cada figurita, representa una persona que ha sufrido por la austeridad, como en España." To which the majority of Spanish interlocutors would respond, "Ay, sí, entiendo." David Cameron and Mariano Rajoy would together claim, later in 2015, that "countries that clean up their public finances, put welfare on a sustainable footing, deliver ambitious structural reforms, and make work pay, create more jobs and restore hope for a better future." Spanish immigrants to London who engaged with *Figures* during the sculpting phase, however, largely appeared to see through such buzz words and to recognize that Crow was attempting to bear witness to those left behind by processes of austerity in the UK very similar to the devastating "reformas estructurales" that Rajoy had implemented in Spain for more than three years. Indeed, as early as 2013, even Rajoy's rivals in the Partido Socialista Obrero Español (PSOE) [Spanish Socialist Workers' Party], despite having initiated the harsh austerity that Rajoy's administration continued, were insisting that "la medicina que le está dando al enfermo le está matando" [the medicine that you are giving the patient is killing him] ("Empecemos a temblar").

Sometimes passersby would descend the ladder to the foreshore themselves (after receiving an initial explanation of what was going on), where they would take photographs or engage in conversations directly with Crow. Scottish comedian Frankie Boyle and the performing artist Mark McGowan (better known for political antiausterity videos he has composed as the "Artist Taxi Driver") were among some of the more well-known visitors who descended the ladder to talk directly with Crow. McGowan composed a short video interviewing Crow that circulated widely through YouTube, Twitter, and other social media. As Crow sculpted, additionally, McGowan tweeted a photograph of Boyle and Crow together on the foreshore to his 55,000 followers; Boyle promptly retweeted it to his 2 million followers. Comedienne and television personality Liz Carr, another wheelchair user and one of the stars of the BBC crime thriller *Silent Witness*, visited and talked with the artistic team on the sidewalk, along with her wife Jo Church, as Crow worked down below. The shelves of the exhibition space behind the Oxo Tower continued to fill with figures over the course of the performance until all 650 were completed [Figure 4.6].

Crow's figures toured the southern UK in a five-day mobile exhibition back to Bristol in the first part of May, immediately before the May 7,

Figure 4.6. *Figures* exhibition space. Photo by Claudio Ahlers/Roaring Girl Productions.

2015 general election, in which (as I explained in the Introduction) the Tories won enough seats in Parliament to govern outright, without the Liberal Democrats who had been their partners in the coalition that had implemented austerity since 2010. Crow noted consistently throughout her performance, however, that she was bringing attention to lives impacted by austerity and urging action against a now-global austerity politics and that this performance was not simply focused on the specific British election. Indeed, Miliband's Labour Party in 2015, despite being charged with socialism and other supposed pejoratives suggesting it was too far Left, had in fact made clear that austerity would not go away if they were to take power, even if austerity under a Labour government would take supposedly "gentler" forms. Crow's performance and tour, therefore, were not simply conceived as putting forward a pre-election critique of the Tories; *Figures* much more comprehensively put forward an analysis of the ways in which a logic of austerity was operative and had material consequences across the UK political spectrum. During the sculpting phase of the performance, passersby generally understood that the Tories and the coalition were sharply targeted by *Figures*, but the flyers and other material did not directly name them. Sometimes the conversations with British citizens turned to topics such as voting for the Greens or another antiausterity party, given that the British first-past-the-post system means (as in US elections) that the winner in a given constituency is the candidate with the most votes (so that many supporters of the Greens worried that their votes would essentially help put a Tory into office, or back into office, in certain constituencies). The failure of Labour to put forward a credible antiausterity platform in Scotland had led to unprecedented levels of support for the antiausterity Scottish National Party (SNP); the prospect of an SNP landslide and the question of what message that would send to Labour nationwide were also topics of debate for some visitors. Crow hoped for these and many other kinds of complex conversations, but did not intend to script them; the performance was conceived from the beginning as in many ways open-ended—what exactly was "accomplished" by *Figures* would be determined by the multiple and unexpected ways that people interacted with it as it unfolded.

Crow's mobile tour was at times deemed too "political" in the days before the election and some of the sites where the team had planned to exhibit as they made their way back to Bristol were thus prohibited. With the general election looming, authorities in at least one London borough and towns where the team planned on parking the truck either refused to issue a booking or revoked it; in at least one instance, the argument was that the tour truck was not "attractive enough" for the town center in question. Exclusion from proper channels generated a necessary and critical impropriety: in response to these challenges, Crow and the team exhibited the figures in what they deemed "guerrilla" sites. These guerrilla sites included Trafalgar Square before leaving London and (later) Cameron's own UK constituency, in the town of Witney (where members of the team left flyers about *Figures* directly at the prime minister's local office).

The team ended up in Trafalgar Square after attaching itself to the end of the May Day workers' parade; they then parked and put *Figures* on display. Trafalgar Square is a particularly edgy and compelling location for a "guerrilla" appearance, given that it is a complicated and multivalent site for "disability" art. Admiral Horatio Nelson, who died in the Battle of Trafalgar in 1805, stands high atop Nelson's Column in the center. He leans upon a sword that some visitors might think is a cane, since it is difficult to make out from the ground. Nelson's actual disabilities, acquired in battle, included an amputed arm (visible in the statue) and blindness in one eye (neither visible nor easily representable in a sculpture). From 2005 until 2007, on the "fourth plinth" of Trafalgar Square (a site where various experimental or contemporary artists are chosen to display their art temporarily), a statue by Marc Quinn called *Alison Lapper Pregnant* appeared. Lapper is a disabled British artist who was born without arms; the beautiful statue of her, pregnant, is notable for its feminist affirmation of a disabled woman's sexuality and was celebrated for its affirmation of disability identity. It quickly became canonical in disability culture and disability studies; an image of the statue in Trafalgar Square appears against a bright, uncharacteristically blue London sky on the cover of the third edition of *The Disability Studies Reader* (Davis). A giant replica of the statue was part of the opening ceremony of the London 2012 Paralympics Games, suggesting that by Summer 2012 it would have been immediately recognizable to many or most members of the audience.

In 2009, Crow herself spent one hour on the fourth plinth, wearing full Nazi regalia in her wheelchair. The performance was connected to her short film *Resistance* (2008), which combined drama and documentary to overview the history of Aktion-T4, a program implemented in 1939 by the Nazis. Thousands of disabled people were murdered as a result of Aktion-T4 and these killings arguably set the stage for the mass extermination of Jewish people, gay people, and others that followed. In 2009, Gormley was commissioned for a hundred-day performance that would place ordinary members of the public on the fourth plinth twenty-four hours a day. The performance was called *One & Other*, and Crow was selected to participate for one hour. The jarring dissonance of the wheelchair and the Nazi regalia was intended to draw attention to *Resistance* and to the seventy-year anniversary of Aktion-T4.

I dwell here momentarily on the varied ways in which "disability" has been central to the space of Trafalgar Square partly to mark the guerrilla appearance of *Figures* there in May 2015 as somewhat different, unlike both the impairments (undoubtedly rarely recognized as such) of the war hero whose battle gives the space its name or the affirmative and substantive celebration of disability identity that was the Quinn statue. Although Lapper too can be understood, like Crow in *Resistance*, as an ordinary member of the public, Quinn's statue is inescapably more substantializing than Crow's ephemeral performance. By noting a certain canonical status for *Alison Lapper Pregnant,* or a certain almost inevitable neoliberal incorporation, my intent is neither to dismiss Quinn's piece nor to discount the importance of a positive affirmation of disabled women's desire. I liked the statue very much in fact, and along with many friends and colleagues, took a great deal of pleasure seeing it on the fourth plinth for more than two years. I do, however, want to suggest that the guerilla appearance of *Figures* in Trafalgar Square, like *Resistance* before it, was a decidedly differently disabled/crip intervention. In *Figures,* "disability" as such, is continually and simultaneously appearing and disappearing, materializing and dematerializing. It could thus in many ways be read as more elusive, challenging, or troubling than a more clearly monumental work. Not unlike Radwanski's photographs, *Figures* offers a Barthesian text of bliss and not of pleasure; according to the logic of the space of Trafalgar Square it is in some ways "untenable" or "impossible" (Barthes 22). Neoliberalism is of course capable of incorporating or domesticating virtually anything; as my analysis of Thatcher's rhetoric already implies, that is one of the key ways in which it has sustained itself for the past four decades. However, it is unlikely that a giant replica of one of Crow's figures or a giant re-creation of Crow in Nazi regalia will be part of a sports spectacle anytime soon.

During the sculpting phase of *Figures,* in the exhibition space members of the public left notes, with drawings, reflections, and messages. One visitor drew a picture of a particular figure and wrote the message:

> Each figure has a different personality. This one caught my eye looking
> elderly and bent, weighed down by life. The elderly are just one of the
> groups who rely on support from the state and public services, particu-
> larly the NHS, who are being affected by austerity. I cared for my granny
> for a year and a half with the support of carer's allowance. Without this
> financial support, what will happen to those who are unable to care for
> themselves?

Clearly, as this and similar messages make clear, the abstraction of Crow's figures allowed them to open up reflections on a wide variety of stories far beyond the 650 stories disseminated as the pieces were completed. Even as new stories of those left behind by austerity were released online as Crow's work continued, there was no direct or necessary connection between an individual story and an individual figure. If disability activism and studies have critiqued the ways in which disabled lives have been objectified as case studies, *Figures* arguably works in another direction, generating a collectivist sense of "we're all in this together" and encouraging the proliferation of personal stories that bore witness to that collective experience. Case studies purport to provide clear, delineated answers ("we know what that means"). *Figures*, in contrast, in Crow's own description, raises only "profound questions" about the world austerity has wrought and about how we might collectively shape alternatives.

Just as they were invited to engage during the sculpting phase of the performance, members of the public were invited to engage during the tour. A woman named Brigitte in Cameron's constituency of Witney cried upon seeing the exhibit, because she had known Mark Wood, one of those whose story is among the 650 narratives. Wood died of starvation in his home. "He was a very kind person," Brigitte told the artistic team. "He's become another figure" (Crow et al., "Meeting") [Figure 4.7]. Other visitors to the touring exhibit left written notes, with messages such as "The role of an artist is to express the tears and the joys of those who are not able to share. Thank you for expressing the pain" (Crow et al., "Comments").

After the tour, *Figures* returned to the riverbank in Bristol, where the 650 sculptures were burned in a bonfire on May 6, the night before the general election. As the fire burned for six hours, all 650 narratives were read aloud; the reading and bonfire were live-streamed and later archived on the We Are Figures site. Eventually, the rising tide of the Avon doused the flames. Crow's team reclaimed the figures after this part of the performance, and they were ground back to dust by a milling machine. On May 27, 2015, the performance concluded. As the Tories took power in the new government in Westminster, the Queen's Speech (read, as tradition would have it, by the monarch but drafted by the prime minister) emphasized the predictable themes that I analyzed in the previous section: "My government," Cameron's text reads, "will legislate in the interests of everyone in our country. It will adopt a one nation approach, helping working people get on, supporting aspiration,

Figure 4.7. Emotional impact of *Figures*. Photo by
Lizzy Maries/Roaring Girl Productions.

giving new opportunities to the most disadvantaged and bringing different parts of our country together." With obfuscating language that
has operated similarly virtually anywhere austerity has taken hold, the
speech insisted that the Tories would "continue to reform welfare, with
legislation encouraging employment by capping benefits and requiring
young people to earn or learn." The full extent of Cameron's updated
plan for capping benefits would be unveiled over the course of Summer
2015; his invocation of young people here was specifically in reference
to his proposed Jobs Bill, excluding anyone under the age of twenty-one
from claiming a range of welfare benefits.

Home ownership clothed in the rhetoric of choice was again put forward as a key component of the speech, as though consumer "choice"
had not been a centerpiece of British neoliberalism for the previous
thirty years: "Legislation will be introduced to support home ownership and give housing association tenants the chance to own their own

homes." More than 150 of the narratives in *Figures* detail stories of so-cial housing tenants or others in extremely precarious housing situa-tions, sometimes losing their homes or actually enduring homelessness; a few narratives detail the stories of those who died in their homes without adequate care, food, or heat. In theory, figures such as these are not (or were not, if we are speaking of those who have died in such circumstances) excluded from the group Cameron describes as hav-ing the "chance" to own their own homes. He does not append to his description of chance in the Queen's Speech the now-famous quotation from Suzanne Collins's *The Hunger Games*, "May the odds be *ever* in your favor" (17); Cameron's talk of "support" for "housing association tenants," nonetheless, can easily if eerily be interpreted as a case of life imitating art. Some in austerity Britain have faced or will face the im-possible "choice" between losing their housing benefits or having the opportunity to purchase their flats for prices decidedly beyond their reach; this is a Cameronian "chance," but it is also a choice that is no choice.[10]

Moreover, even as Cameron opens the Queen's Speech with the supposed recognition of "the most disadvantaged," he had already ap-pointed Justin Tomlinson, earlier in May 2015 following the election, as his new disability minister. While in Parliament, Tomlinson had "voted against protecting benefits for disabled children and cancer patients"; in July 2015 he assisted Iain Duncan Smith, the secretary of state for work and pensions, in cutting an additional £12 billion from the benefits sys-tem (J. Stone). Put differently, then, Cameron in a way opens the Queen's Speech by "recognizing" those whom his administration had already, in official venues and multiple ways, explicitly *not* recognized (with the former move completely contingent on the latter). A little more than a month after the Queen's Speech, moreover, the administration would again officially *not* recognize "the most disadvantaged," as they would be trimmed even further (by Smith's budget). Many instructions for the "healthy growth and flowering" of poppies do, literally, instruct garden-ers to "cut out excess poppy plants once they've started to grow. . . . [C]ut the smaller or weaker plants at the base using garden shears" ("How to"). It is obviously not a logic that should be applied to smaller or weaker human beings. It is, nonetheless, arguably the logic that animated Cam-eron's one nation approach.

As all this was taking place in the Houses of Parliament, on the other side of England *Figures* shifted to a location off the coast at Portishead in North Somerset, about five miles from Crow's home city of Bristol. The ashes from the 650 sculptures were carried by boat out to sea. Once the team reached the open sea, Crow scattered the remains into the waters. There was no soundtrack for the scattering, but it is poetic that the town of Portishead became internationally famous when a local band took the town's name. "Cowboy," the opening track of Portishead's second album, while arguably directly criticizing the United States, poses questions in the first year of New Labour's hold on power in the UK (1997) that are in many ways prescient for the Blameronist years that lay ahead: "Did you feed us tales of deceit/Conceal the tongues who need to speak/ Subtle lies and a soiled coin/The truth is sold, the deal is done" (qtd. in Cinquemani). Thinking about memorialization in relation to *Resistance*, Crow has written about "beautiful faces with boundless untold stories; what were their names, their histories?" ("Resistance"); off the coast of Portishead in May 2015, Crow bears witness to those stories and to the powerful mechanisms that conceal those stories or mask them behind tales of deceit.

The timing of this final element of the performance of *Figures* of course obviously kept attention on the UK, with Crow's poignant performance in the west positioned in stark and direct opposition to, in the east, Cameron's self-congratulatory ascension to full power and lip service suggesting that no one would be left behind in the one nation he planned to materialize. Yet the location of the scattering in the actual sea (not in the River Avon nor in the Thames in front of the Houses of Parliament, which had been the initial plan) was part of Crow's increasing recognition of the many ways that the UK-based stories of austerity she was highlighting through her monthslong performance speak to a politics of austerity that is now global. Crow's figures represent the 650 constituencies in the UK, in other words, but are part of a web of social relations that ties them to innumerable figures elsewhere (figures I have considered throughout *Crip Times*), in Spain, Greece, the United States, Mexico, Chile, and throughout the Global South. Crow insists that the 2015 election results highlight a belief legible in Britain that "some people are more significant than others" (qtd. in "Artist"); the scattering of the ashes from *Figures* in the open sea performatively works to counter that classed belief by looking and pointing outward, to innumerable un-told stories in an age of austerity.

Cameron's language of "reform," "capping benefits," and "earn and learn" in the Queen's Speech would of course have been recognizable to many at the sharp end of austerity as both describing the cuts that the coalition had put in place and as gesturing toward more cuts to come (even if the word *cut* itself, unsurprisingly, never appeared in the speech). In contrast, the 650 stories that accompanied *Figures* and that went online during Crow's performance (and that remain online as part of the digital archive for the project) were brief and poignant, and free from obfuscating language. The stories detailed the effects of austerity and the cuts from 2010 onward to disability benefits, health care, educa-tion, unemployment benefits, and assistance with food or shelter.

A few examples to close this section can help to illustrate the sto-ries' variety. The 626th narrative reads: "Kevin is waiting to go into detox treatment and for surgery for a painful foot condition linked to his time as a homeless person. He is in the Employment and Support Allowance work-related activity group. He failed to attend a mandatory interview because he was caring for his two-year old son and was sanctioned. With a remaining food budget of £3.50, he ended up begging and stealing food." The benefits "sanctions" to which this narrative refers increased astronomically under the coalition's austerity plan. Beyond the cuts that the most disadvantaged in the country were already experiencing, sanc-tions meant that your benefits would not be paid if you missed an ap-pointment, or were late for an appointment, or broke any of a virtually infinite number of rules.

The 632nd narrative reads: "Mark was ruled fit for work against the advice of his GP [general practitioner] and despite having complex mental health conditions. He was left with an income of £40 per week. He weighed five-and-a-half stone when he died of starvation." As I ex-plained in chapter 1, two private companies—the French company Atos and now the US company Maximus—have been contracted to assess whether recipients of disability benefits are or are not "fit to work," through very brief, formulaic, and often degrading interviews. Like so many others, Mark—once declared fit to work—was no longer eligible for the benefits he was receiving. Even though a large number of those deemed fit to work by Atos or Maximus since 2010 have won their cases on appeal, the process can take many months. Mark's story in fact sits alongside more than twenty other narratives in *Figures* that detail the stories of individuals who have died or who took their own lives during the appeals process.

The beauty of Crow's 650 figures to me, lies in their haunting abstraction and the ways in which they both represent *and can never fully represent* the lives of those whose stories are included in the performance. Crow chose the stories working with a number of public sources, including "leading-edge research, Parliamentary records and campaigns in the field of social justice" (*Figures*). Some of the narratives are accompanied by personal names; others are not. For example, the 634th narrative reads: "A woman with depression, anxiety, anorexia and suicidal thoughts, who needs occasional medical treatment during the night, has been hit by bedroom tax. She appealed because she needs the second room for overnight carers, but has been turned down and is now in rent arrears." The source for each narrative accompanies the online text: this narrative is from a local paper in the Wokingham Borough Council (Spencer); Kevin's story comes from the work of a freelance journalist focused on social justice and writing about austerity and food banks (McGauran); Mark's life and death were reported in the *Guardian* (Gentleman). From publicly available sources, in other words, Crow has compiled a record of those left behind by austerity.

By representing these lives *abstractly*, however, Crow attests to the ways in which an individual story of hardship had already been made public while simultaneously allowing the material object or figure that emerges from her sculpting to point in any number of other directions; recall, in this context, that one visitor saw in a particular figure something that conjured up the experience of many elderly people in Britain. *We* are figures, Crow's project insists, in the end. Rather than simply objectifying individuals in a relatively univocal way as a realistic statue or portrait might, *Figures* welcomes a new subjectivity that imagines connections (and modes of caring) across difference. Or, put differently, and more rigorously from a Marxist perspective, *Figures* implicitly recognizes that objectification has multiple and historical meanings. This recognition is simultaneous with its welcoming of new subjectivities. Floyd, in *The Reification of Desire*, examines the queer potentiality of "the legitimacy, within antiheteronormative spaces, of the sexual objectification of bodies" (72); the reification of sexual desire that is Floyd's own object of analysis becomes a condition of possibility for the queer horizons toward which his book moves (horizons which I considered and read as crip, in chapter 1). Floyd points out—in one of many passages in his study that arguably speaks to disability studies as clearly as queer theory—that for Marx,

> bodies are sensory objects impacted, developed, and remade within the ongoing social and historical production of humans by humans. The insistence of the *1844 Manuscripts* [of Marx] on the ongoing objectification, through collective labor, of human desires and capacities in the world, and the resulting historical dynamism of this world, together necessarily imply . . . the manipulation, the re-creation of bodies themselves, the dialectical objectification of bodies *by* the collective social body, whether or not that objectification operates within exploited social relations. (72–73)

Floyd's insight here would suggest that disabled case studies are not essentially (that is, ahistorically) exploitative; insisting as much would deny (to adapt Floyd) the legitimacy, within antiableist spaces, of the disabled or crip objectification of bodies. Crow's project indeed mines journalistic, judicial, and medical locations where disabled and crip bodies are put on display, enfreaked, in ways that should be critiqued. Yet her project is also a clear historical example of (to adapt Floyd once more) the re-creation of crip bodies themselves, the dialectical objectification of bodies *by* the collective social body. Even as *Figures* reaches far beyond disability identity (many, perhaps a majority, of the stories do not directly represent "disability identity" as such), the historical objectification of "disability" and its re-creation by the collective crip social body are conditions of possibility for Crow's critical performance. Her manipulation of literal matter (raw river mud) as the vehicle for that performance only underscores (or actually *figures*) the value and generativity of a genuinely dialectical objectification. "We are figures" is, then, simultaneously a first-person plural pronouncement welcoming new subjectivities and an affirmation of the critical potentiality of crip objectification/figuration.

The initial exhibition space for *Figures* was in the shadow of the South Bank Tower construction project [Figure 4.8], which offers consumers the chance to live the high life in London. It is the result of a partnership

Figure 4.8. South Bank Tower construction site.
Photo by Author.

between London-based private real estate developer CIT and the Saudi
Arabian investment bank Jadwa. The development includes rooms with
floor-to-ceiling windows; it is, in fact, in the words of the developers, "a
building that celebrates light and that makes the spectacular skyline a fea-
ture of every home" (South Bank Tower). In Spring 2015 (with completion
expected in October 2015), a four hundred square foot flat in the South
Bank Tower started at £935,000 (roughly USD $1.4 million at the time).
To say that such a figure is a far cry from Kevin's food budget of £3.50
would be a virtually paradigmatic understatement (the very definition of
understatement, in other words). The two figures side by side (£935,000
and £3.50) illustrate how jaw-droppingly immense income inequality is
in the UK in an age of austerity. It is actually equal to income inequality
in Nigeria (which has been subject to various forms of austerity—under
the guise of World Bank-imposed "Structural Adjustment Programs"—
for going on three decades), and worse than Ethiopia.[11]

A light-filled South Bank Tower flat with a view of the spectacular London skyline is a fitting image, for 2015, of what "aspiration" had become. Aspiration, however, has had other, Marxist valences and I would argue that Crow's performance accesses those valences or allows audiences to access them. An "aspiration to totality," in the Marxist sense Floyd theorizes, attempts to grasp, even if contingently or momentarily (or even while recognizing that thinking "totality" is both necessary and impossible), the complex web of social relations that characterize a given moment. Floyd argues that aspirations to totality "approach the universal . . . from the vantage of a specific location within that web, a vantage that necessarily abstracts that totality in coloring everything it sees, but also makes possible broad understandings of social reality unavailable to other perspectives" (12). Clearly, a disabled person begging or stealing food marks an extremely specific location within the web of neoliberal social relations, but as that person comes to *figure* larger social and economic processes, and as his story is articulated with and to other *figures* ("articulated" both in the sense of spoken and joined together with), crip understandings (Floyd's "broad understandings") of social reality unavailable to other perspectives materialize.

Poppies Redux: Cripping Monumentality

Crow's aspiration to totality makes clear that public art can indeed work to bear witness to the experiences of "the most disadvantaged." Discourses of public art can be used (and are used much more often), however, to subtend Thatcherite aspiration. I'll conclude with a brief example of that subtending before enumerating in conclusion some of the ways in which *Figures* crips austerity. In November 2014, Prime Minister David Cameron himself lauded a public art installation alongside the Tower of London, calling it a "much loved and respected monument" (qtd. in "Tower"). The installation was composed of 888,246 ceramic poppies commemorating Britain's war dead. It was designed by Paul Cummins and Tom Piper and titled, in a way that seemed to conjure up bodily materiality, *Blood Swept Lands and Seas of Red*. The poppies were timed to coincide with Remembrance Day and millions of visitors flocked to the Tower of London to see them.

Blood Swept Lands and Seas of Red was caught up in discord not long after it opened to the public. Writing for the *Guardian*, Jonathan Jones argued that "The first world war was not noble. War is not noble. A meaningful mass memorial to this horror would not be dignified or pretty." In Jones's analysis, however, a meaningful mass memorial was not the point; gesturing toward the only permissible discourse on Britain's war dead, he argued that it is "deeply disturbing that 100 years on from 1914, we can only mark this terrible war as a nationalist tragedy." As this chapter makes clear, a devastating tragedy was (in actual fact) under way across the nation at the same moment and Crow's *Figures* linked that national tragedy to transnational, indeed global, suffering. Suffering, for Cameron and many other public figures, however, was best located in the past and public art provided him an easy vehicle for that act of relocating suffering. Announcing that the exhibition would go on tour, Cameron insisted, "I think the exhibition of the poppies has really caught the public imagination, people have found that incredibly moving. . . . What we've managed to do is find a way of saving part of the exhibition for the nation and making sure it will be seen by many more people" (qtd. in "Parts"). Cleansing, purifying, or stultifying the "we" that Jones's words would interrogate, Cameron's words imply that "we" are in fact dignified and noble; his one nation is deemed worthy only of public art that will bespeak that dignity and nobility. Conjuring up a magnitude that shuts down the possibility of alternative interpretations, leaving one humble and passive before the spectacle, Cameron's culture secretary, Sajid Javid, insisted, "I was left in awe at the sheer scale and strength of the piece. For me this is public art at its most powerful and moving" (qtd. in "Parts"). Javid invoked "the four million or so people who have gone to see" the poppies, bringing into being through that invocation a unity that could only position critiques such as Jones's as illegible or essentially unthinkable. Indeed, a day after Jones's critique, the *Daily Mail* counterposed a unified "many" who "will be astonished that anyone could politicise this magnificent project" to the "sneering, Left-wing art critic" (that is, Jones) who would introduce dissonance into the interpretation of an installation that was, in the tabloid's assessment, of "such a different order and magnitude" that it should "transcend the petty squabbles of Left and Right" (Hardman). For the *Daily Mail*, a self-evident reconciliation of petty differences is achieved in and through *Blood Swept Lands and Seas of Red.*

In a certain sense, public art of the sort that was celebrated in November 2014 by British dignitaries needs an audience that is ironically not aspirational in at least one very specific sense of the word, and the *Daily Mail* dutifully materializes such an audience. The *OED* reminds us that *aspiration*, of course, can refer to the straightforward "action or process of drawing breath." The many who will be "astonished" by the magnificence of *Blood Swept Lands and Seas of Red*, or astonished by anyone who looks critically at it, however, *have had their breath taken away*, to gesture toward a common, idiomatic understanding of *astonishment* in English ("Idiom"). In contrast, public art such as Crow's that aspires to totality encompasses, in theory, anyone who is or has been aspirational in the most literal, corporeal sense. Although Mark's breath has been taken away by austerity, *Figures* testifies that he nonetheless lived, that he was engaged in the action or process of drawing breath.[12]

Seymour's *Against Austerity* details the ways in which New York City was a key site for the emergence of a global austerity politics that is now so particularly pronounced in the UK; a government-sponsored bailout protecting the city's finances in the 1970s was preceded by the explicit construction, by austerians, of the "common sense" that a "fiscal crisis" was under way that required both limiting the power of unions and cutting social services (18–19). Examining "the social services policies of [the] austerity state" that emerged in New York at the moment Seymour surveys, Rosalyn Deutsche makes clear that "public art" played an important role in helping to congeal an austerian common sense (107). Deutsche argues that "new public spaces, materializations of attempts at reconciliation, are the objects of contests over uses and, moreover, are hardly designed for accessibility to all. Rather, they permit, through a multitude of legal, physical, or symbolic means, access by certain social groups for selected purposes while excluding others" (112). For Deutsche, a new "public art" (and arguably a *monumental* public art, in the stupefying and awe-inspiring sense put forward by Javid and others in relation to poppies almost four decades later) helps to lubricate neoliberal reconciliations, masking the ways in which access is actually being curtailed in the name of a seemingly all-inclusive and harmonious public. Discourses of public art in an age of austerity put forward "images of well-managed and beautiful cities" (118), but actively suppress the (classed) antagonisms and contradictions upon which those beautiful cities, or (blood swept) lands, are built.

Extending and specifying Deutsche, I would argue that the compulsory patriotism of Cameron's platitudes on public art obscures the social relations of neoliberalism and austerity in which we are now situated and for which, as *Crip Times* has argued throughout, he was one of the contemporary architects. Which is simply another way of saying that Cameron is someone with a classed investment in ideological obfuscations that would deflect attention away from the material relations of power in the UK today; Marx would say, in fact, that his comments on public art allow "circumstances to appear upside-down, as in a *camera obscura*" (*German* 154). My argument in this chapter is that Crow's aspiration to totality through *Figures* allows for the opposite; to stick with Marx for the moment, *Figures* puts forward life (and vibrant matter) "not determined by consciousness, but consciousness [determined] by life"; that is, *Figures* materializes "real living individuals themselves" whose "consciousness is considered solely as their consciousness," emerging directly from the located, material conditions of their lives (*German* 155).

In contrast to the monumental obfuscation that is *Blood Swept Lands and Seas of Red*, Crow's *Figures* puts forward a very different kind of public art and in the process amplifies the discord that characterizes crip times. Her installation, I want to argue in conclusion, crips austerity in at least four ways. First, perhaps obviously, *Figures* puts forward critically disabled perspectives on austerity; it positions disability as an epistemological or cripistemological site from which we can look critically at austerity and begin to imagine alternatives. Second, and this is merely to gesture again toward the ways in which "crip" has become a more radical term for artists and activists, it forges (or dares to conjure up) a coalition of "left-behinds" who may or may not *identify* as disabled but who can be comprehended as connected somehow through a crip analytic committed to theorizing vulnerability, precarity, and resistance expansively.

Third, *Figures* crips austerity in a perhaps more straightforward sense: it short-circuits austerity, throws a wrench in it, jams the system, or (we might say, more provocatively) works with and against the system simultaneously. In this sense, I love the ways in which Crow's initial proposal for government funding, using obfuscation more consciously and strategically than is evident in "public" art such as *Blood Swept Lands and Seas of Red*, didn't use the word austerity even as the word was everywhere in circulation around the extant performance in 2015; *Figures* was, again, "a mass-sculptural performance that makes visible the human cost of austerity and urges action against it." Finally (and this is simply to make explicit in conclusion what I've already asserted thoughout this chapter), *Figures* crips austerity by aspiring to a vantage point from which we can observe (by which I mean, of course, *attempt* to observe) the totality of austerity's operation. To my knowledge, a century and a half of Marxist theorizing on "totality" has never really taken account of disability; I'm essentially asserting here, however playfully, that one can't aspire to totality without cripping. Thatcherite aspiration, again, was and remains an able-bodied activity: *look after yourself above everything else.* Our crip aspirations to totality, in contrast, are always necessarily, inescapably, disabled: attend to those who are not you, to those who are different from you (different embodiments, different minds, different behaviors), and attempt in that interdependent attending to apprehend the web of social relations in which we are currently located—social relations that can (of course) be figured, and that can (of course) be changed.

Epilogue

Some (Disabled) Aspects of the Immigrant Question

The Cameron years in the United Kingdom came to an end in the Summer of 2016. Austerity, however, did not come to an end, either in the UK or in the other locations that *Crip Times: Disability, Globalization, and Resistance* has considered. The Cameron years came to an end on June 23, 2016, because voters in the UK, by a margin of 52 percent to 48 percent, chose to initiate the process of leaving the European Union. Long before the vote, "Brexit" had materialized as the word for this British exit from the EU. Cameron had campaigned for the country to retain its membership in the EU; he resigned following the outcome, in an acknowledgment of defeat. Theresa May was selected by Conservative members of Parliament as the new prime minister, with the understanding at the time that she would serve as such until the next scheduled general election in 2020. One of May's primary charges was to work with the EU to finalize Brexit.

As she assumed office, May appointed a new cabinet that did not include George Osborne, Cameron's chancellor of the exchequer, who had been one of the primary architects of the austerity plan executed by the coalition government. Although some commentators took this snub as a sign that austerity might be eased, particularly as May abandoned Osborne's aim of running a budget surplus by 2020, others were unconvinced. Prime Minister's Questions are held every Wednesday in the House of Commons; when Labour leader Jeremy Corbyn questioned May about the Tories' austerity agenda in her first appearance there, she responded forcefully, "You talk about austerity. I call it living within our means. You talk about austerity but actually it's about not saddling our children and grandchildren with significant debts to come" (qtd. in Giles). Writing in the *Guardian* not long after May assumed office, Dawn Foster noted that the new prime minister clearly shared the general Tory belief that poverty "is psychological, not material: people live in poverty because they don't have the wherewithal to find a job, aspire to a better paid job, and mismanage their own money. Cuts, sanctions, the bedroom tax and removal of council tax benefit therefore nudge people into action." May voted for all these policies while serving in Cameron's cabinet, and—as this book goes to press—shows no indication that any of them will be reversed in the near future.[1]

Many in the UK who voted in favor of Brexit, however, were clearly feeling the pain of austerity. Although clear majorities in Scotland and Northern Ireland voted to remain, as did London and other urban areas in England such as Manchester, Liverpool, and Bristol, the vote in some of the most impoverished areas elsewhere in the country was in favor of Brexit. The right-wing United Kingdom Independence Party, popularly known as UKIP and led at the time by Nigel Farage, sought to tap into the resentment felt by many in these areas and to direct that resentment toward the form of globalization favored by both the Tory and New Labour establishment and, in particular, toward the levels of foreign immigration to the UK supposedly facilitated by that globalization. Over the course of the Cameron administration, UKIP increasingly exerted pressure, from the nationalist and isolationist Right, on the Tories; Cameron's willingness to hold the June 2016 referendum was, in fact, largely seen as a concession to the Right.

In this Epilogue to *Crip Times*, I briefly consider both UKIP's rhetoric in the final years of Cameron's administration and the ways in which that rhetoric sedimented across the political spectrum. I then turn again to Anne Finger's disability studies analysis of Antonio Gramsci's "Some Aspects of the Southern Question." Focusing on Gramsci's analysis of Italy in the early twentieth century, Finger essentially asks: in what multivalent and intersecting ways does bodily, racial, and regional difference *figure*? And how might difference be made to figure otherwise? These questions of course in many ways animated the previous chapter and my reading of Liz Crow's performance/installation *Figures*. Crow's aspiration to totality enabled us to perceive the ways in which disability is a key component of the larger system of neoliberal capitalism. Disability is always intertwined with other differences and social relations, *and* it can afford a vantage point from which we might imagine alternatives. Crow's crip project thus encouraged action and solidarity in the face of the unjust social relations generated by, and secured through, austerity.

After reviewing Finger's analysis, I complicate the question about how difference figures in crip times through a consideration of one more figure, a very specific disabled figure who was in 2015 arguably also living life at what Crow's installation repeatedly identified as "the sharp end of austerity" (indeed, at the time of this writing, the figure I'll discuss had only fourteen days left of life-saving medication). I'll contend here that this particular specter of disability is both very easy to dismiss or conjure away and is a sign of more to come, certainly as long as we are subject to austerity, but even more generally as long as neoliberal capitalism remains economically and culturally hegemonic. The specter of disability that haunts this Epilogue to *Crip Times*—a specter that perhaps attended many voters as they elected to leave the EU—would encourage us to look inward. I'll conclude, however, where I began, looking outward from the generative indignation of the 15-M movement in Spain (but also outward from the Scottish rejection of austerity) toward what Roderick A. Ferguson, drawing on Toni Morrison, terms "something else to be" (*Aberrations* 132).

Muscular Defenses and Disabled Figures from Elsewhere

In 2014, UKIP won twenty-three seats in the European Parliament, ensuring that it would have the largest representation there of any UK party. This win was, at least on the surface, a significant irony, since UKIP strongly favored breaking with the EU, as the "Independence" in its name suggests. At home, UKIP's anti-EU stance was far broader, manifesting itself in consistent calls for tougher policies on immigration. The racism of these calls ranged from thinly veiled disdain for immigrants articulated as "concern" about "overburdened" state systems to more explicit anger or dismay at how, in UKIP's assessment, uncomfortable or fearful native-born English people feel around immigrants, with their particular customs and religious practices. According to UKIP's view of things, immigrants from the EU (especially eastern Europe), the Caribbean, Asia, the Middle East, and Africa were capriciously migrating to the UK in order to access supposedly generous health and welfare benefits. Congregating by the thousands in urban areas (so the story goes), refusing to speak English, and working (if they worked) for next to nothing, these migrants endangered not only British jobs in a time of economic crisis but, as Farage put it directly, "the makeup of communities and our way of life" (qtd. in Mason, "Immigration"). In interview after interview and appearance after appearance, Farage denounced "claptrap about diversity" and articulated positions affirming that England needed "a much more muscular defence of our Judaeo-Christian heritage" (qtd. in Odone).

The metaphorical invocation of an able-bodied, muscular England defending itself against others is not surprising given the ways in which those foreign others themselves are regularly figured as disabled in some way by UKIP's rhetoric. Indeed, defying any and all evidence, fears of sick and impaired bodies embarking on "benefits tourism" fueled UKIP's anti-immigrant rhetoric; such fears had the effect, in the run-up to the general election of May 2015, of pushing both the Conservative and Labour parties in England even further to the right than they already were. Even within UKIP, Farage himself was at times understood or described as controversial, but the positions he and the party voiced increasingly sedimented across the mainstream political spectrum. Richard Seymour and others have analyzed the broad effect of these racist and anti-immigrant discourses as part of what Seymour terms the "UKIPisation of English politics" ("UKIPisation"). Surveying the situation in the fall of 2014, for example, Seymour illustrated this UKIPisation by writing, not of UKIP itself but of the Labour Party headed at the time by Ed Miliband,

> Every instinct tells them to nod along to the anti-immigrant beat, to acknowledge the "real concerns" behind this racism, to try to deck it in a progressive pallium. . . . They want to say that they are the party that put asylum seekers in detention centres and ratcheted up the "integration" agenda. . . . They want to say that they understood the concerns of ordinary people and will take very tough decisions, very tough decisions indeed, to prevent abuses and protect working people. Indeed, they've more or less said all of this before and will say it again. ("UKIPisation")

In the week before the general election in 2015, in fact, Miliband comically (or tragicomically) unveiled a stone monument with six key principles for the party; the monument was to go in the garden at Number 10 Downing Street were Miliband to become prime minister. "Controls on Immigration" was, unsurprisingly, fourth on the list.

Although low voter turnout for the European Parliament elections in part explained UKIP's success in 2014, the party's gains in that year nonetheless spotlighted the ways in which UKIP, and the concerns it both represented and put into discourse, was becoming a notable influence on British politics between the general elections of 2010 and 2015. By the end of the year in 2014, UKIP had secured two seats in the House of Commons. Douglas Carswell of Clacton switched his membership from the Conservative Party to UKIP and resigned from his seat in Parliament, triggering a by-election, which he won handily (indeed, by a greater margin than any previous British by-election) (Pickard). Later in the year, Mark Reckless, another MP elected as a Tory but who switched parties, won back his own seat as a UKIP representative in Rochester and Strood. Although the party only managed to hang on to Carswell's seat in the general election of May 7, 2015, across England, and dispersed relatively evenly geographically, UKIP secured almost 4 million votes. Except in Scotland, where the antiausterity Scottish National Party (SNP) won virtually every seat, a higher percentage of voters in 2015 swung to UKIP than swung to any other party.

After Carswell's win in October 2014, *Newsweek* magazine asked UKIP's leader who *should* be allowed to migrate into the UK. "People who do not have HIV, to be frank," Farage responded. "That's a good start" (qtd. in Chalmers). Farage's comments were roundly and rationally countered by HIV/AIDS experts; there was no evidence that immigrants with HIV were choosing to migrate to the UK, nor does it "overburden" the system when an immigrant with HIV accesses services (indeed, it is actually less expensive for such a person to be in treatment early and to be educated about ways of preventing the spread of the virus). It is not exactly the falsity of Farage's beliefs about benefits tourism that most interests me here, however—it is, instead, how this *representation* of infected and infectious bodies from elsewhere functions in an age of austerity.

Finger, as I suggested in the Introduction, finds in Gramsci's examination of the ways in which Southern Italian "difference" is both explained away and (paradoxically) sustained a type of nascent, early twentieth-century, disability studies. Gramsci's unfinished essay (left behind in his papers when he was arrested in 1926) overviews descriptions of the South of Italy by criminal anthropologists and others (including

members of the Socialist Party) that basically "discovered" naturally in-
ferior types—"a disabled race," in Finger's analysis. "Reading the works
of these criminal anthropologists," Finger's dissection of Gramsci makes
it possible to understand, "one finds a dizzying number of examples of
the fusion of disability, race, and criminality." This discursive fusion
of stigmatized difference disallowed reading the South-North division
through class (through, that is, histories of uneven development and
capitalist exploitation), effectively using instead supposedly natural corporeal, mental, racial, and regional differences to both account for the
South's supposed "backwardness" and to prevent cross-regional, and
revolutionary, coalitions or blocs from forming. Gramsci of course did
not believe in the innate inferiority of Southerners; he was interested in
tracing the cultural work this "inferiority" performed when it appeared
in discourse.

"Some Aspects of the Southern Question" is an essay in many ways
appropriate to the crip times I have analyzed throughout this book
(times that often call for Gramscian pessimism of the intellect, given
how many forces are in place to block revolutionary alliances). UKIP
in particular makes it possible to apprehend quite easily how and why
the extensive discursive disqualification of disabled people (benefit
scroungers, shirkers, malingerers) has germinated alongside the xenophobic, racialized disqualification of nonwhite bodies in England. This
discursive disqualification draws into its wake immigrants and nonim-
migrants alike, as UKIP's rhetoric materializes a white and able-bodied
British "us" always threatened by "them."[2] "They," moreover, as Farage's
ready-to-hand (and for him, obvious) detection of the human immuno-
deficiency virus in bodies (or hordes) at the border of the UK indicates,
are easily pathologized. The "links between disability and race" that Finger noted in Gramsci's discussion of Italy, in other words, are alive and
well (robust and muscular, we might say) in the establishment's ongoing
consolidation of its power in England and in its successful blockage of
more expansive oppositional alliances.

With the activists and artists who have populated these pages, however, we might imagine, or yearn for, revolutionary alliances that can figure difference in new and transformative ways.[3] We might even, keeping
in purview the cripistemological aspiration to totality from the previous
chapter, imagine a crip figure speaking at and from a situated perspec-

tive where sexuality, race, disability—perhaps even HIV—converge. And indeed, because historical necessity arguably demanded it, such a figure did emerge in the days leading up to the British general election in May 2015. On April 28, 2015, a mixed-race, thirty-year-old, HIV positive man from London wrote a letter to Nigel Farage. Although the man's identity was not revealed at the time, his actual existence was purportedly "verified" by the British press (Barnett). He informs Farage in the letter, in fact, "I can provide you with a passport copy and copy letter from my doctor confirming diagnosis in my name should you wish" (Anonymous).

If it were ever unclear, however, that political affinity does not follow automatically from identity, the HIV positive Londoner's letter clarifies any misconception in that regard. "Dear Mr. Farage," the anonymous Londoner begins, "I am writing in support of your claims and comments regarding HIV services being abused by foreign immigrants." With language that could in other contexts easily position his story alongside the narratives from Crow's *Figures*, he explains, "The reality is I have 14 tablets left, I will run out of medication in 14 days. I must take a tablet each day to stay alive but I can't get blood tests and I can't get to see a doctor and I can't get a prescription which should have resulted in automatic delivery of my Atripla medication to my front door." The far right news outlet Breitbart called the man's letter "heartbreaking" (Edmunds). UKIP itself issued a statement describing it as "an extraordinarily moving email from a young man suffering from HIV."

"Why are the wait times for vital blood tests increasing to unacceptable levels?" the "young man suffering from HIV" asks. "Why are the wait times to see a [sic] HIV specialist doctor massively increasing? Why are the drug home delivery companies so over whelmed [sic] patients have to go back into clinics and are not able to access life-saving medication?" The writer has no doubt about who is responsible for his situation; addressing Farage directly, he affirms, "you are right, there is a steady flow of HIV + immigrants that have directly contributed to this situation which has gone past the point of critical mass."

The man's passport suggests he is himself capable of moving outward (beyond the borders of the UK), but the movement across borders to be feared is of course, in the scenario he stages, not his own movement but rather movement in the opposite direction: "there is a steady flow of HIV + immigrants" into the UK. Farage likewise, regularly and even more forcefully, deployed water imagery, worrying about a "flood" or "deluge" of immigrants. Farage in fact endorsed what he called the "basic principle" (and, implicitly, the imagery) in what is likely the most infamous speech in UK history on immigration: Enoch Powell's 1968 speech decrying immigration that is now widely known as the "Rivers of Blood" speech. The speech, which is obviously grounded in ominous liquid imagery, led to Powell's dismissal from the Conservative shadow cabinet and is widely (and rightly) perceived as viciously racist; many also believe that the racist sentiment articulated in the speech helped deliver the 1970 general election to the Tories (Edward Heath became prime minister). Powell, in the speech (like Margaret Thatcher not long after him), conjured up a disabled Britain to be avoided, arguing that "those whom the gods wish to destroy, they first make mad. We must be mad, literally mad, as a nation to be permitting the annual inflow of some 50,000 dependents, who are for the most part the material of the future growth of the immigrant-descended population." The liquid imagery of "rivers of blood" refers to Powell's allusion to the *Aeneid*, where, "like the Roman, I seem to see 'the River Tiber foaming with much blood.'" When excerpts from the speech were presented to Farage in a television interview (without, at first, being credited to Powell), Farage endorsed them (Graham). Upon learning they were from the Rivers of Blood speech, Farage insisted that "the basic principle" of the speech imagining a deluge of immigrants was correct: "I mean when immigration was being discussed in the 60s and 70s and 80s we were talking about an annual net inflow to the country of between 30,000 and 50,000 people. What we have had in the last 13 years is a net 4 million extra migrants who have come to Britain so we are dealing with something now on a scale that hitherto we couldn't even have conceived" (qtd. in Mason, "Basic Principle").

In the April 28, 2015 letter, however, the spatial imagery is in general somewhat different, presenting closed, nonporous spaces, "past the point of critical mass," unable to contain anything else. Waiting rooms and clinics are bursting with HIV positive bodies from elsewhere, forcing the anonymous letter writer out of the closed space of central London:

The waiting rooms are full with immigrant patients. Not only is this massively increasing cost it is burdening the small specialist system to the point of failure. . . . I moved from a central London clinic at St Thomas' Hospital to another clinic further afield as I was no longer able to access the vital services I needed and should be entitled too [*sic*]. The numbers have increased so dramatically in inner London that I was no longer referred to by my name but given an 8 figure patient number instead!

Despite this eight-figure number, the young man insists, he does have an identity. It is, moreover, *not* a racist one, and according to its own logic, cannot be: "My family are a true diverse representation of British Londoners, half our family are white I am therefore not racist but I am the victim of HIV immigration." The letter does not specify a sexual identity, although news or rumors of one quickly emerged through online reporting and social media, rightfully or wrongfully identifying the man as "gay."[4]

Of course, whether or not this British, mixed-race, disabled figure "really" is gay (*or even "really" exists*, no matter how many British passports or doctor's notes UKIP might be capable of producing on demand) is not the point. What matters for UKIP and the establishment press is the utility and flexibility of the figuration "victim of HIV immigration." As figures, victims of HIV immigration can be white or nonwhite, heterosexual or gay, able-bodied or disabled, even HIV negative or HIV positive. In UKIP's scenario, indeed, "we" are *all* potentially victims of HIV immigration, although as I have implied, UKIP's "we" is very specific and exclusive, insular and threatened. UKIP's inward-looking "we" is *generally* white, able-bodied, and heterosexual. However, it is simultaneously useful to UKIP (and, as I suggested, even historically necessary) to put forward a figure who is *none* of those things, a figure who is (as in the April 28 letter) nonwhite, disabled, perhaps gay. As I have argued throughout *Crip Times*, and in contrast to the historical circumstances Gramsci was analyzing in "Some Aspects of the Southern Question," neoliberalism conjures up spectacularized identities to both dilute the potential critical force of various identities and (more important) to forestall the (antiausterity, antiracist, proimmigrant) alliances that might be generated through and across acknowledged differences. In such times, if UKIP had not had a gay, HIV positive, mixed-race figure, it surely would have needed to invent one.

No Detendrán la Primavera/They Will Not Hold Back the Spring

HIV positive immigrants speaking otherwise, however, exist. In the days leading up to the May 7, 2015, general election, a gay, HIV positive, Nigerian-born British citizen named Bisi Alimi worked tirelessly to counter UKIP's vitriol and to encourage others to vote against them. Obviously not concerned about anonymity (or, rather, narratively constructing an identity where he once had to hide but no longer has to do so), Alimi explained in interviews,

> When I came to this country in 2007 I was running away from being killed. I love [Nigeria] and I want to make change at home, but there was an attempt on my life. I thought, "if I'm going to stay alive I've got to leave my country." I had no idea that I could claim asylum, and that I could have access to treatment. . . . I never talked about my disease. I covered it up because of fear. I knew that if I received treatment people would know about my sexuality. (qtd. in Fearn)

Turning not inward but outward, however, Alimi stressed that free and accessible public health should be a way of uniting, not dividing people: "That poor people and rich people can access the same kind of health-care together is something that British people should be proud of" (qtd. in Fearn). On the day of the 2015 general election, Alimi stood outside a Thanet South polling station on the east coast of England with a placard. Thanet South was where Farage himself was hoping to secure a seat in Parliament (he lost and initially claimed he would resign the UKIP leadership; his resignation came only after Brexit was an established fact). In contrast to the anonymous letter writer's insular confidence, which essentially put forward only easy *answers* in relation to immigration ("you are right, there is a steady flow of HIV + immigrants"), Alimi's placard offered up a space where dialogue and *questions* might be generated: "I'm an immigrant, hug me or ask me a question" (Gadd).

As I have maintained throughout *Crip Times*, and as much queer, and increasingly disabled, thought has demonstrated consistently since the 1990s, identity itself is of course neither necessarily nor automatically radical. Identity is, however, at this point both useful for and in many ways necessary to those continuing to execute austerity and neoliberalism. And we (that is, those of us interested in calling forth with Alimi and others a much more expansive and outward-looking "we") should be vigilant about the uses to which they (the executors of austerity) put it. Alimi certainly claims various identities, but looks outward from them to unpredictable and unexpected connections that might be forged, in contrast to the HIV positive Londoner, who claims various identities to safeguard UKIP's inward-looking, protectionist stance. I noted earlier that the HIV positive Londoner's story could have easily served as one of the narratives for Crow's *Figures*. The UKIP figure's difference, however, is in the rhetorical positioning of himself *alongside* the guardians of austerity (and the border) and *as against* those who have suffered from their policies. Considering the two figures together (the letter writer and Alimi, with his placard in Thanet South) "allows us," as Ferguson might put it, "to refuse the fiction of minority innocence and compels us to develop methodologies for challenging institutional efforts to 'pin down' the meaning of minoritized lives" (*Reorder* 179). In Ferguson's sense, the "us" here potentially materializes as anyone reading Alimi's performance, or any of the performances I have considered in *Crip Times*. As Alimi develops "new ways of entering minority difference, encouraging modes of agency that will make that difference legible and liminal at the same time" (*Reorder* 179), it is easy to position his vision in conclusion alongside the expansive vision of many of the artists and activists analyzed in previous chapters: artists and activists such as Crow, Livia Radwanski, Chilean students on hunger strike, conscientious objectors in Spain, or crips camped out on a traffic island in Berkeley, California.

Of course, especially in the wake of Brexit and ongoing austerity, I'm not at all writing my way toward even the slightest implication that hugging an immigrant will make it all okay. And neither is Alimi; his Thanet South appearance is essentially a performance, and a singular performance can hardly bear the burden of determining, to borrow Lenin's famous phrase, what is to be done. Performance by its nature is evanescent, vanishing even as it appears, and leaving in the wake of its disappearance a space that might be filled, in ways that cannot be fully predicted in advance, by future performances, performances that hold (perhaps) some affinity to the performance that has gone before. In these pages, Crow was quite explicit about conjuring up those future performances; her stated intent with *Figures* was to urge action against austerity as she made its impact visible through her sculptures and performance. In varied ways, however, all the artistic and activist work in *Crip Times* invites performance or action and figures crip futures, often by bearing witness to crip pasts that are vanishing: from Kaliya Franklin's nude self-portrait "Left Out in the Cold" to social medical centers in Greece to the This Is What Disability Looks Like project. El Museo de los Desplazados, the itinerant global installation of which Radwanski's photography is a part, makes the invitation explicit: "Frente a la creación de comunidades cerradas, proponemos el Museo de los Desplazados como una plataforma abierta, incompleta, en continuo proceso de desarrollo y necesariamente colectiva" [In the face of the creation of closed communities, we propose the Museum of the Displaced as an open stage, incomplete, in a continual process of development and necessarily collective] (Left Hand Rotation).

In crip times, however, figures such as the HIV positive Londoner will most certainly enter that stage. It might be easy to dismiss the UKIP letter writer as two-dimensional, but others like him will come forth in the wake of his disappearance. When I asked, at the end of *Crip Theory: Cultural Signs of Queerness and Disability*, "What might it mean to welcome the disability to come, to desire it? What might it mean to shape worlds capable of welcoming the disability to come?" (207), I was not exactly gesturing toward someone who would go on to position himself as an HIV positive "victim of HIV immigration." Welcoming the disability to come in all its unruliness and noninnocence entails, however, recognizing that such figures will inevitably, and even necessarily, come forth. This, too, is what disability looks like; an easy optimism about crip performance and resistance is not sustainable. As long as the redistributive class strategy that is austerity and the larger system of neoliberal capitalism are in place, we will need to grapple with minoritized/disabled figures speaking or being made to speak in ways that endanger the crip futures other minoritized/disabled figures are attempting to access.

But specters of disability are never singular and some disabled aspects of the immigrant question will never be posed in only one place or at one border. The dominant forms of neoliberal capitalist globalization would like to ensure that identity and difference are, in the words of Michael Hardt and Antonio Negri, "corralled into the hierarchical organs of a political body" (*Multitude* 192), but even as that globalizing (and austere) desire and demand for securitization is vouchsafed in one location, indignation, resistance, and excessive desires for connection across borders (desires that this book has read as crip and as queer) are unleashed (or uncorralled) elsewhere.

This opposition was literally in evidence in the UK general election in May 2015 as the consolidation of austerity and racism and anti-immigrant sentiment in England (and in the positions articulated by the three largest parties) was directly countered in Scotland (by the SNP). Seymour's incisive postelection analysis, following the Tories' victory and the shift to the SNP in Scotland, clearly lays out the inward- and outward-looking alternatives:

> And while the Labour Party tailed the Tories on austerity, while they imitated Tory language on welfare, while they copied UKIP on immigration, the SNP defended a simple, civilised position: no austerity, stop demonising people on welfare, and welcome immigrants. In England, Labour aping the Right just leads to its base abstaining, as they have done in growing numbers since 2001. But in Scotland, working class voters had a tried and tested reformist alternative, with an optimistic political identity linked to a profound socio-demographic shift, and were able to rally to it. ("This Is Not")

It remains unclear, at the time of this writing, what will happen in the UK (and especially in England) in relation to these socio-demographic shifts. One of Crow's immediate reactions following the elections was to reflect, sadly, on "those who won't survive a decade of austerity." The Cameron years on which this book has focused are over, but Brexit and the May years ahead do not appear to offer a clear sense that things will improve anytime soon for disabled people and others reeling from austerity's impact. Hope is not, and likely should not be, the dominant sentiment, taking into account the ways in which hopefulness puts at risk what Michel Foucault termed a "hyper- and pessimistic activism" ("Genealogy" 256).

As Foucault's words about hyperactivism imply, however, pessimism need not be austere, and optimism of the will should always keep us pointing both toward an inevitable excess, as well as toward the possibilities that excess affords for new connections and coalitions.[5] Indeed, the "something else to be" that Ferguson theorizes in his overview of black lesbian feminism of the 1970s is always explicitly about anticapitalist coalition *and* excess: artistic and activist "theorizations of coalition," he writes (in a description that can be directly and ironically opposed to the literal UK coalition that initiated austerity from 2010 to 2015), "traced the properties of capital's new phase and sought to address that mode as one that could produce unprecedented possibilities" (*Aberrations* 133). Capitalist globalization at the end of the twentieth century generated simultaneous, interlocking oppressions and modes of exploitation; "coalitions could only challenge these modes of regulation by making gendered, eroticized, and racialized exploitation the basis of political and intellectual intervention" (*Aberrations* 137). The twenty-first century crip times I have surveyed throughout this book likewise call for interventions that make explicit new modes of exploitation. I have obviously been concerned here with the undertheorized centrality of disability to a globalizing austerity politics, but I hope I have consistently and simultaneously been attentive throughout to the ways in which disability oppression is always indissociably caught up in other modes of exploitation, and attentive to the ways in which cultural workers in an age of austerity are, to extend Ferguson, making disabled, gendered, eroticized, and racialized exploitation the basis of political and intellectual intervention.

I'll conclude by letting hang in the air one more phrase from the crip place and time where I began. During the summer of 2011, when I was living near the Puerta del Sol in Madrid, one of the phrases I observed on signs, and at times heard as the square was retaken after being violently cleared by police, was "Podrán cortar algunas flores, pero no detendrán la primavera" [They can cut a few flowers, but they will not hold back the spring]. The valences of *detener* are austere: to interrupt something, to impede its forward movement, to catch someone, to stop or cease the movement or the action (Real Academia Española). But *no detener*, especially in the outward looking future tense naming what *they* will be unable to do (*no detendrán*), points beyond authorities or states that would interrupt, impede, catch, stop, or cut. In this book, I have documented some of the suffering, exploitation, dispossession, and displacement that characterize the crip times in which we are living. But I have also tried to attend to those aspiring toward or articulating a (crip) future tense, insisting that we will not be stopped and conjuring up, in performances and actions that bear witness to that insistence, a world beyond austerity.

NOTES

INTRODUCTION

1 I discuss the influence of other queer theorists—specifically, Licia Fiol-Matta, Lisa Duggan, and Jasbir Puar—in a later section of this Introduction, noting in particular that this sophisticated work has shifted the starting point for queer theory in general. Neither Halberstam nor these other theorists are directly addressing embodiment in an age of austerity, although I hope it will be clear that they have provided me with an indispensable critical vocabulary for doing so. This critically queer work tracing the complex workings of capitalism and imagining alternatives to it should be understood as one of the conditions of possibility for crip theory. At this point, there are indeed numerous books and essays that do bring together queer and disability theory, and I am deeply indebted to all the queer/crip work that has come before me, as should be clear in the pages that follow. Corbett O'Toole has been working at the intersections of sexuality and disability studies for decades; her important memoir recounting much of that academic and activist work, *Fading Scars: My Queer Disability History*, was published in 2015. Eli Clare's groundbreaking 1999 memoir *Exile and Pride: Queerness, Disability, and Liberation* also marked a formative moment for the field and for me personally. An endnote cannot do justice to all the other crip/queer work that has appeared since the late 1990s; a few key titles include Alison Kafer's *Feminist, Queer, Crip*, Mel Y. Chen's *Animacies: Biopolitics, Racial Mattering, and Queer Affect*, Margaret Price's *Mad at School: Rhetorics of Mental Disability and Academic Life*, Margrit Shildrick's *Dangerous Discourses of Disability, Subjectivity and Sexuality*, and Julie Passanante Elman's *Chronic Youth: Disability, Sexuality, and U.S. Media Cultures of Rehabilitation*.

2 This slogan was initially articulated by the group Democracia Real Ya (DRY). DRY was one of several groups that united as "Los Indignados" on May 15, 2011; other groups included Juventud sin Futuro, Plataforma de Coordinación de Grupos Pro-Movilización Ciudadana, Anonymous, No les Votes, Estado del Malester, V de Vivienda (Arenas Conejo and Pié Balaguer 235).

3 I am drawing the phrase "bodies out of bounds" from the title of the important fat studies anthology *Bodies Out of Bounds: Fatness and Transgression*, edited by Jana Evans Braziel and Kathleen LeBesco. Although I am using the phrase in a slightly different context here, I would argue that the foundational fat studies thesis that the radical, unnecessary, and profitable interventions repeatedly in circulation around fat bodies (a global diet industry, bariatric surgery, etc.) are akin to the

radical, unnecessary, and profitable interventions in circulation around all those subject to austerity. For an essay explicitly theorizing these intersections, see Anna Mollow's and my coauthored piece "Fattening Austerity."

4 That circle included, in addition to Moscoso Pérez and Romañach, queer and trans theorist and activist Lucas Platero, who a few years later authored the groundbreaking book *Trans*exualidades: Acompañamiento, factores de salud y recursos educativos* [Trans*exualities: Support, Health Factors and Educational Resources] (2014); Soledad Arnau Ripollés, of the Instituto de Paz, Derechos Humanos y Vida Independiente [Institute for Peace, Human Rights, and Independent Living], a feminist disability activist and sex radical who would go on to create with Irene Navascués Cobo and Rosario Ortega Amador the award-winning short postporno film *Habitación* [Bedroom] (2015), along with other films and recordings; and Paco Guzmán Castillo, one of the central figures in the Foro de Vida Independiente y Divertad [Forum for Independent Living and Diversity/Liberty], which I describe briefly below. Guzmán Castillo died in early 2013.

5 Although my work in *Crip Times* is fundamentally in accord with Judith Butler's work on precarity, especially her argument throughout *Notes toward a Performative Theory of Assembly* that "precarity is enacted and opposed" through "the embodied character of social action and expression, what we might understand as embodied and plural performativity" (22), the place of disability in our work is essentially inverted. Whereas for Butler, disability is always and only an example of a more generalized precarity (she problematically gestures toward the example of "the differently abled" and occasionally notes what we "know from disability studies" [58, 72]), it is for me a primary analytic for theorizing precarity and austerity. The work of Arenas Conejo and Pié Balaguer, implying that a performative theory of assembly in Spain was literally made possible because of the disability movement, underscores both the importance of inverting Butler's positioning of disability here and the ongoing importance of using disability, like feminism, not as exemplum but as analytic.

6 In addition to the books by Blyth and Stuckler and Basu, the major books that have shaped my thinking on austerity in our moment are Owen Jones's *The Establishment: And How They Get Away with It*, Mary O'Hara's *Austerity Bites: A Journey to the Sharp End of Cuts in the UK*, and (especially) Richard Seymour's *Against Austerity: How We Can Fix the Crisis They Made*, with its unparalleled class analysis of the global economic crisis. Of these, O'Hara's is the one study in which disability as such is clearly central to both her book's organization and the stories of suffering that she seeks to convey. Jones's book is important, given its thorough overview of how virtually all UK institutions (the titular "Establishment") are complicit in sustaining the dominant economic order. He has written more directly about the effect of austerity on disabled people in his journalism, including the key 2012 article, "David Cameron Praises Paralympians, but His Policies Will Crush Them." Journalistic accounts of austerity's effect on disabled people have of necessity been important to my study, as have blogs by disabled writers that I will mention as I continue.

7 With the phrase "the cultural logic of neoliberalism," I am intentionally echoing Fredric Jameson's famous description of postmodernism as "the cultural logic of late capitalism"; however, Lisa Duggan's *The Twilight of Equality? Neoliberalism, Cultural Politics, and the Attack on Democracy* remains, in my mind, the best introduction for comprehending the cultural logic of *neoliberalism*. The final two chapters of Kevin Floyd's *The Reification of Desire: Toward a Queer Marxism* have also particularly shaped my understanding of this logic (154–226). For my own related work on the topic, see "Neoliberal Risks: *Million Dollar Baby, Murderball,* and Anti-National Sexual Positions," "Taking It to the Bank: Independence and Inclusion on the World Market," and "Cripping Queer Politics, or the Dangers of Neoliberalism." Long-standing and important critiques of a range of capitalisms (not only capitalism in its neoliberal form) have been developed in disability studies more broadly. The work of Marta Russell, collected in *Beyond Ramps: Disability at the End of the Social Contract*, has played a particularly foundational role in anticapitalist disability theory; Ravi Malhotra's edited 2017 collection, *Disability Politics in a Global Economy: Essays in Honour of Marta Russell* makes explicit Russell's importance to the field. Susan Schweik's *The Ugly Laws: Disability in Public*, Dan Goodley's *Dis/Ability Studies: Theorising Disablism and Ableism,* and Nirmala Erevelles's *Disability and Difference in Global Contexts: Enabling a Transformative Body Politic* also articulate, in varied and brilliant ways, a disability studies critique of capitalism. I engage Erevelles's work more specifically in chapter 2.

8 "Cripping Austerity" was in fact my working title for this project for the first few years of its existence. Examples from the Left of the use of "creeping privatization" or "crippling austerity" are literally innumerable. See, to pick just a few examples directly relevant to *Crip Times*, Rebecca Kolins Givan and Stephen Bach's "Workforce Responses to the Creeping Privatization of the UK National Health Service" (overviewing privatization that commenced under New Labour), and Paul Krugman's repeated critiques of "crippling austerity" ("M.I.T. Gang"; "Greek Regrets").

9 Floyd's overview of the distinction between Fordist and neoliberal production provides one of the foundations for my analysis of neoliberal representation in chapter 1. For more on flexibility in relation to contemporary identities, see Emily Martin's *Flexible Bodies: The Role of Immunity in American Culture from the Days of Polio to the Age of AIDS*, and my discussion of Martin in *Crip Theory: Cultural Signs of Queerness and Disability* (13–19). I use the term "hypostasized" here to emphasize that while target markets have proliferated under neoliberalism, they nonetheless have a longer history. Across the twentieth century, Alexandra Chasin explains in her important study *Selling Out: The Gay and Lesbian Movement Goes to Market*, at key "moments of enfranchisement" for various groups, "movement constituencies became target markets" (xvi).

10 Merriam-Webster determines its words of the year by counting the searches on its website; "socialism," incidentally, was the fourth most sought-after word of 2010.

11 The entire project of Blyth's book is to provide evidence, from the perspectives of political science and economics, that austerity does not work. Krugman, likewise, has consistently asserted that there is a consensus among economists in the UK and the United States about austerity's failure: "British economists have no doubt about the economic damage wrought by austerity. The Centre for Macroeconomics in London regularly surveys a panel of leading UK economists on a variety of questions. When it asked whether the [government]'s policies had promoted growth and employment, those disagreeing outnumbered those agreeing four to one" ("Case for Cuts").

12 As I have already suggested, the long-term influence that the antiausterity party Podemos might have on national politics in Spain remains to be seen. In Greece, the antiausterity party Syriza, under the leadership of Alexis Tsipras, was swept into power in January 2015. After months of struggle with creditors and a national referendum affirming the people's opposition to austerity, Tsipras's government capitulated and imposed even harsher austerity measures on the Greek people. I discuss elements of the Greek situation briefly in chapter 2. In the United States, socialist Bernie Sanders in 2015 mounted an unexpectedly strong (and, essentially, antiausterity) challenge to the eventual 2016 Democratic presidential candidate Hillary Clinton; it remains unclear whether a larger movement challenging (or supplanting) the sedimented neoliberalism of the Democrats will emerge in the wake of Sanders's defeat. Following their own disastrous defeat in the May 2015 general election, Ed Miliband, the leader of the UK Labour Party, resigned. Against all odds and expectations, a socialist and antiausterity member of the party, Jeremy Corbyn, was elected leader by party members in September 2015. Although Labour is likely to remain the opposition party at least through 2020, Corbyn's election is the most visible and powerful sign of serious fractures in the consensus around austerity in the UK. He has been, and remains, opposed by the majority of "New Labour" parliamentarians, who are faithful to the post-Thatcher neoliberal politics and policies of Tony Blair. New Labour parliamentarians have challenged Corbyn's leadership at every turn, especially in late 2016, after the UK voted to leave the European Union in what came to be called "Brexit." Corbyn was opposed to Brexit even as he expressed concern over a lack of real democracy in the EU. He can hardly be blamed in any way for Brexit, and it is clear that New Labour not only used the Brexit vote as a pretext for challenging his leadership but had been planning to do so long before it occurred. I summarize the political situation in the UK from 2010 onward later in this Introduction. It is important to note here that fractures in the neoliberal consensus have also emerged from the Right, in the United States and across Europe. Brexit itself can be read as a protectionist and isolationist rebuke to neoliberal globalization, as can the surprise upset victory of Republican businessman Donald Trump as president of the United States in November 2016. Despite Trump's opposition to some forms of globalization, he has affirmed a clear commitment to slashing the budgets of, or eliminating outright, numerous government agencies and to the radical deregula-

tion of barriers to the free flow of U.S. corporate capital. Trumpism was on the ascendency as *Crip Times* went to press, and I will write more about its disability politics in subsequent publications.

13 For an indispensable analysis of Corbyn's emergence and of what might happen next, see Seymour's book *Corbyn: The Strange Rebirth of Radical Politics.*

14 Some of the material in this section is adapted from my entry "Crip," in the volume *Keywords for Radicals: The Contested Vocabulary of Late-Capitalist Struggle,* and is used here with permission.

15 I am directly adapting here Jeffrey Escoffier's and Allan Bérubé's consideration of the early 1990s activist work of *queer*: "Queer Nationals are torn between affirming a new identity—'I am queer'—and rejecting restrictive identities—'I reject your categories,' between rejecting assimilation—'I don't need your approval, just get out of my face'—and wanting to be recognized by mainstream society—'We queers are gonna get in your face'" (qtd. in Duggan, "Making It" 171). In certain times and places, a range of other words, including *disability* itself, or *gay*, have performed this double move (and will undoubtedly do so in the future). I am making a historical point about the work *crip* appears to be performing now in many locations, not an unsustainable point about its essential radicality.

16 The "supercrip" too, however, has been recently reconsidered. Sami Schalk argues that the supercrip always functions within "a narrative with specific mechanisms and types that can vary by genre and medium" (84). Schalk argues that it is especially important to pay attention to the complex (and nonunitary) appearances of the supercrip because of the figure's ubiquity in "genres of popular cultural representation . . . which tend to have very large audiences" (84).

17 Material associated with the "Cripping Development" conference was published as a special issue of the journal *Somatechnics* in 2016, edited by Kateřina Kolářová and M. Katharina Wiedlack. The desires for new geographies of disability that the 2010 and 2013 conferences spotlighted can of course be traced in many locations; in 2014, for example, the open access and multilingual journal *Disability and the Global South*, edited by Shaun Grech, began publication. In 2016, Grech and Karen Soldatic coedited the important volume *Disability in the Global South: The Critical Handbook.*

18 For other important disability studies critiques of this Puarian move *to* debility *from* disability, see Kay Inckle's "Debilitating Times: Compulsory Ablebodiedness and White Privilege in Theory and Practice," and Margrit Shildrick's "Living On; Not Getting Better." Shildrick is more sympathetic than Inckle to Puar's use of debility; her critique of Puar and debility, however, becomes significantly more pointed when she directly turns toward an analysis of austerity in the UK (17–20).

19 Swantje Köbsell explains that the

"Cripples' Groups" (Krüppelgruppen) . . . were founded from 1978 on by activists Horst Frehe and Franz Christoph [and] had a more political approach to disability [than groups in Germany which had preceded the Krüppelgruppen]. In 1977 the two of them had developed the "cripples' position" on disability. It comprised a perception of disability as the societal suppression of disabled people and the forced conformity to the values, ideals and aesthetics of non-disabled people as a form of cultural enslavement. The best way to develop a "cripples' consciousness" appeared not to be partnership, but opposition to the oppressors.

The Krüppelgruppen did not admit nondisabled participants. While sharing both a systemic critique of oppression and an insistence on the importance of a new consciousness (and of course, the potential that comes from reclaiming language used to demean or marginalize), the activists associated with *Crip Magazine* are both more actively intersectional and more actively anticapitalist than the Krüppelgruppen.

20 *La teoría tullida*, indeed a quite literal translation, appears to function best as a potential translation in Spain; comrades in other Spanish-speaking locations in Latin America, perhaps because *tullido/a* is somewhat archaic there, are less sure about its functionality (*atrofiado/a* [stunted] might be an alternative translation; some activists and theorists have played with the possibilities provided by *cojo* [lame]).

21 I am intentionally echoing here the subtitle to Petra Kuppers's important study *Disability Culture and Community Performance: Find a Strange and Twisted Shape.*

22 I am grateful to Dara Orenstein for a key conversation noting and fleshing out the crip times/New Times connections I discuss in this section.

23 Martin Jacques himself would later remember the ways in which he was living with chronic illness throughout the 1980s: "Basically, my life was lived in a state of permanent emergency. That was what I felt like. It was like camping. No money, working all the hours god sends. I got ill on several occasions. ME-type illness. The first time was '83, the second time was '85. The worst was '87. I was knocked out for a lot of '87" (qtd. in Harris). Although Jacques does not appear to have connected consciously the embodied state of emergency he was experiencing in the 1980s to the issues he and others were theorizing, the ways in which disability was nonetheless inescapably a component of the moment that produced *New Times* is notable. ME refers to myalgic encephalomyelitis and is more commonly termed chronic fatigue syndrome (CFS) in the United States.

24 I am thinking particularly of Alain Badiou's *The Communist Hypothesis*, where he asserts, "The world of global and arrogant capitalism in which we live is taking us back to the 1840s and the birth of capitalism" (66).

25 Although Theresa May appointed a new chancellor of the exchequer, Philip Hammond, and a new work and pensions secretary, Damian Green, her administration left in place the worst components of austerity and particularly those components that were most punitive toward disabled people. May's administration made clear that George Osborne's dream of a "surplus" budget might be untenable as the UK navigated Brexit, but none of the existing cuts were to be

reversed. Moreover, even without any new cuts, as May's government escalated restrictions on immigration, austerity was actually augmented in insidious ways. Immigrants to the UK, contrary to the popular myths about them that I discuss in the Epilogue, actually pay more toward public finances than they draw from them (Chu).

26 The word "scrounger" appeared in the British press a little more than 500 times at the start of the global economic crisis; by 2012, that number had risen to 3,500 (McCloskey). Stuart Hall did note, as early as 1979, the ways in which rhetorical disqualification of benefits recipients was operative for the Tories: "'Thatcherism' has found . . . in the image of the welfare 'scavenger' a well-designed folk devil" ("Great Moving" 17). One of my projects throughout *Crip Times* is thus to trace the contemporary amplification of an ableism that has in fact been structural to neoliberalism from its inception. I analyze Thatcher's own rhetoric in this regard most thoroughly in chapter 4. For a study of the ways in which benefits recipients have long been corporealized, racialized, and disqualified rhetorically in the United States, see Ange-Marie Hancock's *The Politics of Disgust: The Public Identity of the Welfare Queen.*

27 This repeated caveat is infused with what Ellen Samuels has theorized and historicized as "fantasies of identification." Samuels notes that "fantasies of identification are haunted by disability even when disabled bodies are not their immediate focus, for disability functions as the trope and embodiment of true physical difference" (*Fantasies* 3). For an earlier discussion of the capitalist need to identify disability (and anxiety about doing so), see Deborah A. Stone's *The Disabled State*; see also my discussion of Stone in "Disabling Sex."

28 Although specifically focused on the UK and austerity politics, my project here is fundamentally in accord with, and indebted to, Mitchell and Snyder's *The Biopolitics of Disability: Neoliberalism, Ablenationalism, and Peripheral Embodiment.*

29 The popular press piece by Jay Dolmage that I am citing here was published in the wake of global attention in 2015 to the award-winning performances of Julianne Moore in *Still Alice* and Eddie Redmayne in *The Theory of Everything*. Dolmage himself has approached *The King's Speech* somewhat differently in his scholarly study *Disability Rhetoric*, which engages an earlier, unpublished version of this section of my Introduction (225–287).

30 Mia Mingus skillfully affirms key disability concepts such as access, equality, and rights, even as she looks critically at the ways in which they have simultaneously circulated to foreclose certain crip possibilities ("Changing"). Work such as Mingus's should be understood as a condition of possibility for the disidentificatory double moves—working with and through rights, representation, and identity—I am attempting to make in this section.

31 I adapt these brief comments on Fiol-Matta's work from the opening paragraph of my essay "Queer America" (215).

32 The complex and ever-shifting valences of "identity" in relation to both *disability* and *crip* provide me with the main reason for deploying both as central analytics

throughout this study despite the fact that *debility*, as I have indicated, is at times an adequate descriptor for some of the embodied experiences I detail in the pages ahead. Puar's work on "debility," as I have intimated, often puts forward a unidirectional move away from "disability" that to my mind tames its complex political valences (in ways that Julie Livingston's work on "debility"—which sustains a necessary stretchiness due to thinking about languages adequate to the site-specificity of her work in Botswana—does not).

33 Marx's famous essay details the ways in which liberal rights are protected by the same bourgeois, capitalist state that structurally sustains economic inequality.

34 Disabled People Against Cuts was formed after the first wave of austerity cuts and massive protests in the UK in 2011. The Hardest Hit campaign was also formed that year and some have suggested that the May and October marches were the largest disability protests ever. Anticuts activism in general in the UK included the occupation of banks and other locations; queer activists symbolically used such occupations at times to construct makeshift services connected to health care and HIV/AIDS education. The Spartacus Report was largely the work of Sue Marsh, who had for some time composed a blog titled "Diary of a Benefit Scrounger." The report attempted to account for the suffering (and death) that resulted from the coalition government's reform of the welfare system, particularly reductions to the Disability Living Allowance. The Broken of Britain is officially a nonpartisan disability campaign in the UK, although the name, as I discuss briefly in chapter 2, directly and collectively rewrites David Cameron's use of such rhetoric.

CHAPTER 1. AN AUSTERITY OF REPRESENTATION; OR, CRIP/QUEER HORIZONS

1 In his classic study of subculture, Dick Hebdige provides a vocabulary for thinking about the representational foreclosures I am considering here. Hebdige argues that two forms of incorporation threaten to contain resistant subcultures: a commodity form that almost immediately converts subcultural signs into mass-produced (and hence, deadened) objects and an ideological form that dilutes their disruptive force through either (or both) demonization or trivialization, reducing what is different in resistant subcultures to recognizable sameness (92–99).

2 I engage more thoroughly with Muñoz's work in chapter 3. I am particularly indebted, throughout *Crip Times*, to Kateřina Kolářová's crip/queer reading of Muñoz and Lauren Berlant in "The Inarticulate Post-Socialist Crip: On the Cruel Optimism of Neoliberal Transformations in the Czech Republic." Kolářová argues that "the inarticulate crip allows us to revisit and complicate the past to forge different versions of desires for crip futures" (259). Kolářová's direct topic is not the golden age of silent film but rather the postsocialist era in eastern Europe. I would contend, however, that her inarticulate postsocialist crip, a figure who spotlights the crip/queer failure to navigate a compulsory

progress narrative (toward neoliberal capitalism in eastern Europe after 1989), has a range of affinities with Chaplin's little tramp, who is attempting, often in quite bumbling ways, to navigate an earlier transitional moment in the history of capitalism.

3 The material on Oscar Pistorius in this chapter has been significantly revised and expanded from my "Epilogue: Disability, Inc.," and is used here with permission.

4 For an important disability studies article critiquing the extremely sedimented common sense that thinness and health are indissociable, see Anna Mollow's "Disability Studies Gets Fat."

5 Although Hamilton's 1999 autobiography *Landing It: My Life On and Off the Ice* does acknowledge that gay friends who were also skaters helped him overcome discomfort with homosexuality, he writes that "homophobic" had in fact been "an accurate description of my feelings toward gay men" (192). "Frankly," he explains, attempting to account for his bad attitude, "I was sick of people constantly assuming I was gay because I was a figure skater. The fear of being labeled definitely played a role in my decision to radically alter my costumes in my last year of amateur skating" (191).

6 Willitts herself says that she did not knowingly coin "crippspiration," but may have done so. I have not been able to locate an earlier publication using the word.

7 For a good analysis of the events surrounding the removal of *A Fire in My Belly* from the National Portrait Gallery, see the opening to Jennifer Tyburczy's *Sex Museums: The Politics and Performance of Display* (xiii–xvii).

8 Since the imagery I have examined so far in this chapter was denounced by activists as inspiration "pornography," I am interested in alternative deployments of the term that are not used only to *denounce* but instead to *affirm* generative forms of relationality that might be termed pornography. My interest here, of course, does not (and cannot) negate the fact that "pornography" in general exists in a transnational context as big business and is thus always inescapably noninnocent. Reaching beyond the austerity of representation proffered by inspiration pornography, I am ultimately attempting in this chapter and the next to crip the ways in which Floyd theorizes "pornography," working with and against the term simultaneously.

9 A great deal of scholarship in lgbt studies underscores the ways in which activists in the early 1970s were putting forward complex and feminist intersectional critiques of systems of oppression and exploitation that demanded a narrow sameness or normality. John D'Emilio, for example, explains that the Gay Liberation Front

> began to construct a rudimentary analysis of *gay oppression*. It was not a matter of simple prejudice, misinformation, or outmoded beliefs. Rather, the oppression of homosexuals was woven into the fabric of sexism. Institutionalized heterosexuality reinforced a patriarchal nuclear family that socialized men and women into narrow roles and placed homosexuality beyond the pale. These gender dichotomies also reinforced other divisions based on race

and class, and thus allowed an imperial American capitalism to exploit the population and make war around the globe. (242, emphasis in the original) "Gay," as the 1970s continued, was increasingly understood as a term that basically represented only gay *men* (this limited understanding was especially codified by the single-issue activism of the Gay Activists Alliance). "Gay" was understood more expansively, however, when (during the period D'Emilio is considering here) the Gay Liberation Front initially emerged.

10 Hintnaus himself is in fact not gay, although there are certainly a number of openly gay models (such as Mark MacKillop) in the underwear industry today.

11 Again, as I noted in the Introduction, the final chapter of Duggan's *The Twilight of Equality?* likewise traces the taming of "identity" within neoliberalism, but also does so by recognizing its more radical deployments across the new social movements of the late twentieth and early twenty-first centuries (67–88). This taming, she makes clear, happens even on the Left, when forms of sociality and creativity (of the sort Floyd analyzes) are disciplined simply for their imbrication with "identity politics": "The most conservative/neoliberal forms of 'identity politics'—forms that in fact do not offer any political economic critique—are substituted for the radical critiques informing feminist queer, antiracist political creativity" (83). I hope it is again clear that the crip sociality I trace in this chapter (and book) works against, with, and at times through identity while eluding or attempting to elude the capitalist desire or need to still or fix our sociality and creativity.

12 Liz Crow's "Summer of 2012" provides an effective and affective narrative account of these Paralympic contradictions; the classic account of the dispossession of vibrant queer subcultures in and around Times Square is Samuel R. Delany's *Times Square Red, Times Square Blue.*

13 Activist and artistic work has of course arisen to counter this systemic violence. For almost a decade, largely through her acclaimed project "Faces and Phases" (which was published in book form in 2010), black South African photographer Zanele Muholi has particularly documented the lives of black lesbians and transmen in a series of beautiful portraits. Muholi's work directly counters the violence and indignity faced daily by black lesbians and transmen in South Africa.

14 In *Disidentifications: Queers of Color and the Performance of Politics*, Muñoz draws on the work of the French linguist Michel Pêcheuz to put forward a queer understanding of identification, counteridentification, and disidentification: "Instead of buckling under the pressures of dominant ideology (identification, assimilation) or attempting to break free of its inescapable sphere (counter-identification, utopianism), this 'working on and against' is a strategy that tries to transform a cultural logic from within, always laboring to enact permanent structural change while at the same time valuing the importance of local or everyday struggles of resistance" (11–12).

15 For another now-classic disability studies consideration of these issues connected to "invisibility" in relation to both disability *and* sexuality, see Ellen

Samuels's "My Body, My Closet: Invisible Disability and the Limits of Coming-Out Discourse."

16 Alyson Patsavas was extremely influential in helping me work through some of the issues in this paragraph and I am grateful to her for those conversations.

CHAPTER 2. CRIP RESISTANCE

1 Indeed, the cultural studies journal *QED: A Journal in GLBTQ Worldmaking* commenced publication in Fall 2013.

2 Ahmed is specifically addressing new materialisms that position feminist poststructuralism as "matter-phobic," as putting forward a naïve faith in words and thereby avoiding the materiality of things (34). Although the materialism of Erevelles's study is a more traditional Marxist materialism, her representation of poststructuralism at times mirrors what Ahmed terms the "caricature" of poststructuralism legible in some new materialist writing (34).

3 I hope that my description of *Crip Theory* applies equally (perhaps more) to *Crip Times*: "I attempt to put forward a cultural materialist perspective that combines poststructuralist techniques of close reading and literary analysis, or inquiries into how language works to shape and reshape a range of contested meanings, with a materialist commitment to locating (but not fixing) the production of those meanings—and the contradictory texts, identities, and cultures that convey them—within economic structures, processes, and relations. A cultural materialist perspective understands these economic processes as both constraining and enabling culture and social change without being fully or finally determinative" (210). In the context of *Crip Times*, it is worth pointing out that a stark opposition between seemingly individualist literary and cultural production or performance (that is read as immaterial or "ludic" [Erevelles 12]) and other engagements with disabled lives (that are positioned as more material and authentic) might itself be read as inadvertently complicit with a logic of austerity (although this is of course not Erevelles's intent). In most locations, for example, a logic of austerity in higher education has consistently targeted the arts and humanities for trimming, outright cuts, or a mandated reliance on part-time, contingent labor. During the writing of this book, at my own university the Program in Creative Writing and the Department of Music have been the units most devastated by austerity measures.

This explicit disciplinary opposition is less pronounced in Erevelles's study than it is in Don Kulick and Jens Rydström's *Loneliness and Its Opposite: Sex, Disability, and the Ethics of Engagement*, which dismissively gestures toward "professors of literature [and] focuses on representation" in disability studies (10). Kulick and Rydström's two-dimensional representation of crip theory, in particular, opposes it to work on "the actual lives" of disabled people and suggests that crip theory "might deflect or defer a focus on the kinds of serious injustices that many of them face in their day-to-day lives" (15, 17). *Crip Times*, I hope, provides significant evidence to the contrary. *Loneliness and Its Opposite* is a thick and fascinating anthropological study of disabled sexuality in Denmark and Sweden and is a vital contribution to the interdisciplinary field of disability studies. I question, however, the need for the *disciplinary hierarchy* Kulick and Rydström establish at the outset of their book, both because austerity in higher education already depends upon positioning fields associated with creativity and cultural production as essentially more frivolous and because it strikes me as a serious injustice to domesticate the multivalent ways in which the disabled imagination might be expressed.

4 In her brief discussion of the activist group Krips Occupy Wall Street (KOWS), Akemi Nishida points out that despite the fact that Occupy Wall Street had a wheelchair accessible entrance, "this does not mean that it [was] an accessible and safe space for all. The OWS [was] often too crowded to maneuver and over-whelming. Its lack of disability politics [made] some feel unsafe. Also its fast-pace organizing [was] inaccessible and unsustainable to many" (Taylor et al. 25).

5 In chapter 3, I consider some of the ways in which student activists in Mexico used the phrase "Yo Soy" [I Am] in similarly stretchy, nonunitary, collective ways.

6 In the early 1980s, the acronym ADAPT stood for American Disabled for Accessible Public Transport; the acronym shifted in 1990 to American Disabled for Attendant Programs Today (Fleischer and Zames 82). ADAPT's shape-shifting is not at all related to an affinity group in the AIDS Coalition to Unleash Power (ACT UP) that in 1989 used the acronym CHER at a demonstration outside City Hall in New York City. Activists at the action wore T-shirts with silk screens of the performer Cher, but the meaning of the acronym campily shifted over the course of the action, signifying everything from "Commie Homos Engaged in Revolution" to "Cathy Has Extra Rollers" (Crimp and Rolston 20). ADAPT and ACT UP are, however, both products of a moment of embodied activism in the U.S.; even without direct links between the two groups, it's worth noting their parallel, contemporaneous creativity.

7 I am very grateful to Cristián Iturriaga for our several important conversations about the student movement in Chile, as well as for his regular updates about activism and disability in Chile. Any errors of interpretation of the movement are of course my own.

8 The #yoelijoserhumano project, countering austerity mythologies with facts, is not unlike Liz Crow's "In Actual Fact" project in the UK. "In Actual Fact," or #InActualFact, streams numbers intended to counter the disinformation disseminated by the British establishment; for example, "Cuts to public services estimated to hit poorest tenth 13 times harder than richest tenth #InActualFact" (Crow, *In Actual*). Crow's work more generally is the subject of chapter 4.

9 Lennard Davis, in "Nude Venuses, Medusa's Body, and Phantom Limbs: Disability and Visuality," underscores the point about ableist erasures surrounding the Venus de Milo in art history, through an analysis of the work of Duffy. Rosemarie Garland-Thomas has also written about Duffy's performances (Davis 63; Garland-Thomson 36–37).

10 There Is No Alternative, or TINA, is an assertion and ideology that gained wide currency with the rise of Thatcherism in the UK; she used the phrase to justify neoliberal restructurings of state and economy. The phrase has been widely used since that time by defenders of neoliberal capitalism and of the global consensus around austerity.

11 I am certainly not arguing that it is at all easy to resist the ways in which marriage rights and the right to serve in the military have become hegemonic in the mainstream, liberal gay rights movement in the United States or globally. I am suggesting instead that the refusals of "recognition" in lgbt contexts often come with a principled and queer disidentification with the necessity of having one's identity recognized by the state. The demand for "state recognition" at times emanating from people with disabilities or impairments is not necessarily (or always) tied up in mere identity validation and is thus a different kind of ongoing demand that is difficult to wholly reject.

CHAPTER 3. INHABITABLE SPACES

1 An earlier version of this chapter appeared as "Curb Cuts: Crip Displacements and El Edificio de Enfrente," in the special *Cripping Development* issue of *Somatechnics* edited by Kateřina Kolářová and M. Katharina Wiedlack. It has been substantially revised and expanded and is used here with permission.

2 Crossbench peers are officially independent members of the House of Lords in the British Parliament. They speak and vote neither as members of the governing party nor as members of one of the opposition parties.

3 My language here is indebted to a few key conversations with Peter Campbell; I am grateful for the ways in which he helped me clarify my project in this chapter. The chapter has also benefited greatly from regular updates and key sources sent to me by Lucy Burke.

4 This quotation gestures to the fact that the president of Mexico at the time of Clegg's speech to the Senate was Felipe de Jesús Calderón Hinojosa. I will, however, ultimately have more to say in this chapter about Calderón's successor, Enrique Peña Nieto, who assumed office the following year and who was president during the Year of Mexico in the UK and the UK in Mexico. A transcript of Clegg's speech is available in Spanish and English ("New Politics"); I have left diacritical marks off all the letters except the ñ because the UK transcript does not include the marks on other letters. The translation from Spanish to English is Clegg's or a UK official's; all other Spanish translations in this chapter are my own. Clegg speaks seven languages, although Spanish is arguably the most important to him personally: he has been married to a Spanish lawyer, Miriam González Durántez, since 2000; they have three children (Antonio, Alberto, and Miguel) who speak Spanish at home. Mexico was not the only location where Clegg was deployed to speak in Spanish about the coalition government's policies; he appeared on Spanish television in 2010, responding to an interviewer's questions about "recortes" [cuts] by insisting

that *both* the UK and Spain had to address budget crises and attend to debts that must be paid ("Nick Clegg").

5 Biographical information on Livia Radwanski comes both from the artist's website (www.liviaradwanski.com) and from my email correspondence and direct conversations with her in person.

6 My stronger but defensible claim here is that salvage-Marxism is actually contingent on projects such as queer theory, queer of color critique, or crip theory, even as many such projects remain more eclectic, eccentric, and compromised than most traditional Marxist projects would ever allow. A page before arguing "We seek to build a salvage-Marxism. From what we have inherited we keep what we can and reject what we must" ("Perspectives" 4), the editors of the inaugural issue of *Salvage* write that "It is now common, and welcome, to see theories queered, gendered, decolonized, and *Salvage* is committed to such renovation, to learning from those traditionally in the peripheral vision of most of the organised Left" (3). My claim here, reading *Cruising Utopia* and tracing in it a mode of argumentation that would appear six years later in *Salvage*, is not the additive one arguably (if perhaps unintentionally) implied by a salvage-Marxism "learning from" certain formerly peripheral projects; my claim, rather, is that a vibrant (or ironically vibrant) salvage-Marxism must depend upon such projects.

7 Literal travel, incidentally, between the two locations is quite expensive; a direct British Airways flight from London to Mexico City is roughly £750. This is out of reach for the vast majority of Britons; one in five families in the UK (which is, of course, an island nation where access to the ocean should not be difficult) cannot currently afford even a day at the seaside (Smithers).

8 I want to thank Matthew McQuillan for inviting me to this event and for updates on housing activism in London in general.

9 Some of the material in this section is drawn and adapted from my "Epilogue: #YoSoy" and is used here with permission.

10 I discussed the Chilean student movement, particularly considering some of the ways that disability is legible in and around the movement from 2011 to the present, in chapter 2. In 2013, across Brazil, as massive stadiums across the country were being constructed for the 2014 World Cup, protestors took to the streets and demanded, beneath the banner (and hashtag) of #OGiganteAcordou [the giant has awoken], that the state not simply cater to the whims of transnational capital as it prepared for both the World Cup and 2016 Olympic Games, but rather take into account the needs (and intercorporeality) of all its citizens. Brazilians were protesting the fact that total expenditures preparing for the upcoming games could top $3 billion dollars and that such expenditures would benefit only the few while millions of others faced inadequate care and support and lacked basic social services. When the football star Ronaldo Luís Nazário de Lima—popularly known as "il Fenômeno"—crassly suggested that "you host a World Cup with stadiums, not hospitals," one father of a child with disabilities posted his own retort on YouTube, saying that his daughter did not walk, see, or

speak and that it was for citizens such as her that protestors were taking to the streets ("Em video").

11 Nirmala Erevelles has also pointed out that "disability becomes a commodity that has both use value as well as exchange value—both of which are appropriated for profit in transnational markets" (21). My argument is in accord with hers, even as I intend here to make a more specific point about the ways in which commodity fetishism works in relation to what I'm terming neoliberal accessibility.

12 Clegg himself had become a vocal critic of Peña Nieto's record on human rights, but the Mexican president's reception by British dignitaries in 2015 was all about affirming the "natural partnership" the Queen named; yet again, small fractures in the coalition government's general consensus did nothing to disrupt the larger, transnational economic agenda it continued to advance ("UK Deputy").

13 Peña Nieto's reputation continued to deteriorate globally over the course of his administration, most notably following the events of September 26, 2014, when forty-three students studying at the radical Ayotzinapa rural teacher's college were disappeared and presumably murdered. The disappearance and presumed mass murder generated angry protests across the country; these protests continued for months and escalated as evidence of government corruption and cover-up connected to the investigation into the disappearance came to light. Radwanski traveled to Ayotzinapa and photographed everyday life there following the events of September 2014; although an analysis of this photographic project would require an autonomous chapter or article, I want to note its importance here, particularly as it is another project connected to an essentially state-sanctioned failure to recognize and identify the victims (Radwanski, "Ayotzinapa"). The number forty-three has been ubiquitous since 2014; hashtags that have circulated globally in relation to the incidents in Ayotzinapa include #TodosSomosAyotzinapa [we are all Ayotzinapa] and #LosQueremosVivos [we want them alive]. For a good analysis of Ayotzinapa that ultimately ties the incidents to a "rapidly deteriorating" economy and even to the imposition of "harsh austerity measures," see Camilo Ruiz Tassinari's "After Ayotzinapa." In January 2017, massive protests against new government-opposed austerity measures (a 20 percent increase on gasoline protests) broke out across the country; these protests quickly became known as the "gasolinazo" protests.

14 I draw my subtitle here—"The Then and There of Crip Futurity"—from my review of the same name of Alison Kafer's *Feminist, Queer, Crip*.

15 I am extremely grateful to Anastasia Kayiatos, who initiated a conversation with me about the *Trainspotting* T-shirt at my first public presentation of the material in this chapter.

16 My thanks to Ramzi Fawaz for his observation about Spiderman and toxicity in this photograph.

17 For an indispensable discussion, in a US context, of how environmental illness (EI) compelled a search for nontoxic space, and of how that personal experience

is a deeply political one that merits much more attention in disability studies and activism, see Anna Mollow's "No Safe Place."

18 I discuss Alaimo's notion of "trans-corporeality" more at length, alongside this particular Fuentes quotation and some reflections on gay tourism in Mexico City, in my essay "Pink."

CHAPTER 4. CRIP FIGURES

1 I pull the term "rejected body" from Susan Wendell's important study *The Rejected Body: Feminist Philosophical Reflections on Disability*. Wendell writes, "I use the terms 'rejected body' and 'negative body' to refer to those aspects of bodily life (such as illness, disability, weakness, and dying), bodily appearance (usually deviations from the cultural ideals of the body), and bodily experience (including most forms of bodily suffering) that are feared, ignored, despised, and/or rejected in a society and its culture" (85).

2 In "Introduction: Cripistemologies and the Masturbating Girl," Merri Lisa Johnson and I attempt to demonstrate the ways in which deceivingly simplistic phrases such as Ronald Reagan's famous "It's morning again in America" (from a 1984 campaign ad) and Thatcher's "There is no alternative" (commonly abbreviated as TINA) collude in the oppression of disabled people (249–250).

3 For a beautiful disability studies consideration of how tallness does indeed continue to function differently for women, and disabled women in particular, see Georgina Kleege's "On Being Who I Am: My Life as a Tall Blind Woman."

4 The story of schizophrenia's reinvention as dangerous and in need of surveillance, detainment, and incarceration in the 1960s and 1970s (at the precise moment that deinstitutionalization was becoming a common sense of sorts in relation to other disabilities) is detailed in Jonathan M. Metzl's study *The Protest Psychosis: How Schizophrenia Became a Black Disease*. In a different context (critiquing postmodern theory), Catherine Prendergast has written about the ways in which the schizophrenic congealed in the period as "easy to recognize and therefore incarcerate, or celebrate, as the occasion demands" (55).

5 I am drawing on Eve Kosofsky Sedgwick's queer distinction between minoritizing and universalizing approaches in my conclusions here (1–15; cf. Mollow and McRuer 22–25). Sedgwick's argument that *both* minoritizing and universalizing approaches are contingent and thus available for a range of progressive or reactionary uses positions her deployment of "universalizing" apart from bourgeois *universalist* assertions that are removed from the contingencies of history and (thus) supposedly applicable to all. Ending this section with Labour's necessary attention to stigmatizing language (which, of course, they might as easily police in their own party as in the Tories') should underscore the distinctions between my argument, emphasizing the necessary, structural ableism upon which neoliberalism relies, and a more recognizable disability argument that would or could spotlight the compromised language of any politician. Socialists, of course, also put forward unfortunate disability metaphors but socialism is not founded upon

the same, insidious and indispensable, structural ableism. I am grateful to Anna Mollow for conversations about this important distinction.

6 A year after Crow's performance, in 2016 Bristol elected the UK's first black mayor (and indeed, the first black mayor of any city in the whole of Europe), Marvin Rees. Rees himself underscored the diversity of the city following the European Union referendum that resulted in Brexit (in which the city of Bristol decidedly voted "Remain") by tweeting, "Over 90 languages spoken. Over 120 countries of origin amongst residents. We remain welcoming and inclusive."

7 My thanks to Lennard Davis for initially suggesting the Gormley connection to me. In 2009 Crow worked directly with Gormley in connection with her project *Resistance*, described briefly below.

8 I am indebted to generative conversations with Jeffrey J. Cohen for the material in this paragraph and the next.

9 Indeed, as of this writing, more than 200,000 Spanish workers are living in the UK. The Tory foreign secretary, Philip Hammond, however, had indicated that Brexit could require a quota system in the future; the situation of Spanish workers in the UK is thus now even more precarious than it was in 2015 (Benevento).

10 The Collins parallel has in fact been noted by other commentators on British austerity in general; see, for example, Andrew Learmonth, "The Hunger Games: Austerity Is Leaving Pupils So Hungry They Steal from Classmates."

11 My intent here is not to make income inequality in the UK somehow more shocking or surprising simply by placing it alongside income inequality in Nigeria or Ethiopia; my intent, rather, is to historicize income inequality. Put differently, austerity in locations like Nigeria and Ethopia (supported by the UK and other creditors) has sedimented, over the past several decades, income inequality there. With an austerity politics (and its concomitant failures) now firmly rooted in the UK and other locations, it is in fact not surprising to see levels of income inequality equal to locations where those failed policies have long been in place.

12 This paragraph is indebted to key conversations with Anna Mollow and Holly Dugan, both of whom noted the importance of linking *aspiration* with breathing.

EPILOGUE

1 I have of course discussed cuts throughout *Crip Times*; I address the bedroom tax specifically in chapter 3 and benefits sanctions in chapter 4. The removal of council tax benefits refers to a 2013 shift away from a *national* benefit for local councils, aimed at helping people with low incomes or on benefits. Under the new system, local councils were charged with finding the money for this benefit themselves.

2 Eastern European immigrants to the UK, including the large number of Polish immigrants living there, are officially "white" but are nonetheless targets of the racialized disqualification I am citing here. Interestingly, the UK census since 2011 has deployed the liminal category "other white" to comprehend all those who are not white British or white Irish.

3 Yearning as a theoretical concept has traveled across the previous two chapters; I am using it directly here in the sense that Eli Clare uses it in his "Yearning toward Carrie Buck," an essay that traces the classed, raced, gendered, and disabled historical injustices in circulation around Carrie Buck, who was (in a case upheld by the US Supreme Court) forcibly sterilized after being deemed "feeble-minded." Forging connections across time and space, Clare imagines a coalition of the many groups caught up in similar modes of oppression in the United States: "They won't be asking for apologies nor giving absolution, but rather holding remembrance, demanding reparation, planning revolution" (343).

4 A tabloid piece by Helen Barnett in the *Express* was among the news stories reporting that the letter writer was gay. The piece also asserts that the "latest figures from Public Health England show the proportion of men who have sex with other men (both gay and bisexual) who were born abroad has increased from 28 per cent in 2004 to 40 per cent in 2013." It is as though the simple acceptance without commentary of the British writer's identity as gay (and his implicit incorporation as such into the UKIP chorus) is authorizing the residual homophobic (and here xenophobic) sentiment that the act of male homosexual sex itself, or the identity gay or bisexual, are inherent risk factors in the transmission of HIV. Jan Zita Grover's classic essay "AIDS: Keywords" painstakingly excavates the ways in which the language still saturating this 2015 incident (bisexual, general population, spread, and perhaps most notably, victim) was dominant in the 1980s. "Victim" was not a neutral word for Grover, as she demonstrated clearly that "AIDS victims" were generally seen as not simply unlucky or unfortunate, but rather as somehow responsible for their condition. The term *victim*, however, was bifurcated for Grover: "The proof that *victim* is not simply a term applied to the unlucky, to those undeserving and noncomplicit with their fate, is the frequently employed phrase 'innocent victim,' which is *not* seen as redundant" (29). I contend here and in what follows that the HIV positive Londoner, with the help of UKIP, is essentially writing himself into the category of "innocent victim." This suggests a decided shift: although the stigmatizing rhetoric of the 1980s appears to be thriving in this incident, a figure who would have always and only been on the receiving end of that rhetoric is here recruited (*as* gay, mixed-race, and disabled/HIV positive) to redirect it at others. Such a neoliberal cripqueer incorporation would have been unthinkable when Grover wrote her piece.

5 As I explained in the opening to *Crip Times*, Jeremy Corbyn's victory in the September 2015 election for Labour leader, a development that postdates the Scottish shift away from New Labour and to the antiausterity SNP, marks an unexpected fracture in the Tory–New Labour consensus around the class strategy of austerity. Corbyn remains opposition leader at the time of this writing; his platform is akin to the "simple, civilised position" of the SNP that Seymour summarized so effectively immediately following the 2015 general election. As *Crip Times* goes to press, the establishment's attacks on Corbyn in the corporate media remain as unrelenting as his popularity remains high. Corbyn is attempting to sustain a strategy grounded in grassroots activism.

WORKS CITED

"18 de Septiembre, represión y una huelgista detenida: Nada que celebrar!" notascect .wordpress.com. Accessed 24 October 2015.

"2015: El año del Reino Unido en México y del Reino Unido en México." 20 November 2013. www.gov.uk. Accessed 12 December 2015.

"Accessible London: Achieving an Inclusive Environment." Greater London Authority 22 July 2011. www.london.gov.uk. Accessed 9 December 2012.

Ahmed, Sara. "Open Forum Imaginary Prohibitions: Some Preliminary Remarks on the Founding Gestures of the 'New Materalism.'" *European Journal of Women's Studies* 15.1 (2008): 23–39.

Alaimo, Stacy. *Bodily Natures: Science, Environment, and the Material Self.* Bloomington: Indiana University Press, 2010.

Álvarez, Klaudia, Pablo Gallego, Fabio Gándara, and Óscar Rivas. *Nosotros, los indignados: Las voces comprometidas del #15-M.* Madrid: Lectulandia, 2011.

Anonymous. "HIV System Overrun—A Patient's View." d3n8a8pro7vhmx.cloudfront .net. Accessed 20 November 2015.

Arenas Conejo, Míriam, and Asun Pié Balaguer. "Las comisiones de diversidad funcional en el 15M español: Poner el cuerpo en el espacio público." *Política y Sociedad* 51.1 (2014): 227–245.

"Artist Liz Crow's Austerity Mud Figures Ground Up." *BBC News* 2 June 2015. www .bbc.com. Accessed 28 January 2016.

Badiou, Alain. *The Communist Hypothesis.* Trans. David Macey and Steve Corcoran. London: Verso, 2010.

———. "On a Finally Objectless Subject." *Who Comes after the Subject?* Ed. Eduardo Cadava, Peter Connor, and Jean-Luc Nancy, 24–32. Trans. Bruce Fink. New York: Routledge, 1991.

———. *The Rebirth of History.* 2011. Trans. Gregory Elliott. London: Verso, 2012.

Barnett, Helen. "Farage Right on 'HIV Immigrants' Says HIV Positive Brit with Just 14 Days Meds Left." *Daily Express* 30 April 2015. www.express.co.uk. Accessed 20 November 2015.

Barthes, Roland. *The Pleasure of the Text.* 1973. Trans. Richard Miller. New York: Hill and Wang, 1975.

Baynton, Douglas C. "Disability and the Justification of Inequality in American History." *The New Disability History: American Perspectives*, 33–57. Ed. Paul K. Longmore and Lauri Umansky. New York: NYU Press, 2001.

Bearak, Max. "Theresa May Criticized the Term 'Citizen of the World.' But Half the World Identifies That Way." *Washington Post* 5 October 2016. www.washingtonpost .com. Accessed 21 December 2016.

Benedicto, Bobby. *Under Bright Lights: Gay Manila and the Global Scene*. Minneapolis: University of Minnesota Press, 2014.

Benefits Britain: Life on the Dole. Channel 5 Broadcasting Ltd., 2014–2015.

Benefits Street. Channel 4 Broadcasting. Love Productions, 2014.

Benevento, Gina. "Brexit and the View from Spain." *Aljazeera* 27 June 2016. www .aljazeera.com. Accessed 9 July 2016.

Ben-Moshe, Liat, Chris Chapman, and Allison C. Carey, eds. *Disability Incarcerated: Imprisonment and Disability in the United States and Canada*, 273–279. New York: Palgrave, 2014.

Bennett, Jane. *Vibrant Matter: A Political Ecology of Things*. Durham: Duke University Press, 2010.

Benton, Sarah. "The Decline of the Party." Hall and Jacques, eds. 333–346.

Berehulak, Daniel. "Las mujeres de Atenco." *New York Times (es.)* 22 September 2016. www.nytimes.com. Accessed 18 December 2016.

Berlant, Lauren. *Cruel Optimism*. Durham: Duke University Press, 2011.

Berlant, Lauren, and Michael Warner. "Sex in Public." *Critical Inquiry* 24.2 (Winter 1998): 547–566.

Besana, Bruno. "The Subject." *Alain Badiou: Key Concepts*, 38–47. Ed. A. J. Bartlett and Justin Clemens. Durham, UK: Acumen Publishing, 2010.

Best, Richard. "Better Retirement Housing Would Be More Effective Than a 'Bedroom Tax.'" *Guardian* 21 November 2012. www.theguardian.com. Accessed 1 December 2015.

Blyth, Mark. *Austerity: The History of a Dangerous Idea*. Oxford: Oxford University Press, 2013.

Bogdan, Robert. *Freak Show: Presenting Human Oddities for Amusement and Profit*. Chicago: University of Chicago Press, 1988.

Bose, Shumi. "Meet the Architect Who Wants to Return Mexico City to Its Ancient Lakes." *Guardian* 13 November 2015. www.theguardian.com. Accessed 13 December 2015.

Boxer, Andrew. "The Establishment of the Post-War Consensus, 1945–64." *History Review* 66 (March 2010): 38–43.

Boyle, Danny, dir. *Trainspotting*. London: Channel Four Films, 1996.

Braziel, Jana Evans, and Kathleen LeBesco, eds. *Bodies Out of Bounds: Fatness and Transgression*. Berkeley: University of California Press, 2001.

Brown, Carl. "Peer Defends 'Bedroom Tax' Term." *Inside Housing* 6 March 2013. www .insidehousing.co.uk. Accessed 1 December 2015.

Brown, Oliver. "Oscar Pistorius Says the World Will Be Amazed by the London Paralympic Games." *Telegraph* 29 August 2012. www.telegraph.co.uk. Accessed 14 October 2015.

Brunt, Rosalind. "The Politics of Identity." Hall and Jacques, eds. 150–159.

Butler, Judith. *Bodies That Matter: On the Discursive Limits of "Sex."* New York: Routledge, 1993.

———. *Notes toward a Performative Theory of Assembly.* Cambridge: Harvard University Press, 2015.

Butler, Judith, and Athena Athanasiou. *Dispossession: The Performative in the Political.* Cambridge: Polity, 2013.

Butler, Patrick. "Bedroom Tax: One in Seven Households 'Face Eviction.'" *Guardian* 11 February 2014. www.theguardian.com. Accessed 6 December 2015.

Cameron, David. Queen's Speech 2015: Full Text. *New Statesman* 27 May 2015. www .newstatesman.com. Accessed 27 January 2016.

Cameron, David, and Mariano Rajoy. "Jobs and Growth in Europe." 4 September 2015. www.gov.uk. Accessed 25 January 2016.

Campbell, Beatrix. "New Times Towns." Hall and Jacques, eds. 279–299.

Campbell, Fiona Kumari. *Contours of Ableism: The Production of Disabilty and Abledness.* New York: Palgrave, 2009.

Canaday, Margot. *The Straight State: Sexuality and Citizenship in Twentieth-Century America.* Princeton: Princeton University Press, 2009.

Carney, Steve. "National Public Radio to Cut Shows, Personnel." *Los Angeles Times* 10 December 2008. latimesblogs.latimes.com. Accessed 13 September 2015.

Carrell, Severin. "Scotland Will Give £20m to Mitigate Effects of Bedroom Tax." *Guardian* 11 September 2013. www.theguardian.com. Accessed 7 December 2015.

Catanzaro, Michele. "Spanish Physicist Brings Radical Politics to Brussels." *Nature: International Weekly Journal of Science* 12 June 2014. www.nature.com. Accessed 19 August 2016.

"Cena de Estado en honor del Presidente Peña Nieto, ofrece S.M. la Reina Isabel II." Gobierno de la República Mexicana. 3 March 2015. www.youtube.com /watch?v=oaYN_-flP2A. Accessed 12 December 2015.

Chalmers, Robert. "Inside the Mind of Nigel Farage: 'I Want to Be Minister for Europe.'" *Newsweek* 9 October 2014. www.newsweek.com. Accessed 18 November 2015.

Chasin, Alexandra. *Selling Out: The Gay and Lesbian Movement Goes to Market.* New York: St. Martin's, 2000.

Chen, Mel Y. *Animacies: Biopolitics, Racial Mattering, and Queer Affect.* Durham: Duke University Press, 2012.

Child, Ben. "Meryl Streep Praises Margaret Thatcher as 'Figure of Awe.'" *Guardian* 9 April 2013. www.theguardian.com. Accessed 21 January 2016.

Chrisman, Wendy L. "A Reflection on Inspiration: A Recuperative Call for Emotion in Disability Studies." *Journal of Literary and Cultural Disability Studies* 5.2 (2011): 173–184.

Chu, Ben. "Damian Green Says There Won't Be Any More Austerity Cuts under Theresa May—But He's Going to Sneak Them In Anyway." *Independent* 20 September 2016. www.independent.co.uk. Accessed 14 November 2016.

Cinquemani, Sal. "Portishead." *Slant* 11 September 2007. www.slantmagazine.com. Accessed 28 January 2016.

"Ciudades para tod@s: Embajada Británica y Nuestras Realidades A.C. promueven ciudades más accesibles." 26 March 2013. www.gov.uk. Accessed 7 December 2015.

Clare, Eli. *Exile and Pride: Disability, Queerness, and Liberation.* Cambridge: South End Press, 1999.

———. "Yearning toward Carrie Buck." *Journal of Literary and Cultural Disability Studies* 8.3 (2014): 335–344.

COHA (Council on Hemispheric Affairs). "Business as Usual? The United Kingdom's Relationship with Latin America in 2011." 11 November 2011. www.coha.org. Accessed 29 July 2016.

Cohen, Jeffrey Jerome. "Stories of Stone." *Postmedieval: A Journal of Medieval Cultural Studies* 1.1–2 (2010): 56–63.

Collins, Suzanne. *The Hunger Games, Book 1.* 2008. Reprint ed. New York: Scholastic Press, 2010.

Conway-Smith, Erin. "Judge Who Found Oscar Pistorius Not Guilty of Murder under Police Protection." *Telegraph* 16 September 2014. www.telegraph.co.uk. Accessed 17 September 2016.

Coogan, Tom. "The 'Hunchback' across Cultures and Times." *Changing Social Attitudes toward Disability: Perspectives from Historical, Cultural and Educational Studies,* 71–79. Ed. David Bolt. Abingdon, UK: Routledge, 2014.

Crimp, Douglas. *Melancholia and Moralism: Essays on AIDS and Queer Politics.* Cambridge: MIT Press, 2004.

Crimp, Douglas, and Adam Rolston. *AIDS DemoGraphics.* Seattle: Bay Press, 1990.

cripteori. lambda nordica 17.1–2 (2012).

Crow, Liz. *Figures.* Mass-sculptural durational performance. 2015. wearefigures.co.uk. Accessed 28 January 2016.

———. *In Actual Fact.* inactualfact.org.uk. Accessed 25 October 2015.

———. *Resistance.* Filmed drama and documentary and live durational performance. 2008/2009. www.roaring-girl.com. Accessed 21 October 2016.

———. "Resistance Conversations: Behind the Scenes." www.roaring-girl.com. Accessed 28 January 2016.

———. "Summer of 2012: Paralympic Legacy and the Welfare Benefit Scandal." *Review of Disability Studies: An International Journal* 10.3–4 (2014): 62–76.

Crow, Liz, et al. "Comments in Witney." Instagram. www.instagram.com. Accessed 27 January 2016.

———. "Meeting Brigitte in Witney Was an Emotional Experience." Instagram. www.instagram.com. Accessed 27 January 2016.

CUIDO (Communities United in Defense of Olmstead). cuido-arnieville.blogspot.com. Accessed 23 October 2015.

Davis, Lennard, ed. *The Disability Studies Reader.* 3rd ed. New York: Routledge, 1997.

———. *Enforcing Normalcy: Disability, Deafness, and the Body.* London: Verso, 1995.

———. "Nude Venuses, Medusa's Body, and Phanton Limbs: Disability and Visuality." *The Body and Physical Difference: Discourses of Disability*, 51–70. Ed. David T. Mitchell and Sharon L. Snyder. Ann Arbor: University of Michigan Press, 1997.

de Certeau, Michel. *The Practice of Everday Life*. Trans. Steven Rendall. Berkeley: University of California Press, 1984.

Delany, Samuel R. *Times Square Red, Times Square Blue*. New York: NYU Press, 1999.

Deutsche, Rosalyn. *Evictions: Art and Spatial Politics*. Cambridge: MIT Press, 1996.

D'Emilio, John. *Making Trouble: Essays on Gay History, Politics, and the University*. New York: Routledge, 1992.

Disability Bitch. "Disability Bitch Isn't Angry at Colin Firth." *BBC—Ouch!* 13 January 2011. www.bbc.co.uk. Accessed 24 September 2015.

Disabled People Against Cuts (DPAC). "About DPAC." campaigndpac.wordpress.com. Accessed 1 October 2015.

Dolmage, Jay. *Disability Rhetoric*. Syracuse: Syracuse University Press, 2014.

———. "Hollywood Mustn't Shut Out Disabled." *Waterloo Region Record* 13 March 2015. www.therecord.com. Accessed 18 February 2017.

Dorset Orthopaedic. "Company Overview." www.dorset-ortho.com. Accessed 14 October 2015.

———. "Ellie-May Challis Features in Little Hero's Photo Shoot!" www.dorset-ortho.com. Accessed 14 October 2015.

Douzinas, Costas. "*Adikia*: On Communism and Rights." *The Idea of Communism*, 81–100. Ed. Costas Douzinas and Slavoj Žižek. London: Verso, 2010.

Doward, Jamie. "Disabled People in Britain Face a Hidden Housing Crisis, Charity Warns." *Guardian* 26 July 2014. www.theguardian.com. Accesssed 9 December 2015.

"Dual Year." Mexico-United Kingdom 2015. mexicouk2015.mx. Accessed 1 December 2015.

Duggan, Lisa. "Making It Perfectly Queer." *Sex Wars: Sexual Dissent and Political Culture* by Lisa Duggan and Nan D. Hunter, 155–172. New York: Routledge, 1995.

———. "The New Homonormativity: The Sexual Politics of Neoliberalism." *Materializing Democracy: Toward a Revitalized Cultural Politics*, 175–194. Ed. Russ Castronovo and Dana D. Nelson. Durham: Duke University Press, 2002.

———. *The Twilight of Equality? Neoliberalism, Cultural Politics, and the Attack on Democracy*. Boston: Beacon Press, 2003.

Duggan, Lisa, and José Esteban Muñoz. "Hope and Hopelessness: A Dialogue." *Women and Performance: A Journal of Feminist Theory* 19.2 (2009): 275–283.

Durington, Matthew. "Pistorius and South Africa's Culture of Fear." *Baltimore Sun* 22 February 2013. www.baltimoresun.com. Accessed 19 October 2015.

Edelman, Lee. *No Future: Queer Theory and the Death Drive*. Durham: Duke University Press, 2004.

Edmunds, Donna Rachel. "HIV Positive Londoner Unable to Access Care Gives Human Face to Cost of Health Tourism." *Breitbart* 1 May 2015. www.breitbart.com. Accessed 20 November 2015.

Elman, Julie Passanante. *Chronic Youth: Disability, Sexuality, and U.S.Media Cultures of Rehabilitation*. New York: NYU Press, 2014.

Elman, Julie Passanante, and Robert McRuer. "The Gifts of Mobility: Disability Exceptionalism, Queerness and Rehabilitation in the Emergent Global Order." Unpublished manuscript.

"Empecemos a temblar: Rajoy anuncia nuevo paquetes de 'reformas estructurales.'" *El Plural* 14 April 2013. www.elplural.com. Accessed 25 January 2016.

"Em video, pai dá resposta comovente à polêmica declaração de Ronaldo 'Fenômeno.'" *Hoje em Dia* 6 June 2013. www.hojeemdia.com.br. Accessed 12 December 2015.

"Entregan PND en Los Pinos." *Vanguardia* 2 December 2012. www.vanguardia.com.mx. Accessed 12 December 2015.

Erevelles, Nirmala. *Disability and Difference in Global Contexts: Enabling a Transformative Body Politic.* New York: Palgrave, 2011.

Evans, Natalie. "Oscar Pistorius's Girlfriend Condemned Violence against Women Days before She Was Shot Dead." *Mirror* (South Africa) 14 February 2013. www.mirror.co.uk. Accessed 7 December 2016.

Fearn, Hannah. "HIV-Positive Man Slams Nigel Farage for 'Deeply Offensive' Remarks." *Independent* 3 April 2015. www.independent.co.uk. Accessed 22 November 2015.

Feeney, David. "Labour Must Return to 'Aspirational Blair Years,' Say Senior Party Figures." *Guardian* 9 May 2015. www.theguardian.com. Accessed 22 January 2016.

Ferguson, John. "Atos Scandal: Benefits Bosses Admit Over Half of People Ruled Fit to Work Ended Up Destitute." *Daily Record and Sunday Mail* 26 September 2012. www.dailyrecord.co.uk. Accessed 15 October 2015.

Ferguson, Roderick A. *Aberrations in Black: Toward a Queer of Color Critique.* Minneapolis: University of Minnesota Press, 2004.

———. *The Reorder of Things: The University and Its Pedagogy of Minority Difference.* Minneapolis: University of Minnesota Press, 2012.

Fernández-Rivas, Aranzazu, and Miguel Angel González-Torres. "The Economic Crisis in Spain and Its Impact on the Mental Health of Children and Adolescents." *European Child and Adolescent Psychiatry (ECAP)* 22 (September 2013): 583–586.

Finger, Anne. "Antonio Gramsci's South . . . or . . . Some Aspects of the Disability Question." *New Politics* 14.1 (Summer 2012). newpol.org. Accessed 19 September 2015.

Fiol-Matta, Licia. *A Queer Mother for the Nation: The State and Gabriela Mistral.* Minneapolis: University of Minnesota Press, 2009.

Fleischer, Doris Zames, and Frieda Zames. *The Disability Rights Movement: From Charity to Confrontation.* Philadelphia: Temple University Press, 2001.

Floyd, Kevin. *The Reification of Desire: Toward a Queer Marxism.* Minneapolis: University of Minnesota Press, 2009.

Foster, Dawn. "Theresa May Is No Breath of Fresh Air on Poverty." *Guardian* 19 July 2016. www.theguardian.com. Accessed 10 September 2016.

Foucault, Michel. *The History of Sexuality, Volume 1: An Introduction.* 1976. Trans. Robert Hurley. New York: Vintage-Random House, 1978.

———. "On the Genealogy of Ethics: An Overview of Work in Progress." 1983. *Michel Foucault: Ethics: Subjectivity and Truth*, 253–280. Ed. Paul Rabinow. New York: New Press, 1994.

Fritsch, Kelly. "The Neoliberal Circulation of Affects: Happiness, Accessibility and the Capacitation of Disability as Wheelchair." *Health, Culture and Society* 5.1 (2013): 1–17.

Fuentes, Carlos. *Christopher Unborn*. Trans. Alfred MacAdam and Carlos Fuentes. Champaign, Ill. Dalkey Archive, 2005.

Gadd, Sophie. "HIV Positive Immigrant Convinces Ukip Supporters NOT to Vote for Nigel Farage." *Mirror* 5 May 2015. www.mirror.co.uk. Accessed 22 November 2015.

Galeano, Eduardo. *Las venas abiertas de América Latina*. 1971. 2nd ed. Madrid: Siglo, 2003.

Garland-Thomson, Rosemarie. "Dares to Stares: Disabled Women Performance Artists and the Dynamics of Staring." *Bodies in Commotion: Disability and Performance*, 30–41. Ed. Carrie Sandahl and Philip Auslander. Ann Arbor: University of Michigan Press, 2005.

Gentleman, Amelia. "Vulnerable Man Starved to Death after Benefits Were Cut." *Guardian* 28 February 2014. www.theguardian.com. Accessed 28 January 2016.

Gibson, Owen. "London 2012 Olympics Will Cost a Total of £8.921bn, Says Minister." *Guardian* 23 October 2012. www.theguardian.com. Accessed 27 September 2015.

Giles, Chris. "Theresa May Commits to a Balanced Budget." *Financial Times* 20 July 2016. www.ft.com. Accessed 10 September 2016.

Givan, Rebecca Kolins, and Stephen Bach. "Workforce Responses to the Creeping Privatization of the UK National Health Service." *International Labor and Working-Class History* 71.1 (Spring 2007): 133–153.

Glass, Charles. "Time for Outrage!" *Nation* 16 February 2011. www.thenation.com. Accessed 16 August 2016.

Goldstein, Jacob. "Top 10 Words of the Year Include 'Austerity,' 'Socialism.'" *NPR* 22 December 2010. www.npr.org. Accessed 13 September 2015.

Goodley, Dan. *Dis/Ability Studies: Theorising Disablism and Ableism*. London: Routledge, 2014.

Gould, Deborah B. *Moving Politics: Emotion and ACT UP's Fight against AIDS*. Chicago: University of Chicago Press, 2009.

Govan, Fiona. "Spanish Doctors and Nurses Protest over Health Care Law for Immigrants." *Telegraph* 6 August 2012. www.telegraph.co.uk. Accessed 25 October 2015.

Graham, Georgia. "Nigel Farage: 'The Basic Principle' of Enoch Powell's River of Blood Speech Is Right." *Telegraph* 5 January 2014. www.telegraph.co.uk. Accessed 21 November 2015.

Grech, Shaun, and Karen Soldatic, eds. *Disability in the Global South*. New York: Springer, 2016.

"Greece and the Euro's Future: Go Ahead, Angela, Make My Day." *Economist* 31 January 2015. www.economist.com. Accessed 27 October 2015.

Grover, Jan Zita. "AIDS: Keywords." *AIDS: Cultural Analysis, Cultural Activism*, 17–30. Ed. Douglas Crimp. Cambridge: MIT Press, 1988.

Gunne, Sorcha. *Space, Place, and Gendered Violence in South African Writing*. New York: Palgrave Macmillan, 2016.

Hadjimatheou, Chloe. "The Disabled Children Locked Up in Cages." *BBC News* 14 November 2014. www.bbc.com. Accessed 27 October 2015.

Halberstam, J. Jack. *Gaga Feminism: Sex, Gender, and the End of Normal*. Boston: Beacon Press, 2012.

——. *In a Queer Time and Place: Transgender Bodies, Subcultural Lives*. New York: NYU Press, 2005.

——. *The Queer Art of Failure*. Durham: Duke University Press, 2011.

Hall, Stuart. "Cultural Studies and Its Theoretical Legacies." Morley and Chen, eds. 261–274.

——. "The Great Moving Right Show." *Marxism Today* (January 1979): 14–20.

——. "The Meaning of New Times." Hall and Jacques, eds. 116–134.

——. "New Ethnicities." Morley and Chen, eds. 441–449.

——. "The Work of Representation." *Representation: Cultural Representations and Signifying Practices*, 13–74. Ed. Stuart Hall. London: Sage, 1997.

Hall, Stuart, and Martin Jacques. "Introduction." Hall and Jacques, eds. 11–20.

——, eds. *New Times: The Changing Face of Politics in the 1990s*. London: Lawrence and Wishart, 1989.

Halperin, David M. *Saint Foucault: Towards a Gay Hagiography*. Oxford: Oxford University Press, 1995.

Hamilton, Scott. "I Am Second." www.iamsecond.com. Accessed 14 October 2015.

——, with Lorenzo Benet. *Landing It: My Life On and Off the Ice*. Kensington, Md.: Kensington Books, 1999.

Hancock, Ange-Marie. *The Politics of Disgust: The Public Identity of the Welfare Queen*. New York: NYU Press, 2004.

Hardman, Robert. "Why DO the Left Despise Patriotism? Sneering Left-Wing Art Critic Brands the Poppy Tribute Seen by Millions at the Tower as a 'UKIP-Type Memorial.'" *Daily Mail* 29 October 2014.. Accessed 1 February 2016.

Hardt, Michael, and Antonio Negri. *Commonwealth*. Cambridge: Harvard University Press, 2009.

——. *Multitude*. New York: Penguin, 2004.

Harper, Douglas. "Debris." *Online Etymology Dictionary*. www.etymonline.com. Accessed 14 January 2016.

Harris, John. "Marxism Today: The Forgotten Visionaries Whose Ideas Could Save Labour." *Guardian* 29 September 2015. www.theguardian.com. Accessed 1 October 2015.

Harvey, David. *The Enigma of Capital and the Crises of Capitalism*. Oxford: Oxford University Press, 2010.

——. *The New Imperialism*. Oxford: Oxford University Press, 2005.

Health and Social Care Act of 2012. www.legislation.gov.uk. Accessed 22 September 2015.

Hebdige, Dick. *Subculture: The Meaning of Style*. London: Routledge, 1979.

Henley, Jon. "Greece's Solidarity Movement: 'It's a Whole New Model—and It's Working.'" *Guardian* 23 January 2015. www.theguardian.com. Accessed 29 October 2015.

Hessel, Stéphane. *Time for Outrage/Indignez-vous!* 2010. Trans. Marion Duvert. New York: Twelve-Hatchette Book Group, 2011.

Holehouse, Matthew. "Blair's Warning to Miliband: Please the Voters, Not Your Ideological Ghosts." *Telegraph* 21 July 2014. www.telegraph.co.uk. Accessed 22 January 2016.

Hooper, Tom. "Academy Awards Acceptance Speech." aaspeechesdb.oscars.org. Accessed 25 September 2015.

———. dir. *The King's Speech*. London: UK Film Council, 2010.

"How to Grow Poppies." www.wikihow.com. Accessed 27 January 2016.

"Huelga de hambre: Huelgistas marcharon por Santiago." *El Chileno*. elchileno.cl. Accessed 24 October 2015.

"Idiom: Take Your Breath Away." *UsingEnglish.com* www.usingenglish.com. Accessed 10 July 2016.

Inckle, Kay. "Debilitating Times: Compulsory Ablebodiedness and White Privilege in Theory and Practice." *Feminist Review* 111 (2015): 42–58.

Jameson, Fredric. *Postmodernism, or, The Cultural Logic of Late Capitalism*. Durham: Duke University Press, 1991.

Johnson, Merri Lisa. *Girl in Need of a Tourniquet: Memoir of a Borderline Personality*. Berkeley: Seal Press, 2010.

Johnson, Merri Lisa, and Robert McRuer, eds. "Cripistemologies." *Journal of Literary and Cultural Disability Studies* 8.2–3 (2014).

———. "Introduction: Cripistemologies and the Masturbating Girl." *Journal of Literary and Cultural Disability Studies* 8.3 (2014): 245–255.

Johnson, Tim. "Mexico City Copes with That Sinking Feeling." *Seattle Times* 24 September 2011. www.seattletimes.com. Accessed 3 December 2015.

Jones, Jonathan. "The Tower of London Poppies Are Fake, Trite and Inward-Looking—A UKIP-Style Memorial." *Guardian* 28 October 2014. www.theguardian.com. Accessed 1 February 2016.

Jones, Owen. *Chavs: The Demonization of the Working Class*. London: Verso, 2011.

———. "David Cameron Praises Paralympians but His Policies Will Crush Them." *Independent* 26 August 2012. www.independent.co.uk. Accessed 12 September 2015.

———. *The Establishment: And How They Get Away with It*. London: Penguin, 2014.

Kafer, Alison. *Feminist, Queer, Crip*. Bloomington: Indiana University Press, 2013.

Kelley, Robin D. G. *Freedom Dreams: The Black Radical Imagination*. Boston: Beacon Press, 2002.

Kleege, Georgina. "On Being Who I Am: My Life as a Tall Blind Woman." *Toast* 2 March 2016. the-toast.net. Accessed 13 October 2016.

Klein, Naomi. *The Shock Doctrine: The Rise of Disaster Capitalism.* New York: Picador, 2007.

Köbsell, Swantje. "Towards Self-Determination and Equalization: A Short History of the German Disability Rights Movement." *Disability Studies Quarterly* 26.2 (2006). dsq-sds.org. Accessed 17 September 2015.

Koksall, Izzy. "Can't Pay, Won't Move: Resisting the Bedroom Tax." *Red Pepper* 189 (April/May 2013): 22–23.

Kolářová, Kateřina. "The Inarticulate Post-Socialist Crip: On the Cruel Optimism of Neoliberal Transformations in the Czech Republic." *Journal of Literary and Cultural Disability Studies* 8.3 (2014): 257–274.

Kolářová, Kateřina, and M. Katharina Wiedlack, eds. "Cripping Development." *Somatechnics* 16.2 (September 2016).

Kouvelakis, Stathis. "The Alternative in Greece." *Jacobin Magazine.* 24 February 2015. www.jacobinmag.com/. Accessed 27 October 2015.

Krugman, Paul. "The Case for Cuts Was a Lie. Why Does Britain Still Believe It? The Austerity Delusion." *Guardian* 29 April 2015. www.theguardian.com. Accessed 13 September 2015.

———. "Greek Regrets." *New York Times* 5 June 2013. krugman.blogs.nytimes.com. Accessed 13 September 2015.

———. "The M.I.T. Gang." *New York Times* 24 June 2015. www.nytimes.com. Accessed 13 September 2015.

Kulick, Don, and Jens Rydström. *Loneliness and Its Opposite: Sex, Disability, and the Ethics of Engagement.* Durham: Duke University Press, 2015.

Kuppers, Petra. *Disability Culture and Community Performance: Find a Strange and Twisted Shape.* New York: Palgrave, 2011.

———. "Introduction." *Somatic Engagement*, 9–18. Ed. Petra Kuppers. Oakland: Chain-Links, 2011.

———. "Social Somatics." *Performance Studies: Keywords, Concepts and Theories*, 185–192. Ed. Bryan Reynolds. London: Palgrave, 2014.

Lansley, Stewart. *Life in the Middle: The Untold Story of Britain's Average Earners.* London: Trades Union Congress (TUC), 2009.

Leadbeater, Charlie. "Power to the Person." Hall and Jacques, eds. 137–149.

Learmonth, Andrew. "The Hunger Games: Austerity Is Leaving Pupils So Hungry They Steal from Classmates." *National* 30 December 2015. www.thenational.scot. Accessed 9 July 2016.

Left Hand Rotation. Museo de los Desplazados. www.museodelosdesplazados.com. Accessed 23 November 2015.

"Left Out in the Cold—PRESS RELEASE." thebrokenofbritain.blogspot.com.br. Accessed 29 May 2017.

Lenin, Vladimir Ilyich. "The Irish Rebellion of 1916." 1916. *Lenin on Britain*, 256–260. Moscow: Progress Publishers, 1979.

Leonard Cheshire Disability. "No Place Like Home: 5 Million Reasons to Make Housing Disabled-Friendly." www.leonardcheshire.org. Accessed 9 December 2015.

Livingston, Julie. "Insights from an African History of Disability." *Radical History Review* 94 (Winter 2006): 111–126.

Lloyd, Phyllida, dir. *The Iron Lady*. London: UK Film Council, 2011.

"London 2012 Paralympics: Build Up to Paralympic Games." *Evening Standard* 24 August 2012. www.standard.co.uk. Accessed 15 October 2015.

London Aquatics Centre. queenelizabetholympicpark.co.uk. Accessed 9 December 2015.

Lorde, Audre. *Sister Outsider: Essays and Speeches*. Freedom, Calif.: Crossing Press, 1984.

"Los machetes de Atenco vuelven al DF en marcha contra el nuevo aeropuerto." *CNN México* 8 September 2014. mexico.cnn.com. Accessed 13 December 2015.

Lyons, James. "Charity Bosses Claim David Cameron Has Misled Disabled People about the Bedroom Tax." *Mirror* 2 December 2013. www.mirror.co.uk. Accessed 7 December 2015.

Magrath, Andrea. "X Marks the Spot! Dazzling Plans by British Architect Lord Norman Foster for Mexico City's New £5.5BILLION Airport Unveiled." *Daily Mail* 4 September 2014. www.dailymail.co.uk. Accessed 13 December 2015.

Malhotra, Ravi, ed. *Disability Politics in a Global Economy: Essays in Honour of Marta Russell*. London: Routledge, 2017.

Maltezou, Renee. "Greece Pushes for Austerity Deal as Time Runs Short." *Reuters* 2 October 2012. www.reuters.com. Accessed 29 October 2015.

Marquand, David. "Beyond Left and Right: The Need for a New Politics." Hall and Jacques, eds. 371–378.

Martin, Emily. *Flexible Bodies: The Role of Immunity in American Culture from the Days of Polio to the Age of AIDS*. Boston: Beacon Press, 1994.

Marx, Karl. *Capital, Volume One*. 1867. Tucker 294–438.

———. "Contribution to the Critique of Hegel's *Philosophy of Right*: Introduction." 1844. Tucker 53–65.

———. *The German Ideology*. 1845. Tucker 146–200.

———. "On the Jewish Question." 1843. Tucker 26–52.

Marx, Karl, and Friedrich Engels. "Manifesto of the Communist Party." 1848. Tucker 469–500.

Mason, Rowena. "Boris Johnson's IQ Comments Met with Outrage." *Guardian* 28 November 2013. www.theguardian.com. Accessed 6 December 2015.

———. "Liberal Democrat Activists Condemn Bedroom Tax." *Guardian* 16 September 2013. www.theguardian.com. Accessed 7 December 2015.

———. "Nigel Farage Backs 'Basic Principle' of Enoch Powell's Immigration Warning." *Guardian* 5 January 2014. www.theguardian.com. Accessed 21 November 2015.

———. "Nigel Farage: Immigration Has Left Britain Almost Unrecognisable." *Guardian* 31 March 2015. www.theguardian.com. Accessed 17 November 2015.

Mason, Rowena, and Nicholas Watt. "Boris Johnson IQ Comments Reveal 'Unpleasant, Careless Elitism,' says Clegg." *Guardian* 28 November 2013. www.theguardian.com/politics. Accessed 7 December 2015.

McCloskey, Stephen. "Stereotyping the Poor: Why Development Educators Need to Challenge the Myths of Austerity." *Policy and Practice: A Development Education Review* (Autumn 2013). www.developmenteducationreview.com. Accessed 22 September 2015.

McGauran, Ann. "An Exercise in Hope: The Biscuit Fund Steps to Help Kevin after His Benefits Are Sanctioned." annmcgauran.org.uk. Accessed 28 January 2016.

McRuer, Robert. "Crip." *Keywords for Radicals: The Contested Vocabulary of Late-Capitalist Struggle.* Chico, Calif.: AK Press, 2016. 119–125.

———. "Cripping Queer Politics, or the Dangers of Neoliberalism." *Scholar and Feminist Online* 10.1–2 (Spring 2012). sfonline.barnard.edu. Accessed 12 September 2015.

———. *Crip Theory: Cultural Signs of Queerness and Disability.* New York: NYU Press, 2006.

———. "Curb Cuts: Crip Displacements and El Edificio de Enfrente." Special issue on *Cripping Development.* Ed. Kateřina Kolářová and M. Katharina Wiedlack. *Somatechnics* 6.2 (2016): 198–215.

———. "Disabling Sex: Notes for a Crip Theory of Sexuality." *GLQ: A Journal of Lesbian and Gay Studies* 17.1 (2011): 107–117.

———. "Epilogue: #YoSoy." *Libre Acesso: Latin American Literature and Film through Disability Studies,* 259–264. Ed. Susan Antebi and Beth E. Jörgensen. Albany: SUNY Press, 2016.

———. "Epilogue: Disability, Inc." Ben-Moshe, Chapman, and Carey 273–279.

———. "Neoliberal Risks: *Million Dollar Baby, Murderball,* and Anti-National Sexual Positions." *The Problem Body: Projecting Disability on Film,* 159–177. Ed. Sally Chivers and Nicole Markotić. Columbus: Ohio State University Press, 2010.

———. "Pink." *Prismatic Ecology: Ecotheory beyond Green,* 63–82. Ed. Jeffrey Jerome Cohen. Minneapolis: University of Minnesota Press, 2013.

———. "Queer America." *The Cambridge Companion to Modern American Culture,* 215–234. Ed. Christopher Bigsby. Cambridge: Cambridge University Press, 2006.

———. "Taking It to the Bank: Independence and Inclusion on the World Market." *Journal of Literary Disability* 1.2 (2007): 5–14.

———. "The Then and There of Crip Futurity." Review of Alison Kafer's *Feminist, Queer, Crip. GLQ: A Journal of Lesbian and Gay Studies* 20.4 (2014): 532–534.

"Meaning of Symbol." www.3elove.com. Accessed 22 October 2015.

Medwave. "Huelga de hambre de estudiantes: Diario de una lucha." *Revista Biomédica Revisada Por Pares.* www.medwave.cl. Accessed 24 October 2015.

Metzl, Jonathan M. *The Protest Psychosis: How Schizophrenia Became a Black Disease.* Boston: Beacon Press, 2009.

"Mexican Government Announces Fresh Austerity Measures." *Telesur* 18 February 2016. www.telesurtv.net. Accessed 6 August 2016.

"Mexican President Delivers State of the Union Address." *Telesur* 3 September 2015. www.telesurtv.net. Accessed 6 August 2016.

"Mexican President Flaunts $430 Million 'Palace in the Sky.'" *Telesur* 7 January 2016. www.telesurtv.net. Accessed 6 August 2016.

"Mexico City for Everyone: The Accessibility Legacy of London 2012." 26 March 2013. www.gov.uk. Accessed 7 December 2015.

Miles, Kathleen. "The State with the Most Rich People Also Has the Highest Poverty Rate." *Huffington Post* 15 November 2013. www.huffingtonpost.com. Accessed 23 October 2015.

Mingus, Mia. "Changing the Framework: Disability Justice." *RESIST* Newsletter (November 2010). leavingevidence.wordpress.com. Accessed 17 September 2015.

———. "Wherever You Are Is Where I Want to Be: Crip Solidarity." *Leaving Evidence* 3 May 2010. leavingevidence.wordpress.com. Accessed 22 August 2016.

Minich, Julie Avril. *Accessible Citizenships: Disability, Nation, and the Cultural Politics of Greater Mexico*. Philadelphia: Temple University Press, 2014.

Mitchell, David T. "Gay Pasts and Disability Future(s) Tense: Heteronormative Trauma and Parasitism in *Midnight Cowboy*." *Journal of Literary and Cultural Disability Studies* 8.1 (2014): 1–16.

Mitchell, David T., and Sharon L. Snyder. *The Biopolitics of Disability: Neoliberalism, Ablenationalism, and Peripheral Embodiment*. Ann Arbor: University of Michigan Press, 2015.

———, dir. *Vital Signs: Crip Culture Talks Back*. United States: Fanlight Productions, 1995.

Mollow, Anna. "Criphystemologies: What Disability Theory Needs to Know about Hysteria." *Journal of Literary and Cultural Disability Studies* 8.2 (2014): 185–201.

———. "Disability Studies Gets Fat." *Hypatia: Journal of Feminist Philosophy* 30.3 (Fall 2014): 199–216.

———. "Is Sex Disability? Queer Theory and the Disability Drive." *Sex and Disability*, 285–312. Ed. Robert McRuer and Anna Mollow. Durham: Duke University Press, 2012.

———. "No Safe Place." *Women's Studies Quarterly* 39.1–2 (Spring/Summer 2011): 188–199.

Mollow, Anna, and Robert McRuer. "Fattening Austerity." *Body Politics: Zeitschrift für Körpergeschichte* 5 (2015): 25–49.

———. "Introduction." *Sex and Disability*, 1–36. Ed. Robert McRuer and Anna Mollow. Durham: Duke University Press, 2012.

Montgomery, Cal. "A Hard Look at Invisible Disability." *Ragged Edge Online* 2 (2001). www.raggededgemagazine.com. Accessed 8 December 2016.

Morley, David, and Kuan-Hsing Chen, eds. *Stuart Hall: Critical Dialogues in Cultural Studies*. New York: Routledge, 1996.

Moscoso, Melania. "'De aquí no se va nadie': Del uso del discapacitado para el aleccionamiento moral." *Constelaciones: Revista de Teoría Crítica* 5 (2013): 170–183.

Muholi, Zanele. *Zanele Muholi: Faces and Phases*. New York: Prestel Publishing, 2010.

Mulgan, Geoff. "The Changing Shape of the City." Hall and Jacques, eds. 262–278.

Muñoz, José Esteban. *Cruising Utopia: The Then and There of Queer Futurity*. New York: NYU Press, 2009.

———. *Disidentifications: Queers of Color and the Performance of Politics*. Minneapolis: University of Minnesota Press, 1999.

Murphy, Richard. "Collect the Evaded Tax, Avoid the Cuts." *Guardian* 25 November 2011. www.theguardian.com. Accessed 27 September 2015.

Murray, Robin. "Benetton Britain." Hall and Jacques, eds. 54–64.

Naidu, Ereshnee, Sadiyya Haffejee, Lisa Vetten, and Samantha Hargreaves. "On the Margins: Violence against Women with Disabilities." CSVR: Centre for the Study of Violence and Reconciliation. April 2005. www.csvr.org.za. Accessed 7 December 2016.

Navascués Cobo, Irene, and Rosario Ortega Amador, dir. *Habitación*. Perf. Soledad Arnau Ripollés. Spain, 2015.

"New Politics at Home, New Partnerships Abroad." 29 March 2011. www.gov.uk. Accessed 29 July 2013.

"Nick Clegg Speaks Spanish." YouTube 29 June 2010. www.youtube.com/watch?v =CypvKvKLfk8. Accessed 29 July 2016.

Northover, Kylie. "Melbourne Comedy Festival Causes Nervous Laughs." *Sydney Morning Herald* 15 March 2014. www.smh.com.au. Accessed 14 September 2015.

Núñez, María Paz. "Rodrigo Avilés es dado de alta tras de recuperar la memoria y casi toda la movilidad del cuerpo." *La Tercera* 21 July 2015. www.latercera.com. Accessed 24 October 2015.

Oborne, Peter. "This Infatuation with Blair Will Damage David Cameron's Reputation." *Telegraph* 18 December 2014. www.telegraph.co.uk. Accessed 17 January 2016.

Odone, Cristina. "Nigel Farage: We Must Defend Christian Heritage." *Telegraph* 1 November 2013. www.telegraph.co.uk. Accessed 17 November 2015.

O'Hara, Mary. *Austerity Bites: A Journey to the Sharp End of Cuts in the UK*. Bristol: Policy Press, 2014.

"Oscar Pistorius: Six Years for Reeva Steenkamp Murder." *BBC News* 6 July 2016. www.bbc.com. Accessed 17 September 2016.

O'Toole, Corbett Joan. *Fading Scars: My Queer Disability History*. Fort Worth: Autonomous Press, 2015.

Owen, Paul. "Hardest Hit: Disabled People March in London—Wednesday 11 May 2011." *Guardian* 11 May 2011. www.theguardian.com. Accessed 26 September 2015.

"Panagiotis Kouroublis." Hellenic Parliament Biography. www.hellenicparliament.gr. Accessed 27 October 2015.

"Paro. Rajoy pide 'mantener las mismas politicas' para alcanzar 20 millones de trabajadores la próxima legislatura." *Siglo XXI* 5 May 2015. www.diariosigloxxi.com. Accessed 7 July 2016.

"Parts of Tower of London Poppy Display Reprieved." *Guardian* 7 November 2014. www.theguardian.com. Accessed 1 February 2016.

"Peña Nieto es recibido con protestas en su visita oficial al Reino Unido." *El Mundo* 3 March 2015. www.elmundo.es. Accessed 12 December 2015.

Perraudin, Frances. "Osborne's 'Lost Marbles' Taunt Reinforces Mental Health Stigma, Says Labour." *Guardian* 19 January 2016. www.theguardian.com. Accessed 22 January 2016.

Perring, Rebecca. "Queen Hails UK and Mexico as 'Natural Partners' at Banquet with Mexican President." *Daily Express* 3 March 2015. www.express.co.uk. Accessed 12 December 2015.

Peterson, Brittany. "Chilean Student Hunger Strikers Hold President Piñera Accountable." *Nation* 22 August 2011. www.thenation.com. Accessed 24 October 2015.

Peterson, Latoya. "Corrective Rape: The Epidemic of Violence against South Africa's LGBT Community." *Root* 23 May 2015. www.theroot.com. Accessed 7 December 2016.

Pickard, Jim. "Ukip Gains First Elected MP after Douglas Carswell Wins in Clacton." *Financial Times* 14 October 2014. www.ft.com. Accessed 18 November 2015.

Pinsker, Joe. "The Financial Perks of Being Tall." *Atlantic* 18 May 2015. www.theatlantic .com. Accessed 8 July 2016.

"Pistorius Eligible for Olympics." *BBC Sport* 16 May 2008. news.bbc.co.uk. Accessed 13 October 2015.

"Pistorius's Home on Estate Voted Most Secure in South Africa." *Guardian* 14 February 2013. www.theguardian.com. Accessed 19 October 2015.

Platero, Lucas. "Las políticas neoliberales contra los derechos sexuales." *Fundación Betiko* (2014). http://fundacionbetiko.org. Accessed 17 September 2015.

———. *Trans*exualidades: Acompañamiento, factores de salud y recursos educativos.* Barcelona: Edicions Bellaterra, 2014.

Portavoz, Profeta Marginal, M. C. Erko, and Raza Humana. "Ni Un Minúto Solos." www.rimasrebeldes.com.ar. Accessed 24 October 2015.

Powell, Enoch. "Rivers of Blood." 1968. *Telegraph* 6 November 2007. www.telegraph .co.uk. Accessed 21 November 2014.

Prendergast, Catherine. "The Unexceptional Schizophrenic: A Post-Postmodern Introduction." *Journal of Literary and Cultural Disability Studies* 2.1 (2008): 55–62.

Price, Margaret. *Mad at School: Rhetorics of Mental Disability and Academic Life.* Ann Arbor: University of Michigan Press, 2011.

Pring, John. "'Damning' Research on WCA Deaths Is 'Timely' Reminder of Government's Shame." *Disability News Service* 20 November 2015. www.disabilitynewsservice .com. Accessed 9 July 2016.

———. "Disability Poverty Rose Sharply in Fourth Year of Coalition." *Disability News Service* 3 July 2015. www.disabilitynewsservice.com. Accessed 26 September 2015.

Puar, Jasbir K. "Prognosis Time." *Women & Performance: A Journal of Feminist Theory* 19.2 (July 2009): 161–172.

———. *Terrorist Assemblages: Homonationalism in Queer Times.* Durham: Duke University Press, 2006.

Purnell, James, and Jim Murphy. "The Battle Lines Are Aspiration versus Conservation." *London Times* 26 March 2007. www.thetimes.co.uk. Accessed 22 January 2016.

Radwanski, Livia. "Ayotzinapa." liviaradwanski.com. Accessed 12 December 2015.

———. *Mérida9o.* Mexico City: Tumbona Ediciones, 2011.

———. *Unos Otros Méxicos.* Mexico City: Tumbona Ediciones, 2011.

Ramesh, Randeep. "Welfare Reform: 'Most Radical Shake-Up for 60 Years.'" *Guardian* 17 February 2011. www.theguardian.com. Accessed 26 September 2015.

Ramiro, Joana. "Wish We Were Here: A Melancholy Postcard." *Salvage* 1 (July 2015): 101–105.

Raphaely, Carolyn. "Disabled Inmates in Oscar Pistorius Prison Speak Out against Poor Treatment." *Guardian* 22 October 2014. www.theguardian.com. Accessed 13 October 2015.

Roaring Girl Productions (RGP). "About." www.roaring-girl.com. Accessed 14 January 2016.

———. "Bedding Out." www.roaring-girl.com. Accessed 16 January 2016.

———. "#InActualFact." www.roaring-girl.com. Accessed 16 January 2016.

Robinson, Andrew. "Alain Badiou: Truth, Subjectivity, and Fidelity." *Ceasefire* 15 January 2015. ceasefiremagazine.co.uk. Accessed 12 October 2015.

Robinson, Sadie. "800 Meet to Unite the Resistance for 30 June Strike." *Socialist Worker* 2257 (23 June 2011). socialistworker.co.uk. Accessed 23 September 2015.

Russell, Marta. *Beyond Ramps: Disability at the End of the Social Contract*. Monroe, Maine: Common Courage Press, 1998.

Salvage editorial board. "Perspectives 1: Amid This Stony Rubbish." *Salvage: A Quarterly of Revolutionary Arts and Letters* (July 2014): Insert, 1–15.

———. "Pessimism after Corbyn." *Salvage: A Quarterly of Revolutionary Arts and Letters* 14 September 2015. salvage.zone. Accessed 17 September 2015.

Sample, Ian. "Why Is Mexico City Sinking?" *Guardian* 6 May 2004. www.theguardian.com. Accessed 3 December 2015.

Samuels, Ellen. *Fantasies of Identification: Disability, Gender, Race*. New York: NYU Press, 2014.

———. "My Body, My Closet: Invisible Disability and the Limits of Coming-Out Discourse." *GLQ: A Journal of Lesbian and Gay Studies* 9.1–2 (2003): 233–255.

Sandahl, Carrie. "Queering the Crip or Cripping the Queer? Intersections of Queer and Crip Identities in Solo Autobiographical Performance." *GLQ: A Journal of Lesbian and Gay Identities* 9.1–2 (2003): 25–56.

Schalk, Sami. "Reevaluating the Supercrip." *Journal of Literary and Cultural Disability Studies* 10.1 (2016): 71–86.

Schwarz, Hunter. "If Britain Were a U.S. State, It Would Be the Second Poorest, behind Alabama and before Mississippi." *Washington Post* 26 August 2014. www.washingtonpost.com. Accessed 7 December 2015.

Schweik, Susan M. *The Ugly Laws: Disability in Public*. New York: NYU Press, 2009.

Scott, Darieck. *Extravagant Abjection: Blackness, Power, and Sexuality in the African American Literary Imagination*. New York: NYU Press, 2010.

Sedgwick, Eve Kosofsky. *Epistemology of the Closet*. Berkeley: University of California Press, 1990.

Seidler, David. "How the 'Naughty Word' Cured the King's Stutter (and Mine)." *Daily Mail* 20 December 2010. www.dailymail.co.uk. Accessed 24 September 2015.

Seymour, Richard. *Against Austerity: How We Can Fix the Crisis They Made*. London: Pluto Press, 2014.

———. "Austerity Has Hit Politicians Hard." *Guardian* 21 June 2011. www.theguardian.com. Accessed 23 September 2015.

———. *Corbyn: The Strange Rebirth of Radical Politics*. London: Verson, 2016.

———. "This Is Not 1992." *Lenin's Tomb* 8 May 2015. www.leninology.co.uk. Accessed 25 November 2015.

———. "The UKIPisation of English Politics." *Lenin's Tomb* 10 October 2014. www.leninology.co.uk. Accessed 27 October 2015.

Shildrick, Margrit. *Dangerous Discourses of Disability, Subjectivity and Sexuality*. New York: Palgrave, 2009.

———. "Living On; Not Getting Better." *Feminist Review* 111 (2015): 10–24.

Siebers, Tobin. *Disability Theory*. Ann Arbor: University of Michigan Press, 2008.

Smith, Helena, and Ian Traynor. "Greek PM Alexis Tsipras Unveils Cabinet of Mavericks and Visionaries." *Guardian* 27 January 2015. www.theguardian.com. Accessed 27 October 2015.

Smith, Michael. "Black Lesbians Shot without Judgment." *Times Live* (South Africa) 20 September 2016. m.timeslive.co.za. Accessed 7 December 2016.

Smithers, Rebecca. "One in Five UK Families Can't Afford Seaside Day Out." *Guardian* 25 August 2014. www.theguardian.com. Accessed 7 December 2015.

Snyder, Sharon L., and David T. Mitchell. *Cultural Locations of Disability*. Chicago: University of Chicago Press, 2006.

———, dir. *Self-Preservation: The Art of Riva Lehrer*. Chicago: Brace Yourself Productions, 2004.

South Bank Tower. southbanktower.com. Accessed 30 January 2016.

Spencer, Julie. "Mentally Ill Patients Victimised by Bedroom Tax Rules, Says Campaigner." *Get Reading* 16 May 2014. www.getreading.co.uk. Accessed 28 July 2016.

Stockton, Kathryn Bond. *The Queer Child; or Growing Sideways in the Twentieth Century*. Durham: Duke University Press, 2009.

Stone, Deborah A. *The Disabled State*. Philadelphia: Temple University Press, 1984.

Stone, Jon. "David Cameron's New Disabilities Minister Voted against Protecting Disabled Children's Benefits." *Independent* 13 May 2015. www.independent.co.uk. Accessed 27 January 2016.

Stuckler, David, and Sanjay Basu. *The Body Economic: Why Austerity Kills—Recessions, Budget Battles and the Politics of Life and Death*. New York: Basic Books, 2013.

"Supporting Business to Increase UK Exports and Attract Inward Investment in Mexico." 19 March 2013. www.gov.uk. Accessed 12 December 2015.

Tassinari, Camilo Ruiz. "After Ayotzinapa." *Jacobin Magazine* 1 March 2015. www.jacobinmag.com. Accessed 12 December 2015.

Taylor, Sunaura, et al. "Krips, Cops and Occupy: Reflections from Oscar Grant Plaza." *Occupying Disability: Critical Approaches to Community, Justice and Decolonizing Disability*, 15–30. Ed. Pamela Block et al. New York: Springer, 2016.

Téllez, Magali. "Maltrato en 'anexos': Sin control, los centros de rehabilitación de adictos." *El Universal* 12 August 2014. archivo.eluniversal.com.mx. Accessed 15 December 2015.

Thatcher, Margaret. "Interview for *Woman's Own*." 23 September 1987. Margaret Thatcher Foundation: Speeches, Interviews & Other Statements. www.margaretthatcher .org. Accessed 19 January 2016.

———. "The Renewal of Britain: Speech to the Conservative Political Centre Summer School." 6 July 1979. Margaret Thatcher Foundation: Speeches, Interviews & Other Statements. www.margaretthatcher.org. Accessed 21 January 2016.

———. "Speech in Mexico." 25 March 1994. Margaret Thatcher Foundation: Speeches, Interviews & Other Statements. www.margaretthatcher.org. Accessed 4 August 2016.

———. "Speech to the Conservative Party Conference." 8 October 1976. Margaret Thatcher Foundation: Speeches, Interviews & Other Statements. www.margaretthatcher .org. Accessed 21 January 2016.

———. "Speech to Greater London Young Conservatives (Iain Macleod Memorial Lecture—'Dimensions of Conservatism')." 4 July 1977. Margaret Thatcher Foundation: Speeches, Interviews & other Statements. www.margaretthatcher.org. Accessed 8 July 2016.

Titchkosky, Tanya. *The Question of Access: Disability, Space, Meaning.* Toronto: University of Toronto Press, 2011.

———. *Reading and Writing Disability Differently: The Textured Life of Embodiment.* Toronto: University of Toronto Press, 2007.

"Toddler's Best Ever Christmas Gift." *Sky News* 26 December 2006. news.sky.com. Accessed 14 October 2015.

Topping, Alexandra. "Locog Hails Biggest and Best Paralympics in History." *Guardian* 6 September 2012. www.theguardian.com. Accessed 14 October 2015.

"Tower of London Poppies: Thousands to Go on Tour." *BBC News* 9 November 2014. www.bbc.com. Accessed 1 February 2016.

Tremain, Shelley. "Foucault, Governmentality, and Critical Disability Theory: An Introduction." *Foucault and the Government of Disability*, 1–24. Ann Arbor: University of Michigan Press, 2005.

Tucker, Robert C. *The Marx-Engels Reader.* 2nd ed. New York: Norton, 1978.

Tyburczy, Jennifer. *Sex Museums: The Politics and Performance of Display.* Chicago: University of Chicago Press, 2016.

"UK and Mexico Celebrate Closer Economic and Academic Ties during Mexico State Visit." 1 March 2015. www.gov.uk. Accessed 12 December 2015.

"UK Deputy Prime Minister Slams Mexico during Peña Nieto Visit." *Telesur* 4 March 2015. www.telesurtv.net. Accessed 5 August 2016.

United Kingdom Independence Party [UKIP]. "The Human Cost of Uninsured Health Tourists." 29 April 2015. www.ukip.org. Accessed 20 November 2015.

Undurraga, Eduardo A., et al. "The Perceived Benefits of Height: Strength, Dominance, Social Concern, and Knowledge among Bolivian Native Amazonians." *PLOS ONE* 4 May 2012. journals.plos.org. Accessed 19 January 2016.

Vale, Paul. "Austerity in the United Kingdom Leaves Disabled in Fear for Their Lives." *Huffington Post* 17 July 2012. www.huffingtonpost.com. Accessed 15 October 2015.

Walters, Ben. "What *The King's Speech* Can Teach Prince William and Kate Middleton." *Guardian* 12 January 2011. www.theguardian.com. Accessed 25 September 2015.

Watt, Nicholas. "Ed Miliband Moves on from Criticism with Housing Pledge." *Guardian* 12 June 2011. www.theguardian.com. Accessed 26 September 2015.

Wehrwein, Peter. "Oscar or Not, *The King's Speech* Teaches about Stuttering." *Harvard Health Publications* 27 February 2011. www.health.harvard.edu. Accessed 24 September 2015.

Wendell, Susan. *The Rejected Body: Feminist Philosophical Reflections on Disability.* New York: Routledge, 1996.

"Why Silver Woods: Silver Woods Country Estate—Class, Style, Distinction." www .silverwoods.co.za. Accessed 19 October 2015.

Wiginton, Melissa. "'*The King's Speech*' and Feminism." *Faith and Leadership* 4 March 2011. www.faithandleadership.com. Accessed 24 September 2015.

Williams, Raymond. *Keywords: A Vocabulary of Culture and Society.* Rev. ed. New York: Oxford University Press, 1983.

———. *Marxism and Literature.* Oxford: Oxford University Press, 1977.

Willitts, Philippa. "Bad Attitudes Do Not Cause Disability Any More Than Good Attitudes Guarantee Health." *Independent* 1 August 2012. blogs.independent.co.uk. Accessed 15 October 2015.

Wilson, Eric. "Stretching a Six-Pack." *New York Times* 12 May 2010. www.nytimes.com. Accessed 16 October 2015.

Wintour, Patrick, and Denis Campbell. "Cameron Should Apologise for NHS Reforms, Says Miliband." *Guardian* 6 February 2015. www.theguardian.com. Accessed 13 October 2015.

Wojnarowicz, David. *Close to the Knives: A Memoir of Disintegration.* New York: Vintage-Random House, 1991.

———, dir. *A Fire in My Belly.* New York: unfinished, 1986–1987.

Wood, Caitlin. "Tales from the Crip: This Is What Disability Looks Like." *Bitch Media* 2 October 2012. bitchmedia.org. Accessed 19 October 2015.

Young, Stella. "We're Not Here for Your Inspiration." *Drum* 2 July 2012. www.abc.net .au. Accessed 15 September 2015.

Zirión, Antonio. "El Edificio de Enfrente." Radwanski, *Mérida90* 75–81.

INDEX

ABOUT THE AUTHOR

Robert McRuer is Professor of English at the George Washington University. He is the author of *Crip Theory: Cultural Signs of Queerness and Disability* and *The Queer Renaissance: Contemporary American Literature and the Reinvention of Lesbian and Gay Identities* (both also available from NYU Press). With Anna Mollow, he co-edited the anthology *Sex and Disability*.